DATE DUE

DEMCO 38-296

Industrial Economics

Also by Paul R. Ferguson and Glenys J. Ferguson
BUSINESS ECONOMICS: The Application of Economic Theory
(*with R. Rothschild*)

Industrial Economics

Issues and Perspectives

SECOND EDITION

Paul R. Ferguson and Glenys J. Ferguson

NEW YORK UNIVERSITY PRESS
Washington Square, New York

HD 2326 .F47 1994

Ferguson, Paul R.

Industrial economics

. Ferguson

p.   cm.
Includes bibliographical references and indexes.
ISBN 0-8147-2624-0 — ISBN 0-8147-2625-9 (paperback)
1. Industrial organization (Economic theory)   2. Transaction
costs.   I. Ferguson, Glenys J.   II. Title.
HD2326.F47 1994
338.5-dc20   93-45506
                                                         CIP

Printed in Great Britain

Contents

List of Figures

List of Tables

Acknowledgements

The authors and publishers wish to thank the following who have kindly given permission for the use of copyright material:

The Advertising Association for material from Waterson (1992) and *Advertising Statistics Yearbook* (1992, 1993).

The Economist for material from 15 March 1986 issue of *The Economist*.

Every effort has been made to trace all copyright-holders, but if any have been inadvertently overlooked the publishers will be pleased to make the necessary arrangement at the first opportunity.

Preface to the First Edition

The industrial economics courses taught at the University of Lancaster have always been rather heretical. Philip Andrews and Elizabeth Brunner had an enduring belief in the strength of competition and were sceptical of the relevance of the 'structure–conduct–performance' (SCP) approach which dominated the subject. Harry Townsend, following the eclectic tradition of the London School of Economics, had a similar distaste for this paradigm, believing it to be too constraining. As long ago as 1972, he introduced transaction costs as a key element of the undergraduate industrial economics course, but even today this topic is ignored (or given scant attention) in many such courses elsewhere. Hence, as both a student and a lecturer at Lancaster, I have been made aware of alternative interpretations and approaches to the study of industrial economics which are only now beginning to receive wider recognition.

The Lancaster tradition of non-conformity is continued in this book which differs in scope from other texts in the field of industrial economics. It covers the mainstream analysis, but challenges this approach – and the resulting policy conclusions – by introducing many of the less well-known developments in the area.

Without the help of many friends and colleagues, this book would have taken much longer to write. Andrea Pezzoli made many valuable comments while Harry Townsend gave enthusiastic support and help. Ron Bowen's lack of knowledge of economics, but careful attention to detail, removed much of the jargon. The boundless energy and enthusiasm of Professor Balasubramanyam led me to discover that I could work twice as hard as I had previously thought possible. My greatest debts are to Gerry Steele, who amazed me by his capacity to examine meticulously every draft I produced (and, furthermore, by his claim to enjoy such an onerous task) and to my wife, Glenys. As the book slowly advanced, she decided that the fastest way to rediscover leisure would be to help me. She finished up spending as long on the book as I did, and, in this sense, it is as much her effort as mine. Nevertheless, any remaining errors are my own responsibility.

This is the point where authors traditionally thank their secretary for her miraculous ability to decipher almost illegible handwriting; in this case thanks must go to my word-processor. Furthermore I believe that I could have dispensed with the technical skills of the publisher and typeset the book myself. In fact, I could have performed all the publisher's tasks equally well, given the assumption that information is perfect, and in the absence of uncertainty and transaction costs. But if that were the case there would also have been no need for me to write this book, and I would be doing a different job.

PAUL R. FERGUSON

Preface to the Second Edition

Since writing the first edition, we have become more aware of the great differences between individual firms, both within and across markets and industries. An advantage of writing a second edition is that it requires the authors to find the time to become immersed in the recent literature. Among other things, it became evident that we are by no means alone in realising that individual firms deserve more consideration in analysis.

Whilst the first edition presented the work of the Austrian School as the main counter to the traditional (neoclassical) paradigm, the second edition widens the theoretical approaches considered. It now encompasses all the major variants of what is becoming known as the *new institutional economics*, with, in particular, more attention being given to transaction cost economics (associated principally with Williamson and North). Not only does the second edition adopt a wider theoretical compass, but the discussion of empirical work, the tables and examples have been thoroughly updated. All the chapters have been rewritten, but some have changed more than others. For instance, those on industry policy in practice and state against private control are now substantially different.

The re-writing of this book was hastened by the addition of a second author. Glenys Ferguson shouldered a substantial proportion of the work, and this is reflected in the joint authorship. As with the first edition, considerable credit must be given to Gerry Steele, who re-examined every word with diligence. John Finch provided valuable comments on the various theoretical paradigms introduced in Chapter 1.

PAUL R. and GLENYS J. FERGUSON

■ *Chapter 1* ■

Introduction

> The main concern of economics is thus with human beings who are impelled, for good and evil, to change and progress. Fragmentary statical hypotheses are used as temporary auxiliaries to dynamic – or rather biological – conceptions: but the central idea of economics even when its Foundations alone are under discussion must be that of living force and movement (A. Marshall,1920, p. xiii).

■ *1.1* Introduction

Industrial economics is at an important stage in its development. Increasing refinements to the techniques first developed in the late nineteenth century (marginal analysis) led many economists to believe that they had an analytical framework capable of providing answers to most of the problems of industrial economics. In recent years, doubts have crept in. Controversies now surround many of the central areas of investigation, and the 'traditional' approach increasingly faces re-examination and re-evaluation.

Many economists are searching for an alternative way forward: for theoretical frameworks that better explain the issues of industrial economics. Developments are taking many directions and it may be that no one approach will provide all the answers. This book will introduce students to the debate. More recent developments will be set against a critical exposition of the traditional approach.

■ *1.2* What is industrial economics?

Industrial economics is best defined as the application of micro-economic theory to the analysis of firms, markets and industries. Stigler

1

(1968) argues that industrial economics does not really exist as a separate discipline, that it is simply differentiated microeconomics. This misses the point. The distinction arises from the overriding emphasis, in industrial economics, on empirical work and on implications for policy. Although the main focus has been on the secondary (or industrial) sector of the economy, there is no reason why study of the primary (agricultural) or tertiary (service) sectors of the economy should not also be included.

The term *industrial organisation* is commonly viewed as synonymous with *industrial economics*. It is more useful to follow Carlsson (1985, 1989) in distinguishing between them. He reasons that the main concern of industrial organisation has become the structure of 'industries' at a particular point of time. Concern with industrial organisation stems from the work of Chamberlin on monopolistic competition in the early 1930s. Mason and Bain then developed the structure–conduct–performance (SCP) paradigm, based on the neoclassical theory of the firm (essentially the models of perfect competition, monopoly and monopolistic competition together with the various models of oligopoly).

By contrast, industrial economics encompasses both industrial organisation and what Carlsson terms *industrial dynamics*, which is:

> primarily concerned with the evolution of industry as a process in time at both the macro level, the sector or industry level, and the firm level (1985, p. 6).

Industrial dynamics has its basis both in the work of Alfred Marshall and that of the Austrian School. It differs from industrial organisation in that its main focus of attention can vary from the firm, to relationships between firms, to the links between microeconomics and the macro economy. Carlsson argues that there are four main themes which encompass the subject matter of industrial dynamics:

1. The nature of economic activity in the firm and its connection to the *dynamics of supply* and therefore economic growth, particularly the role of knowledge.

2. How the *boundaries of the firm* ... and the *degree of interdependence among firms* change over time and what role this interdependence plays in economic growth.

3. The role of *technological change and the institutional framework* conducive to technological progress at both macro and micro levels.

4. The role of economic policy in facilitating or obstructing adjustment of the economy to changing circumstances (domestically as well as internationally) at both micro and macro levels – *industrial policy* (1989, p. 3).

When the economist turns the attention to industrial dynamics the area of investigation is widened to analyse topics where change is central (such as innovation) and a different perspective is taken on many of the issues of industrial organisation. For instance, where industrial organisation would be concerned with the extent to which the presence of monopoly in the economy reduces society's welfare, industrial dynamics addresses itself to the reasons why monopoly has developed, and the question of how long it might persist. To do this, analysis must draw on theories outside the neoclassical paradigm.

1.3 Theoretical foundations of industrial economics

Most 'industrial economics' texts are misnamed since they usually focus on industrial organisation. Few dwell on industrial dynamics. This book aims to cover developments in both areas of industrial economics. To do this, it will draw on a variety of theoretical approaches. To set the context for subsequent chapters it is important to identify their basic characteristics.

Table 1.1 is based on a typology suggested by Knudsen (1993). This differentiates according to whether the focus of analysis is on the decision-maker or the transaction. When considering the *decision-maker* (the entrepreneur, household, or individual), the main interest is in how groups of decision-makers interact and respond to changes in market circumstances. Williamson offers several definitions of a *transaction*, the most useful being:

when a good or service is transferred across a technologically-separable interface. One stage of processing or assembly activity terminates and another begins (1986, p. 139).

Of particular interest are those transactions which involve agreements between economic agents. The concern is with the nature of the agreement: whom it involves (managers, owners, other firms, the government), the form it takes, and the extent to which it can be monitored and policed effectively.

Table 1.1 *Economic approaches employed in this book*

Concept of rationality	Focus	
	Decision-makers	Transactions
Maximisation rationality	Neoclassical theory (SCP approach; new industrial organisation; Chicago School; public choice theory)	Principal–agent theory
Bounded rationality		Transaction cost theory (Williamson)
Procedural rationality	Austrian School; evolutionary economics	Transaction cost theory (North)

Knudsen also differentiates between economic approaches according to their treatment of *rationality*. This describes the extent to which individuals possess information and are able to process it effectively. *Maximisation rationality* implies that individuals have all the information relevant to any decision, which they are able to utilise effectively, so as to maximise profits or utility. This differs from the concept of *bounded rationality*; according to Simon:

The capacity of the human mind for formulating and solving complex problems is very small compared with the size of the problems whose solution is required for objectively rational behaviour in the real world (1957, p. 198).

This implies that individuals make decisions on the basis of partial information. However, each decision is made separately on the basis of current information. This contrasts with *procedural rationality* where general behavioural 'rules' (either innate, cultural or learned) are established and the lessons of the past are carried forward to help solve current problems. The availability of standard responses to certain types of situation facilitates decisions by providing a device for coping with a complex and changing environment.

Combining the two types of focus with the three concepts of rationality allows different theoretical approaches to be distinguished. The neoclassical approach focuses on the decision-maker in a world in which

maximisation rationality is possible. Decision-makers are able to maximise their objectives subject to the constraints imposed by technology
and market prices. This implies that decisions are made with perfect
information. Decision-makers pursue the maximisation of utility or
profits, and their objectives are attained. The logical conclusion is that
markets are forced into equilibrium. As Stigler notes:

> If the entrepreneurs in a competitive industry correctly anticipated all
> relevant future events and if they were fully able to adjust their plans,
> no disequilibrium could arise: the markets would be in full
> equilibrium at every moment of time (1963, p. 64).

If the assumption of perfect information appears extreme – and, consequently, unhelpful – it can be defended by interpreting it to mean that
decision-makers act *as if* they had perfect knowledge. Lucas argues that
where an economy has been unchanged for many years (that is, it has
achieved a steady state) decision-makers will have evolved an efficient
set of decision rules:

> I think of economics as studying decision rules that are steady states
> of some adaptive process, decision rules that are found to work over
> a range of situations and hence are no longer revised appreciably as
> more experience accumulates (1987, p. 218).

The logic of the neoclassical approach therefore makes it best suited
to the analysis of markets and economies in – or very close to –
equilibrium.

1.4 Developments within the neoclassical paradigm

The neoclassical structure–conduct–performance (SCP) approach dominated the study of industrial economics in the period after the Second
World War. Since the 1970s there has been increasing recognition that
SCP fails to give adequate insights into many issues within the field of
industrial economics. In seeking to establish a more appropriate theoretical basis, economists have followed several different paths. A résumé of
the main developments is given here and in the next section; more
detailed analysis will be introduced at appropriate junctures in the book.

Many developments have remained within the neoclassical
framework. One is the *new industrial organisation* (sometimes termed
the *new industrial economics*, or the *new empirical industrial*

organisation (Bresnahan, 1989)), which tries to sharpen the SCP approach by relating it more rigorously to neoclassical theory. Of particular note is the accommodation of advances in oligopoly and game theory. Work in this area includes that of Spence, Dixit and Stiglitz in the USA, and Cowling, Clarke and Waterson in the UK. Their refinements are widely accepted and have found their way into several recent texts with an industrial organisation focus (for instance, Tirole, 1988).

Baumol's concept of *contestability* and the contribution to industrial economics of the *Chicago School* (economists such as Stigler, Demsetz, Peltzman and Brozen) have attracted wide attention. Neither approach can be described as radical, since each still adheres firmly to the neoclassical paradigm. However, SCP and the new industrial organisation highlight monopolistic 'excesses' in various degrees. In contrast, Baumol and the Chicago School see the world as one in which competitive forces generally hold sway. As a result, they offer alternative explanations which argue that monopoly may be benign, or even beneficial, to economic welfare.

Public choice theory introduces a different element into the policy debate. Prominent in this field are Tullock and the Nobel Laureate, James Buchanan. They extend neoclassical theory to the politicians and bureaucrats responsible for the formulation and implementation of policy. Those in power are assumed to seek to maximise their own welfare. Traditionally, economists have argued that benevolent action by government can correct market failures. Analysis by public choice theorists suggests that politicians' and bureaucrats' motivations and objectives are not always altruistic. This introduces the concept of *government failure*: government intervention cannot be guaranteed to improve economic welfare.

1.5 Developments outside the neoclassical paradigm

A text on industrial economics which focuses on interactions between decision-makers and the subsequent consequences for economic welfare is useful, but incomplete. The firm of neoclassical theory is merely an abstraction (a 'black box') to aid investigation of the workings of the price mechanism. It is more useful if it can be developed into a closer approximation of a typical real-world firm: owned by shareholders, but run by a team of professional managers who face an uncertain future and take decisions based on information which is far from perfect. To provide a comprehensive treatment of industrial economics, the neoclassical theory of the firm needs to be supplemented. Developments outside the neoclassical paradigm (see **Table 1.1**) introduce significant insights into a wide range of issues and have made a notable contribution in particular areas (such as the study of innovation). Despite this, they have received limited attention and remain outside the mainstream of industrial economics.

Principal–agent theory (associated with Fama, Jensen and Meckling) lies closest to the neoclassical paradigm. It retains the assumption of maximisation rationality, while focusing on transactions in the form of contracts between the principal and his agent. The principal hires an agent to act on his behalf (for example, shareholders hire managers to run the firm profitably). However, the agent may seek to pursue different objectives from the principal. The theory assumes that both agent and principal are well informed, but that each has a different set of partial information. The world is presumed to be *risky*, such that objective probabilities can be attached to future outcomes. Surprises do not occur. The world changes about the steady state in a regular and predictable manner. Consequently, over time, the principal is able to infer the extent to which his interests are being pursued. The theory analyses the contracts which can be drawn up in order to align the agent's interests with those of the principal (for instance, tying a manager's salary to the profit performance of the firm). This approach is consistent with maximisation rationality in that it assumes contracts can be designed to achieve equilibrium solutions, with principals maximising their objectives.

The four remaining cells in **Table 1.1** list more radical developments. Collectively, they are described as *new institutional economics*. To the price and technology constraints recognised by the neoclassical approach, a third is introduced: *institutions*, which are the 'formal and informal social rules' (Knudsen, 1993, p. 269) or:

> humanly devised constraints that shape human interaction so that when we wish to greet friends on the street, drive an automobile, buy oranges, borrow money, form a business, bury our dead, or whatever, we know or can learn how to do these things (North, 1993, p. 242).

It is useful to distinguish between the institutional environment and institutional arrangements. The *institutional environment* comprises those political, social and legal groundrules that underpin production, exchange and distribution. Examples are property rights and the right of contract. *Institutional arrangements* (such as firms, clubs and political parties) exist and evolve within the institutional environment. They assist economic agents in coping efficiently in the institutional environment. For instance, by combining activities within a firm, economies of scale and scope may be achieved. All institutional arrangements are limited in the scope of their actions by the institutional environment. In the new institutional economics, institutions of both types are important. Explicit consideration is given to how they emerge and evolve, and to the ways in which they constrain the choices of economic agents.

The new institutional economics incorporates two other common themes (Langlois, 1986). Maximisation rationality is rejected, because *uncertainty* is assumed. This is fundamentally different from the concept of *risk* (sometimes, confusingly, referred to as *parametric uncertainty*). Uncertainty (sometimes termed *structural uncertainty*) means that surprises can occur because the future is unknown and unknowable. Economic agents may seek to maximise profits or utility, but surprises prevent them from attaining their goals. Secondly, attention is moved away from the analysis of equilibrium states to consideration of the process of change over time. In addition, proponents of the new institutional economics argue that the institutions themselves merit study.

Transaction cost theory is one element of the new institutional economics. Transaction costs are defined by Arrow as the 'costs of running the economic system' (1969, p. 48). Such costs contain two main elements. There are the costs involved in acquiring information and those involved in effecting transactions. Consider the case of a house purchase. Transaction costs include those incurred in locating suitable accommodation, and in arranging a structural survey to check on its 'quality', obtaining the finance, engaging a solicitor to deal with the legal aspects and hiring a removal firm. The work of Coase (and, more recently, Williamson, Kay and the 1993 Nobel Laureate, Douglass North) shows that explicit consideration of such costs offers important new perspectives. Williamson implicitly works within an unchanging institutional environment, which makes his analysis fairly static. In neoclassical theory, the firm would aim to minimise the production costs of a particular level of output; in Williamson's approach, the firm aims to minimise the sum of production and transaction costs. North takes a broader focus, arguing that the institutional environment determines – and is determined by – institutional arrangements. (For instance, firms may lobby the government for protection against foreign competition.) North's version gives more emphasis to the process of change, and more prominence to the concept of uncertainty.

The most comprehensive critique of neoclassical analysis comes from the work of the *Austrian School*. The ideas of the Austrian School originate in Menger and proponents include Mises and Hayek. Reekie and Littlechild are amongst those who have applied the Austrian approach to problems of industrial economics since the late 1970s. Austrians see competition as a process rather than as the static market structure of perfect competition. They focus on the processes by which economic agents seek to enhance their welfare through time in an uncertain and changing world. These agents' decisions are facilitated by recourse to 'rules' of behaviour, although individual economic agents may modify or reject these in the light of the specific problem. Whilst allocated to the 'procedural rationality' cell in **Table 1.1**, their analysis also recognises bounded rationality. Like the Chicago School, Austrians contend that markets are generally competitive. Such treatment can often lead to analytical conclusions and policy prescriptions which differ markedly from those of SCP analysis.

Evolutionary economics has many similarities with Austrian economics. The essential difference is the greater emphasis placed on the role of *routines* (defined as the repositories of knowledge about how to undertake various tasks), and the lesser emphasis on the actions of individual economic agents. Under pressure from its environment, a firm should develop more efficient routines over time. Firms which do not evolve become uncompetitive and may fail. The theory's principal contribution has been to the study of innovation (through the work of Schumpeter, Nelson and Winter) and of the links between the micro- and macroeconomy (through the work of Eliasson).

■ *1.6* Evaluation criteria

The aim of the industrial economist is essentially the same as that of economists working in other fields. It is to describe, to explain and to draw inferences about the effectiveness with which scarce resources are used; to consider how the coordination of diverse economic activity is achieved; and to comment on policies. This requires the establishment of criteria against which changes can be judged.

The yardstick invariably chosen is the impact of each change on the economic welfare of society as a whole. This book is no exception. Adopting the *potential Pareto improvement (PPI) criterion*, overall welfare is enhanced by change as long as those who benefit are (theoretically) capable of compensating the losers while, themselves, remaining better off. In most neoclassically-based texts, the concern is with the allocation of resources in a framework in which tastes, techniques and resources are constant and known. This approach glosses over the change and uncertainty that characterise the real world of industrial economics: the future cannot be predicted with confidence; unforeseen developments may occur. In all such circumstances, the static approach to welfare is inappropriate, and, if applied, may give rise to misleading conclusions.

Uncertainty rules out any precise measurement of the magnitude and direction of changes in welfare. Indeed Austrian economists argue that since it is impossible to anticipate the entire consequences of any action, any attempt to calculate the effect on overall economic welfare is pointless. However, a qualitative analysis can still give important guidelines to policy-makers. By showing some of the ways in which changes will affect the operation of industry, it may be possible to deduce some of the costs and benefits of such changes.

The different theoretical approaches detailed in **Table 1.1** suggest other criteria that can be employed in any attempt to appraise economic welfare and contribute to the formulation of policy. North's transaction cost approach would look to the structure of the institutional environment, and how conducive it is to the formation of institutional arrangements beneficial to society. For instance, does the institutional environment provide incentives to individuals to invest in the acquisition of socially useful knowledge and skills? Austrian economists argue that the purpose of an economic system is to permit each individual to make the fullest use of his talents or, as Kirzner puts it, by 'the degree to which currently known information is optimally deployed' (1973, p. 235). Austrians consider that anything which prevents innovation and change is undesirable, and that the economic system should encourage economic agents to collect information and use it effectively.

■ *1.7* Issues discussed in this book

This book considers major issues within the field of industrial economics. Issues related to industrial dynamics can be rigorously explored by using other theories in parallel with the neoclassical approach. Although this places greater demands on readers, it permits the book to include more explicit consideration of advertising and the process of innovation, and offers a more coherent framework for the discussion of industry policy and deindustrialisation than is found in texts with an industrial organisation focus. Moreover, incorporating a variety of theoretical perspectives means that there may be a number of rival solutions to any particular problem, and a range of policy implications can be drawn.

Chapter 2 introduces in detail the SCP approach to industrial economics, the contribution of the Chicago School, the concept of contestability, developments made by the new industrial organisation, and the work of the Austrian School – several of the main theoretical approaches which recur throughout the book. Following an exposition of the established SCP paradigm, the chapter focuses on the limitations of this technique, many of which can be traced back to its foundation in neoclassical theory. This leads to a more detailed consideration of the alternative theoretical approach of Austrian economics.

Market concentration plays a central part in the SCP approach. Chapter 3 critically appraises the most widely used of the measures of market concentration, and considers the extent to which market concentration levels are altered by incorporating the effects of international competition. The widespread reliance on these measures is questioned from the perspectives of the Chicago and Austrian Schools.

It has traditionally been accepted that advertising and monopoly reduce economic welfare. Chapters 4 and 5 reconsider this viewpoint and argue that such a conclusion is crucially dependent on the theoretical approach adopted. In particular, Austrian theory can present both phenomena as welfare-enhancing – advertising performing a worthwhile role by providing information, whilst monopoly may be simply the result of beneficial product or process innovation.

Chapter 6 concentrates on the role and effects of innovation. Innovation is difficult to incorporate within the static neoclassical framework. In contrast, analysis of change under conditions of uncertainty is central to both Austrian and to evolutionary economics and the chapter discusses their important contributions in this area. The book then moves to a more explicit discussion of policy. Chapter 7 considers the theoretical case for industry policy, and shows that 'market failure' arguments are critically dependent on the recognition of transaction costs. Chapter 8 considers the types of industry policy adopted in the UK, USA and European Community (EC) in the areas of competition policy, regional development, innovation and trade. In identifying and evaluating the various stances on industry policy, these chapters draw on the theoretical work of earlier chapters. The contributions of public choice theory are also included here.

Chapters 9 and 10 focus on topical issues of the 1990s. Traditional arguments for state control of certain sectors of industry are re-examined in Chapter 9. The economic rationale for the reduction of state control (privatisation) is considered in detail. Chapter 10 confronts the issue of deindustrialisation. This subject has typically been analysed at a macroeconomic level, and with limited attention given to developments in the service sector. Consideration of the decline in the manufacturing base from the viewpoint of industrial economics introduces additional insights. This is another area where the relevance of neoclassical analysis is questioned and where the Austrian view is more illuminating because of its ability to incorporate change.

■ *1.8* Guide to further reading

It is presumed that readers will already have a grounding in neoclassical microeconomics, particularly with regard to the theory of the firm. The book will extend this understanding, and introduce other theoretical treatments. However, this text aims to apply theories, rather than to present a comprehensive exposition. Readers wishing to deepen their theoretical understanding are referred to the books listed below.

There are a number of articles relevant to the various methodologies listed in Table 1.1. in U. Mäki, B. Gustafsson and C. Knudsen (eds.), *Rationality, Institutions and Economic Methodology* (London: Routledge, 1993). U. Mäki's article 'Social Theories of Science and the Fate of Institutionalism in Economics' provides an interesting explanation of the dominance of the neoclassical paradigm. The article by R. N. Langlois and L. Csontos, 'Optimisation, Rule-following and the Methodology of Situational Analysis', develops the different concepts of rationality.

Principal–agent theory is surveyed in M. Jensen, 'Organisation Theory and Methodology', *Accounting Review*, vol. 50 (1983) pp. 319–39.

A basic introduction to transaction cost economics is given in P. R. Ferguson, G. J. Ferguson and R. Rothschild, *Business Economics* (Basingstoke: Macmillan, 1993). A full exposition of Williamson's ideas is found in O. E. Williamson, *Markets and Hierarchies: Analysis and Antitrust Implications* (New York: Free Press, 1975) and O. E. Williamson, *The Economic Institutions of Capitalism* (New York: Free Press, 1985). A critique of Williamson, and a different perspective on transaction costs is given in N. M. Kay, *The Emergent Firm* (London: Macmillan, 1984) and N. M. Kay, 'Markets, False Hierarchies and the Evolution of the Modern Firm', *Journal of Economic Behaviour and Organisation*, vol. 17 (1992) pp. 315–33. North's views on transaction costs are developed in D. North, *Institutions, Institutional Change and Economic Performance* (Cambridge: University Press, 1990).

An easy and comprehensive introduction to Austrian economics is to be found in A. H. Shand, *The Capitalist Alternative* (Brighton: Wheatsheaf, 1984). A shorter introduction is contained in S. C. Littlechild, *The Fallacy of the Mixed Economy*, 2nd ed. (London: Institute of Economic Affairs, 1986a).

Two good applications of evolutionary economics are found in R. R. Nelson and S. G. Winter, *An Evolutionary Theory of Economic Change* (Cambridge, Mass.:Harvard University Press, 1982) and G. Eliasson, 'Modelling the Experimentally Organised Economy', *Journal of Economic Behaviour and Organisation*, vol. 16 (1991) pp. 153–82.

■ *Chapter 2* ■

The Structure–Conduct–Performance Paradigm

Economics, like every other science, started with the investigation of 'local' relations between two or more economic quantities ... It was but slowly that the fact began to dawn upon analysts that there is a pervading interdependence between all economic phenomena, that they all hang together somehow (J. Schumpeter, 1954, p. 242).

■ 2.1 Introduction

The structure–conduct–performance (SCP) approach – based exclusively upon neoclassical theory – has long been central to the study of industrial organisation (**Section 1.2**). SCP postulates causal relationships between the structure of a market, the conduct of firms in that market and economic performance. It has been used to provide the theoretical justification for competition policy (**Sections 8.3–8.9**). Here SCP has provided the rationale for measures intended to modify (or to prevent) the development of market structures likely to promote behaviour and performance detrimental to the public interest.

In recent years, the SCP approach has been subject to widespread criticism. Some suggest that the relationships between structure, conduct and performance are more complex than originally envisaged. It is argued that the technique is too loosely derived from its theoretical underpinnings, and this has led to various developments, including attempts to link SCP more rigorously (if more narrowly) back to neoclassical theory. Others have disputed the relevance of neoclassical microeconomics to the study of industry. They consider that the SCP approach gives too limited a perspective on the operations of markets, and that it provides a poor (and even misleading) basis for policy formulation.

■ 2.2 What is structure?

Structure describes the characteristics and composition of markets and industries in an economy. At its most aggregated level, it relates to the relative importance of broadly defined sectors of the economy. Here the focus is on the relative sizes of (and trends in) the primary (agriculture and the extractive industries), secondary (industrial) and tertiary (service) sectors. This is the view of structure adopted in Chapter 10, which examines the recent decline in the industrial sectors of many advanced economies.

Secondly, structure can refer to the number and size distribution of firms in the economy as a whole. For instance, in the UK data are collected on the share of total output provided by the largest 100 firms. *Fortune* magazine provides an annual directory of the largest 500 firms in the USA, whilst the UK's *Financial Times* ranks Europe's top 500 firms in terms of market capitalisation. There could be far-reaching political and economic implications if such firms became progressively more dominant. The economic consequences are the subject of Chapter 5.

Structure also relates to the importance and characteristics of individual markets within the economy. This is the sense of the term within the SCP approach. Structure describes the environment within which firms in a particular market operate. It can be identified by considering the number and size distribution of buyers and sellers (*market concentration*), the extent to which products are differentiated, how easy it is for other firms to enter the market, and the extent to which firms are integrated or diversified. These are just the principal structural characteristics; McKie (1970, p. 9) cites more than twenty factors.

■ 2.3 Conduct and performance

Conduct refers to the behaviour (actions) of the firms in a market: to the decisions firms make and to the way in which decisions are taken. It focuses on how firms set prices, whether independently or in collusion with others in the market. How firms decide on their advertising and research budgets, and how much expenditure is devoted to these activities, are also typical considerations. These factors are often more difficult to identify empirically than either structural or performance characteristics.

The economist's concern is with the *performance* of firms. The essential question is whether or not firms' operations enhance economic welfare. The usual consideration is how well firms satisfy consumer requirements in the current time period. That is, are they being *productively efficient*, avoiding wasteful use of available factors of production? Also, are they being *allocatively efficient* in producing the 'right' goods and in the 'right' quantities? Light may be shed on these issues by considering aspects of performance such as the relationship between prices and costs, and the level of profits earned.

In a world where tastes do not change and where consumers and producers are perfectly informed, economic welfare would be maximised when the Pareto marginal conditions are fulfilled (see, for instance, George and Shorey (1978) for an exposition of these criteria). This requires firms to set price equal to marginal cost. In the neoclassical model of perfect competition, firms maximise profits by equating price and marginal cost, which results in a price and output combination that is both productively and allocatively efficient.

Inferior performance is expected in markets that match the neoclassical models of monopoly, oligopoly or monopolistic competition. Although firms may be productively efficient, the level of output is unlikely to meet the requirements of allocative efficiency. This arises because firms in such markets possess a degree of *market* (or *monopoly*) *power*: that is, they have some discretion in determining the price at which to sell their output. Unlike in the model of perfect competition, they are able to raise price above the level of marginal cost. The *Lerner index* (1934) or *price–cost margin* presents one theoretical measure of market power:

Lerner index = (Price – Marginal cost) / Price

A Lerner index of zero would be recorded by a perfectly competitive firm; the closer the index is to 1, the greater the market power.

High profits are another sign of market power and poor economic performance. Despite data complications, appropriate measures can usually be constructed (**Section 2.9**). But, as with pricing, it is an indicator of current (or past) performance, yielding few insights into how well firms will perform in satisfying consumer wants over time. Although early proponents paid lip-service to technological progressiveness as a desirable performance characteristic, the essential concern of the SCP approach has been with effects on current economic welfare.

■ 2.4 The SCP approach explained

The SCP approach argues that performance is determined by the conduct of firms, which in turn is determined by the structural characteristics of the market (**Figure 2.1**). The linkage between structure, conduct and performance then turns on 'matching' the structural characteristics against the models of perfect competition, monopoly, monopolistic competition and oligopoly. This technique was first formalised by Mason (1939). His detailed case study approach was modified by Bain (1951) who sought to draw more generalised conclusions from large sample, cross-section studies.

As an illustration, **Table 2.1** contrasts the structures of two different markets. Market 1 displays the characteristics expected under perfect competition. From this, deductions can be made about conduct. The large number of competitors leaves firms with no choice but to act independently in determining price and output levels. Individual firms will be unable to influence (and have no reason to depart from) the price determined by the market. This suggests that price will tend towards marginal cost and, in the long run, firms will earn normal profits. Production is allocatively and productively efficient to the greater benefit of current economic welfare.

The attractiveness of this approach lies in the straightforwardness of the chain of reasoning and the relative ease with which structural characteristics can be identified. Furthermore, it gives clear guidance to policy-makers; performance can be improved by actions designed to

Figure 2.1   *The traditional SCP approach*

Table 2.1 *Comparison of the structures of two hypothetical markets*

Structural characteristics	Market 1	Market 2
Number of firms	Many firms each with a small market share	Four firms with similar market shares
Number of buyers	Many	Few
Nature of product	Homogeneous	Differentiated
Entry barriers	Low	Substantial

influence the structure of particular markets. In some cases, analysis of conduct is superfluous (for instance, in Market 1). Performance can be predicted directly from a consideration of market structure because structural conditions yield sufficient information to deduce how firms *must* behave. Similar considerations apply where markets approximate conditions of monopoly.

Bypassing conduct in all situations can lead to misleading inferences where markets display the features of oligopoly. This is the case with Market 2 (**Table 2.1**) where the small number of equal-sized firms suggests that price, advertising and other aspects of firm behaviour are likely to be decided collusively. This would produce a higher price and lower level of output compared with the perfectly competitive situation. But the structure of the market does not guarantee collusive behaviour. The oligopolists may compete for increased market share with the result that price is kept close to the perfectly competitive level, to give an acceptable level of economic performance. In oligopolistic markets, analysis of conduct is an essential component of the SCP approach. Otherwise only limited conclusions can be drawn; certain types of market structure are more likely to suggest beneficial or adverse performance.

2.5 Relationships between structure, conduct and performance

The traditional premise that market structure is exogenously determined is unsound. Performance – and more particularly conduct – affect structure. For instance, mergers directly affect the number and size distribution of firms in the market, innovation and advertising may raise entry barriers, predatory pricing could force competitors out of the market. If market structure gives rise to conduct which raises prices and

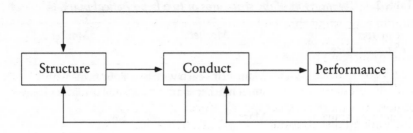

Figure 2.2 *More complex relationship between structure, conduct and performance*

enhances profits, then this may attract entry, modifying the structure of the market. Furthermore, the various structural elements are unlikely to be independent so that, for example, market concentration is likely to bear some relationship to the height of the entry barriers. Recognising these complications, Koch modifies the definition of structure:

> the relatively permanent strategic elements of the environment of a firm that influence, and are influenced by, the conduct and performance of the firm in the market in which it operates (1980, p. 90).

Figure 2.2 shows how the SCP approach may be adapted to incorporate these more complex linkages, but the essential causality still flows from structural criteria.

 ## 2.6 Neoclassical developments of the SCP approach

Baumol (1982) casts another light on the relationships between structure, conduct and performance. His idea of *contestable markets* implies that a particular market structure does not necessarily equate with a particular type of performance. Markets are contestable where the costs facing new entrants are similar to those of firms already in the market and where a firm leaving the market is able to salvage its capital costs, minus depreciation (hence, there are no *sunk costs*). The implication is that there are no barriers to entry or exit, so monopoly profits cannot exist. The mere threat of entry forces existing firms to minimise their production and distribution costs and, thereby, influences the structure of the market. Regardless of the structure that emerges, contestability automatically ensures that good performance will result.

Earlier, Demsetz (1973) (Chicago School) came to a similar conclusion in suggesting that high profits may be a sign not of market power but of efficiency. Since, in any market, the firm with the lowest costs will tend to increase in size and market share over time, there will be a tendency for market concentration to increase but, at the same time, there will be pressure on all firms to be efficient. Consequently, Demsetz argues that market structure will develop into that which enables production and distribution to be undertaken at least cost.

Proponents of the new industrial organisation (**Section 1.4**) seek to integrate industrial economics more closely with neoclassical theory (for instance, Cowling and Waterson, 1976; Clarke and Davies, 1982; Tirole, 1988). In so doing, they have moved away from the emphasis upon structure, arguing that conduct is the key element, interacting both with structure (through the choice of output level) and performance. Nevertheless, the structural measure of market concentration is accorded a central role. Donsimoni *et al.* note that: 'it is *the only* piece of information needed to proxy performance' (1984, p. 424).

The new industrial organisation makes use of precisely specified neoclassical models, particularly those of oligopoly. They adopt quite a narrow view of performance, being primarily concerned with the static consideration of the extent to which prices are elevated above costs as encapsulated by the Lerner index. (Analysis of the Cournot model in Appendix 1 offers an introduction to the methodology of this approach.) These studies are more rigorously grounded in economic theory than the traditional SCP approach, but as a result they take a very narrow focus. For instance, innovation is often modelled using game theory by making the strong assumptions that the number of firms, the state of consumer tastes, and – more significantly – the profits to be gained from successful innovation are all known. The ability of the new industrial organisation to yield insights into many real world problems is limited by the restrictive nature of the models. However it does introduce an extra element into the policy debate by suggesting that government efforts to improve performance by manipulating structure are misplaced: they will fail to produce the requisite (but subtle) changes in conduct.

■ 2.7 Entry barriers

Even where it is accepted that structure determines performance in some predictable way, the validity of the SCP approach is undermined if there is no unanimity over which structural characteristics are important, or how the presence of particular characteristics is to be interpreted. These points can be illustrated by considering the various views of entry barriers. (Market concentration, the structural characteristic most frequently used in empirical studies, forms the subject of Chapter 3.)

The concept of entry barriers was pioneered by Bain (1956). He defined a *barrier to entry* as anything which places potential entrants at a competitive disadvantage compared with established firms, so that established firms are able to earn abnormal profits over the long run. The height of the entry barrier determines the magnitude of such long-run profits. Bain identified three main types of barrier: *absolute cost*, *economies of scale* and *product differentiation*. Patents, access to superior resources, or lower-cost finance are sources of absolute cost advantage. Even where cost functions are similar, economies of scale may give the established firm an advantage. First, the new entrant may operate at a scale which is too small to realise fully potential cost savings. Secondly, an entrant which is able to operate at sufficient scale to realise such economies may find that the consequent increase in market output (assuming established firms maintain their pre-entry output levels) depresses the market price below average cost. Here, the established firms' advantage will depend upon the height of the entry barriers and the extent to which they convince a potential entrant that its extra output will have a large effect on price. Bain's third barrier – product differentiation – arises from the existing firms having established products which have built up consumer goodwill. While new entrants may be capable of producing functionally identical products at similar cost, they will be at a disadvantage because they must either spend more on promotion, or reduce their price to gain custom.

Stigler (Chicago School) suggested that entry barriers are generally less formidable. This follows from his alternative definition of entry barriers:

> a cost of producing ... which must be borne by a firm which seeks to enter an industry but is not borne by firms already in the industry (1968, p. 67).

This means that product differentiation, for instance, is unlikely to act as a barrier because firms already in the market must, themselves, have previously incurred the costs of establishing goodwill. Similarly, scale economies accruing to an established firm are the result of being first in the field. Many of Bain's barriers simply reflect the date of a firm's entry (and are more precisely termed first-mover advantages).

First-mover advantages cause barriers of the Bain and, sometimes, the Stigler type. First-mover advantages occur when the innovating firm retains a competitive advantage from being first in the field (for a survey, see Lieberman and Montgomery, 1988). Ownership of patents and the pre-emption of scarce resources are examples, as are reputation effects. Being a pioneer – as in the case of Hoover with the vacuum cleaner – may generate a favourable reputation which endures over time and carries over to the firm's other products, forcing the later entrant to incur even greater expenditure if it is to overcome this disadvantage. Even where reputation effects are absent, first-mover advantages introduce a cost asymmetry between the incumbent and the potential entrant. The first firm to enter a market may face low promotion costs because it has no rivals. Later entrants' promotion costs may be higher because they have to face a competitor. The incumbent has already invested in assets whose function is specific to its market (such as highly specialised machinery). If the firm chose to leave the market, such assets would have no value (*asset specificity* gives rise to sunk costs). To enter a market where asset-specific investments are important, the new firm will have to make a major commitment. This has an important implication: the profits from operating in the market are not the only consideration for the entrant; it will also take into account the degree to which costs can be recovered if entry proves unsuccessful.

Established firms may themselves undertake measures to raise entry barriers (conduct impinging on structure). Incumbent firms realise that for entry to occur a potential entrant has to believe abnormal profits will be earned. This depends on how the post-entry price compares with the potential entrant's unit costs. Incumbents may reduce the entrant's potential to earn abnormal profits by lowering price to the *limit-price*, defined by Bain as:

> the extent to which, in the long run, established firms can elevate their selling prices above the minimal average costs ... without inducing potential entrants to enter an industry (1968, p. 252).

The higher the entry barriers, the higher the limit-price.

However, incumbents forgo certain profits by limit-pricing. Other actions to reduce the entrant's profit expectations may prove less costly. A mixture of threats and bluffs may be used. To estimate the market price post entry, a potential entrant needs to gauge the likely response of established firms. The post-entry price will fall if incumbents maintain their existing output levels; it will fall even more if they expand their output levels. However such a threat has to be made credible to be effective since, unless committed to high rates of output, established firms will find it more profitable to accommodate the entrant by cutting production. This is a subject widely investigated in the new industrial organisation literature. Dixit (1982) suggests that, if established firms choose capital intensive production methods (which involve large sunk costs) whose profitability depends on high rates of capacity utilisation, they are making a commitment that will give credibility to threats to deter entry. Likewise Spence (1977) argues that credibility can be enhanced by building excess capacity. First, this may generate less favourable expectations of profitable entry. Secondly, it may strengthen the established firms' ability to engage in a price war.

The extent to which any of these factors acts a barrier to entry depends on the nature of the entrant. Bain's work implicitly assumes that those seeking to enter a market will typically be new, small firms building their own facilities. However, access to a market may prove easier for a newly formed firm if it takes over the facilities of an incumbent. In opposition to Bain, Andrews (1964) argued that entry is much more likely to come from established multi-product firms (probably already in the same industry) which decide to add an extra product to their range by entering a new market. The entry barriers facing such firms will be much lower. Such a firm's prospects may still vary according to the way in which it chooses to enter the market (by altering the product mix of its existing plant, by building new plant or by takeover). These different entry routes are also open to foreign firms, who have the additional option of serving the market by exporting from their home base.

■ 2.8 Tests of SCP

The SCP approach has spawned a wide variety of empirical work. The principal tests have sought to relate profits (or price) to:

1. market concentration;
2. market concentration plus entry barriers;
3. differences in relative or absolute firm size causing differences in efficiency or in the rate of innovation;
4. differential growth rates which imply that markets are in disequilibrium;
5. the level of advertising relative to sales (*advertising intensity*).

Empirical work on relationship 5 is considered in Chapter 4; relationships 1–4 are considered in Chapter 5. Many of the tests using regression analysis purport to show significant results. However there is a problem as to their interpretation: a significant relationship says nothing about the direction of causation. A strong positive relationship between profits and, say, advertising intensity may be evidence of market power, the causation running from structure to performance. Equally it could be consistent with an argument that higher profits result in a larger advertising budget (Chapter 4).

In addition, doubt has been cast on the validity of the empirical tests undertaken. Donsimoni *et al.* (1984) suggest that exercises seeking to relate profits to several structural variables are certain to yield some correlation. On the other hand, tests that focus on particular aspects of market structure may yield results that are not robust. Minor changes to the specification of the other characteristics of the model may produce quite contrary results because the researcher has failed to specify carefully the rest of the model. In checking for sensitivity in the specification of the model, Bothwell *et al.* (1984) charge that only the relative firm size and advertising hypotheses could be supported. Likewise, Koch (1974) notes that a strong relationship between concentration and price–cost margins may even disappear when other structural variables are introduced.

■ 2.9 Problems of measuring variables

Any tests of SCP face a number of practical problems. For instance, in studies of profitability there is the difficulty that profit by itself is an incomplete measure. Some businesses experience greater variability of earnings (usually measured by *beta* – **Section 5.12**), and so require higher returns to compensate (Sharpe, 1964; Lintner, 1965). Empirical studies should take this into account when studying the relationship with profit. If earnings variability is positively related to concentration, then any positive relationship between profits and concentration may reflect this influence rather than market power.

The choice of profit measure is itself a fundamental issue. Empirical studies have used *accounting rate of return on assets*, *accounting rate of return on equity*, the *Census price–cost margin* (the value of sales less the costs of bought-in materials and the wage bill divided by the value of sales) and *Tobin's q* (the ratio of a firm's stock market value to its replacement value). A firm's entry to (or exit from) a market is in response to differences in returns on assets (after adjustment for variability in earnings), so theoretically this should be the profit measure of choice. However, the treatment of depreciation means that accounting measures may bear little resemblance to the true return (Fisher and McGowan, 1983). Another serious deficiency occurs where a firm's main source of competitive advantage comes from the deployment of long-lived intangible assets, such as reputation and brands. Accounting standards prevent the real value of these assets being incorporated into company accounts, which can bias profitability estimates in cross-section studies and overstate the stability of profits over time.

The greater a firm's ability to earn profits on a given set of assets, the more attractive it will be to equity-holders. This will raise the firm's market value, increasing its Tobin's q. However, this measure of profitability suffers from the serious drawback of having to estimate a firm's replacement value. The Census price–cost margin has the advantage of being closely related to the Lerner index (**Section 2.3**). Its disadvantage is that the exclusion of capital costs and advertising expenses inflates margins in those industries where capital and advertising intensities are high. Moreover Liebowitz (1982) observed that when this problem was corrected, the price–cost margin failed to correlate well with other measures of profitability.

A plausible measure of entry barriers has proved particularly elusive. Bain (1956) relied upon subjective judgement, Orr (1974) constructed an index, Kessides (1990, 1991) considered the ratio of sunk to total costs, but sunk costs are a function of the degree of asset specificity (**Section 2.7**) and this presents considerable measurement problems. Andersen and Rynning (1991) used the novel approach of asking firms' chief executives to rank entry barriers subjectively on a five-point scale.

There is the related problem of measuring entry. Is it the number of new firms, their market penetration, net entry (number of entrants minus the number of exits) or net market penetration (the market share of new entrants minus the share of those firms leaving) that is important? In part it depends on the impact of entrants upon the market structure. The net measures may be more appropriate if entrants simply displace existing small firms, since the traditional concept of entry envisages an increase in the number of suppliers. However, if the interest is with the potential extent of competition, then the number of new firms alone is relevant. Market penetration is appropriate for judging the influence on the market new entrants are likely to exert. This is linked to a further issue: the identity of the new entrant (**Section 2.7**). Bain's entrant (the newly formed business setting up from scratch) is likely to find entry far harder than a multinational entering a new geographical market by taking over the facilities of an existing producer.

■ 2.10 Markets and industries

In empirical tests of the SCP approach it is important to distinguish between 'markets' and 'industries'. *Markets* group together firms whose products are close substitutes from the buyers' point of view (product demand side). Cross-elasticity of demand would be high between products within the market and low against products of other markets. However, it is not always easy to identify clear boundaries. Cars of all types can be considered to belong to the same basic market – that for motorised, personal transport – but a medium-sized family saloon is hardly a close substitute for a sports car or a luxury saloon. To buyers, a Fiat Cinquecento is not in the same market as a Porsche 968 and a low cross-elasticity would be expected. As competition authorities have found, 'the market' needs to be defined with care. The European Commission's interpretation of dominance in the market for metal containers in the Continental Can case was over-ruled by the European Court on the grounds that plastic and glass containers belong to the same market (Swann, 1983).

There is also a geographic dimension to the market. Petrol stations in Paris will serve different customers from those in Lyon, but for gold bullion the market is worldwide. In implementing competition policy, the Commission of the European Communities considers:

> The definition of the geographic reference market in particular aims to group together those undertakings capable of exerting an effective competitive constraint on the market behaviour of firms (1992a, p. 43).

The competition authorities in the USA delineate the market according to whether a hypothetical, profit-maximising supplier would find it profitable to raise the price of the products by a 'small, but significant and non-transitory' amount, which is usually taken to be 5 per cent.

In contrast, the term *industry* is best used to refer to product groups which are close substitutes from the suppliers' viewpoint (product supply side). All car types plus buses, coaches and trucks may be grouped into the same industry because such products are fairly close substitutes in production, using similar processes, similar raw materials and requiring similar employee skills. If truck manufacturers thought bus production profitable they could easily extend their product range. An industry, therefore, can be defined as comprising firms which have the ability to produce, relatively rapidly, the products of any of the other firms in the group. These are usually (but not always) broader groupings than markets. One exception is the energy market which covers firms in the coal, electricity supply, gas and oil industries.

For purposes of analysing the price and output levels of a particular product, the market will be the more relevant concept. When considering new entry into a market, this is most likely to come from firms which are closely related on the production side (the industry).

These are the firms which are most likely to identify abnormal profits, and against which barriers to entry are likely to be low. For instance, Jones and Cockerill (1984) noted that there was considerable entry into pharmaceuticals in the period 1950–66, mainly from other parts of the chemical industry, such as organic chemicals, dyestuffs and cosmetics.

■ 2.11 Use of data at the level of the firm

Research into industrial economics has recently tended to switch attention from the use of data at the level of the industry to firm-level data. However, this trend is questionable when the intention is to analyse the market. Studies using firm-level data have focused on medium and large firms (for example, Mueller, 1986; Cubbin and Geroski, 1987a). These are typically multi-product and multi-market, so that, in raw form, such data give a poor approximation to the theoretical concept of the market. Researchers studying the USA can minimise this problem if they can gain access to the Federal Trade Commission's Line of Business Survey. For certain years, information on pre-tax profit, advertising, research and development, assets, market share and the extent of integration/diversification is available for each area of the multi-product firm's operations.

Another difficulty with data at the level of the firm is the lack of standardisation in accounting conventions which complicates direct comparisons. For example, a firm reporting high profits in its accounts may not be earning abnormal economic profits. Fisher and McGowan argue:

> there is no way in which one can look at accounting rates of return and infer anything about relative economic profitability or, a fortiori, about the presence or absence of monopoly profits (1983, p. 90).

For example, the UK retailer, Marks and Spencer, has had a high rate of return on capital employed for many years, but few would deny that it operates in a competitive environment. Some of its main assets – such as the goodwill of its customers and the value of the *St Michael* brand – are excluded from the accounts.

Until it is possible to overcome such deficiencies, the use of firm-level data does not offer obvious advantages over industry data as a means to approximate the market. However, the particular focus of the empirical work itself influences the choice of data source. For instance, industry data are more relevant to the study of market profitability, since the fact that one or two firms within the market may have persistent high profits is not of direct interest to the question in hand. For a study of the relationship between efficiency and firm size, the more useful data are at the level of the firm.

■ *2.12* Changes in market structure

Many empirical studies of SCP use cross-section data. This is appropriate only if the structure of the market is stable, otherwise some firms are in disequilibrium, which creates difficulties in tracing the causal linkages between structure, conduct and performance. In practice, market stability is unlikely. Barriers to entry and the extent of product differentiation alter continuously over time. Moreover, the number and size distribution of firms in a market also change. Of the largest 100 firms in the UK in 1968, 36 had not been in the top 100 ten years earlier, and 52 had not been in the top 100 in 1948 (Whittington, 1972). Likewise, for the USA, Caves (1980) notes that of the 50 largest companies in 1972, only half had been in that group in 1947, and five had not even been in the largest 200. Such changes can be brought about by mergers and differential rates of firm growth caused by different responses to technological developments and to changes in the pattern of demand. In addition, there may be a purely stochastic explanation for changes in relative firm sizes: if a fixed number of firms were to face the same probability distribution of growth rates (which are independent of past growth rates) then Gibrat's Law (1931) will apply. This states that, even where all firms are initially identical in size, chance application of randomly selected growth rates will eventually produce a size distribution that is log normal. In other words, markets will become progressively dominated by fewer firms.

■ *2.13* The neoclassical basis

The inability to handle changes in market structure is but one limitation of the SCP approach. Others relate specifically to its neoclassical foundations. In the models of perfect competition, monopolistic competition, oligopoly (with some exceptions) and monopoly, the usual objective of the firm is to maximise profits subject to cost and revenue constraints. These models are static. They show the equilibrium properties of markets, but fail to show the paths by which new equilibria are reached. This focus stems automatically from the assumptions that producers and consumers are perfectly informed (of both current and future states of the world) and that tastes are constant. In such a framework, there can be no uncertainty, and, implicitly, no transaction costs. Demsetz catalogues the limitations of the model of perfect competition:

> It ignores *technological competition* by taking technology as given. It neglects *competition by size of firm* by assuming that the atomistically sized firm is the efficiently sized firm. It offers no productive role for *reputational competition* because it assumes full knowledge of prices and goods, and it ignores *competition to change demands* by taking tastes as given and fully known (1992, p. 209).

This seriously limits the applicability of the SCP models.

Furthermore, in focusing on these different models, the SCP approach implicitly incorporates the neoclassical view that competition implies a certain market structure. This generally leads to the recommendation that good performance can be encouraged by an industry policy which favours the perfectly competitive ideal. This view is blinkered because of its narrow concept of 'good' performance. How well an economy satisfies current consumer wants is important, but so too is future economic welfare. People generally wish to enjoy a stream of satisfaction over time. The achievement of this objective may well require policy recommendations at variance with those designed to maximise satisfaction in any particular time period.

Attention can be drawn to these aspects by taking a wider view of competition. The term can also describe rivalrous behaviour but, more significantly, it can describe *the process* by which efficient firms grow and prosper. Early economists were well aware both of this concept of competition and of the wider view of performance. For instance, Blaug notes about Adam Smith:

> It is true to say, however, that his [Smith's] own faith in the benefits of 'the invisible hand' rested very little upon static considerations of allocative efficiency. A decentralised price system was held to be desirable because of its dynamic effects in widening the scope of the market and extending the advantages of the division of labour – in short, because it was a powerful engine for promoting the accumulation of capital and the growth of income (1968, p. 62).

Similarly, Marshall's insight into competition was much clearer than many of his successors':

> it is especially needful to remember that economic problems are imperfectly presented when they are treated as problems of statical equilibrium, and not of organic growth. For though the statical

treatment alone can give us definiteness and precision of thought, and is therefore a necessary introduction to a more philosophic treatment of society as an organism, it is yet only an introduction (1920, p. 382).

More recently this view of competition has been propounded by Clark and Andrews and by many new institutional economists, particularly proponents of the Austrian School, but (as yet) without seriously threatening the central status accorded to the neoclassical view of competition as a market structure.

▌ 2.14 The contributions of Clark and Andrews

Clark (1940) realised the limitations of the perfect competition model and the dangers of using it as a yardstick for judging markets. He argued that economic welfare would generally be enhanced by markets whose structure departs from the perfectly competitive reference, because they were likely to generate a superior level of performance over time. Inferior current want satisfaction (because of the presence of allocative inefficiency) is tolerable if the current reduction in welfare can be more than compensated for by future gains. Recognising this, Clark introduced the concept of *workable competition*, by which he meant the conditions necessary for competition as a process to exist. Various authors have suggested characteristics required to ensure that dynamic or workable competition can take place. These have been summarised by Sosnick (1958) and the most important are shown in **Table 2.2**.

Clark attempted to work within the framework of conventional analysis, with modifications to create a broader view of competition. Perhaps he would have been more successful if he had rejected the neoclassical paradigm. His modifications are such that the resultant criteria for a desirable market structure are unworkable. In a world of uncertainty the form of market structure which would maximise welfare over time is unknown. It is impossible to say of any existing market structure what is 'excessive', or what counts as 'unfair'. Consequently, workable competition has been abandoned.

Andrews's critique of neoclassical theory was more substantial, but still made little impression. He believed this view hampered the development of industrial economics and suggested that:

A theory of industrial structure must, indeed, get entangled with the flux and stresses of the real world which orthodox constructions of

Table 2.2 *The characteristics of workable competition*

Structure

1.   An appreciable number of firms with no single firm dominant

2.   Moderate quality differentials that are sensitive to price changes

3.   No artificial barriers to entry or exit, including the absence of legal restrictions

4.   Reasonable information flows

Conduct

1.   No collusion, but rivalry between firms

2.   No unfair, exclusionary or predatory behaviour

3.   No misleading promotional activity

Performance

1.   Productive and allocative efficiency

2.   Promotion expenses kept to reasonable levels

3.   Profits should be sufficient to reward investment and encourage innovation

4.   Responsive to possibilities for improving products and processes

static marginalist equilibrium theories have kept outside their analysis (1964, p. 84).

By limiting economists' perceptions of the world, the neoclassical approach results in failure to recognise the forms of competition actually present. Extending the ideas of Alfred Marshall, Andrews regarded competition as a process, coining the term *open competition* to describe an industry open to the entry of new competition. From this different interpretation of competition and Andrews's view that entry barriers would generally be low, can the conclusion be drawn that competition would be widespread:

Once recognised, instead of such markets ... being analytically differentiated into little monopolies in the orthodox fashion, we are forced to regard each as subject to strong competition (1964, p. 78).

Clark's and Andrews's critiques (discussed more fully in Reid, 1987) were valid in many respects. However, they did not cause economists to question the relevance of the neoclassical models.

■ *2.15* The Austrian critique

Andrews's view has similarities with that of Austrian theorists. This school of thought dates from the marginal revolution of the 1870s. Attention shifted from concern with factors leading to economic growth and development to the use of marginal concepts and to maximisation within a static framework. The simultaneous originators of this shift were Jevons, Walras and Menger. Ironically, whilst these developments were the start of neoclassical economics, Karl Menger (1840–1921) was the first member of the Austrian School, which now presents a comprehensive critique of this 'traditional' approach.

The Austrian approach differs from neoclassical mainstream thought in three crucial respects. First, Austrians reject the assumption that economic agents possess perfect knowledge of all aspects relevant to their decisions. Instead, knowledge is assumed to be only partial. For instance, consumers are aware of their own tastes but may be unaware of the full range of available consumption possibilities. Producers may know the costs associated with current processes, but may be unaware of the costs of alternative techniques. Likewise they may have only a hazy impression of the true nature of demand for their product. Secondly, Austrians reject the neoclassical concern with the state of equilibrium and its mathematical properties. Although the economy may be expected to move in the direction of equilibrium, the characteristics of this equilibrium are constantly changing, and the state of equilibrium is never attained. The economy is argued to be continuously in flux, so that analysis of a stable and static equilibrium is misplaced effort.

Thirdly, the Austrians reject the neoclassical view of competition. Where knowledge is perfect, competition as a process or an activity cannot exist. Hence it is impossible to explain the mechanisms by which economic advance is attained. To Austrians, the major issue is the *competitive process*, the forces that move the economy towards equilibrium. They are interested in the ways by which economies evolve through time and how decisions are made in conditions of uncertainty and limited information. As Littlechild notes:

> Austrian economics, by contrast, sees the [economic] problem as including the *discovery* of those preferences, techniques and resource availabilities ... [and] sees the economy as involved in a continual *process* of discovery, coordination and change (1986a, p. 12).

The process of exchange is central to Austrian economics (frequent use is made of the term *catallactics*, which means the science of exchanges).

This focuses attention on markets where the entrepreneur, or *acting man*, is the key factor. (Consumers, as well as producers, are regarded as acting men in the sense that they respond to and seek out changes in the market: price changes, product changes, new employment prospects for the factors of production they command, and new sources of information.) The actions of entrepreneurs, spurred by the pursuit of self-interest, drive the competitive process. Entrepreneurs have to make choices on the basis of their own limited information and according to their perception of current (and future) states of the world. Once made, these choices lead to changes in the prices and quantities of goods sold. In turn, these changes will be incorporated as new information, so that every choice affects the actions of other entrepreneurs. Entrepreneurs' responses to conditions in the market move the economy towards equilibrium. Even though information is incomplete, the market mechanism works to coordinate decisions, to make the best use of available information, and to enhance economic welfare.

Entrepreneurs can make mistakes in the Austrian world. If their perceptions are faulty, their choices may leave them worse off. As acting men, however, they learn from mistakes as much as they learn from successes. New information will be assimilated, altering entrepreneurs' perceptions of the world and influencing subsequent decisions. Hayek (1945) used the analogy of a pebble hitting the surface of a pond. Initially only a tiny area is disturbed, but eventually the ripples spread across the whole surface. So it is with markets; the reasons for a change in one market may be known only to a handful of people, but the market responds. Via changes in relative prices, this leads to repercussions throughout the economy.

2.16 An example of the Austrian approach

An example will illustrate the Austrian approach and show how limited information is mobilised. A producer sees a new opportunity for making a profit. This involves transforming oranges into orange juice, a new – and, he believes, more highly valued – product. To act on this belief he must purchase factor inputs and determine methods of production, promotion and distribution. These decisions must be made against the background of limited information. However, markets enable him to economise on information: for instance, if oranges from Brazil are cheaper than those of similar quality from Spain, this information (the price of oranges) is sufficient for the entrepreneur to decide to use Brazilian oranges. It is immaterial why Brazilian oranges are cheaper.

Entrepreneurial decisions are unlikely ever to be 'optimal' from the neoclassical viewpoint of perfect knowledge, especially since the pioneer's knowledge of production, promotion and distribution will be very limited. However, correctly identifying an unexploited opportunity (oranges) and transforming it into a more highly valued product (orange juice) will be rewarded by abnormal (entrepreneurial) profit. His success will be observed by others. As Mises notes:

> The market that catallactics deals with is filled with people who are to different degrees aware of changes in data and who, even if they have the same information, appraise it differently (1949, p. 325).

Some will be aware of the new product, others of the promotional activity or perhaps of the increased price of the factors of production being used to make orange juice. This will cause other entrepreneurs to change their perception of the world. A few may see the prospect of profit for themselves in the production of orange juice. Imitators will face fewer problems in setting up, since the pioneer's activities present them with better information on production methods, promotion and distribution networks. The activities of the pioneer thus stimulate further entrepreneurial action. High profits will be a temporary phenomenon as others decide to enter the market. Increased demand for inputs drives up the costs of orange juice production. At the same time, the price of orange juice falls as entrants undercut the pioneer to gain sales. Eventually the workings of competition as a process will eliminate entrepreneurial profits. The greater the pioneer's initial success, the more rapidly his profits (and those of subsequent imitators) will be eroded.

Entrepreneurial profits exist in the first place because the pioneer identifies an unsatisfied demand. When others see this opportunity, profits are eliminated by the operation of the competitive process. Economic welfare is enhanced because inputs are transformed into outputs that are more highly valued than those they were previously producing. Such opportunities may arise from the development of new products to meet existing tastes more fully, as a result of a change in tastes, or from developing new techniques that reduce the costs of existing products. The essence of the competitive process is entrepreneurial action working through the market mechanism to transfer resources to superior uses.

In the neoclassical world of perfect knowledge there would be no need for entrepreneurial activity, and no competitive process. A change in tastes creating the demand for a new product would instantaneously attract new producers because everyone would be immediately aware of the new, higher valued use. The simultaneous increase in factor prices would combine to eliminate any opportunity for entrepreneurial profit.

The Austrians' rejection of perfect knowledge focuses attention upon the ability of a market economy to operate when individuals have only partial information and upon the dynamic processes by which it moves towards equilibrium.

■ *2.17* The transaction cost critique

Transaction cost economics has developed from the work of Coase (1937). He showed that, without explicit transaction costs, there is no reason why firms should exist. All the activities undertaken by firms can be explained only if transaction costs are recognised. With limited information, and within an uncertain environment, economic agents seek the most cost-effective way of attaining their objectives.

Williamson's work (1975, 1985) is the most developed aspect of transaction cost economics. He extended Coase's analysis to identify those factors which favour undertaking activities within the firm, as opposed to using the market. For instance, a firm must decide whether to employ its own advertising specialists or to contract out to an agency. Williamson confusingly uses the term 'transaction costs' to refer to firm–market *or* intra-firm exchanges, whereas others confine the term to the costs which arise when using the market (those of arranging, monitoring and policing contracts). Following the latter approach, *management costs* are incurred when activities are internalised within the firm, transferring such tasks to managers. The firm's decision whether or not to internalise activities turns on the relative magnitude of the transaction and management costs.

Williamson's analysis is built on three main factors: *bounded rationality, uncertainty* (**Sections 1.3** and **1.5**) and *opportunism* ('a lack of candor or honesty in transactions, to include self-interest seeking with guile' (Williamson, 1975, p. 9)). The presence of any one of these factors makes long-term contracting prohibitively expensive, and so explains the existence of firms. However, these factors also affect the relative costs of short-term contracting compared with coordination of the particular activity within the firm. For instance, the sanctions and reward systems available within a firm may prove more effective than the market in curbing opportunistic behaviour. Moreover, the greater the degree to which assets involved in a transaction are specific (**Section 2.7**), the more likely it is that coordination within the firm is preferred.

Recognition of transaction costs permits another slant on relationships between market structure and performance. Like Demsetz (**Section 2.6**), transaction cost economists could argue that high profits signify efficiency rather than market power. Firms may become large and profitable, not simply because of lower production and distribution costs, but because of organisational economies which reduce management costs (Williamson, 1975).

This is but a minor aspect of the transaction cost critique of SCP and the neoclassical approach. Neoclassical theory implicitly assumes that firms are perfect substitutes for each other: they deploy homogeneous resources using universally available production functions and all select that combination of resources and products which maximises profits. As a result, the neoclassical focus is entirely upon markets. Whilst the Austrian approach, too, generally conducts analysis at the level of the market, there is an acceptance that each firm is distinct as a consequence of the differential knowledge of the entrepreneur. Transaction cost economics places even more emphasis on the individual firm and its uniqueness: it may produce products which compete with those of other firms, but it is likely to be organised differently, or use proprietary technology in production, or use different distribution methods. Firm-specific advantages and asset specificity (**Section 2.7**) endow each firm with its own *strategic core* (all assets, both tangible and intangible, which give the firm a competitive advantage in a particular activity). At any time, and depending upon the market it contests, each firm will therefore have differential advantages and/or disadvantages with respect to others. In transaction cost economics, analysing the market may be misleading: market structure is only one influence on the conduct and performance of individual firms.

■ 2.18 Implications for empirical work

Austrian economists' interest in the process of competition and changes over time make statistical testing difficult. Moreover, Austrian theorists have a tendency to eschew empirical work, regarding it as an irrelevancy. Despite this, both the Austrian and transaction cost approaches have important implications for what is tested in empirical work, as well as for the appropriate level of study. In neoclassical economics, the focus is on identifying relationships with profits or price (**Section 2.8**) as a means of distinguishing areas of the economy where current performance is poor. Transaction cost economists argue that attention should be turned to investigation of costs. This should incorporate analysis of both transaction and management costs and how they are affected by factors such as vertical integration, asset specificity, product complexity and the frequency with which consumers purchase the product (see Ravenscraft and Wagner, 1991). To economists concerned with dynamic as well static efficiency, current relationships may be of less interest than how these change over time. For instance, for how long do observed high profits persist?

Rather than the whole market, it may be more meaningful to undertake analysis at the level of the firm, or for groups of firms with similar characteristics. A *strategic group* comprises firms which follow a similar strategy and hence possess similar differential advantages. For instance, Amel and Rhoades (1988) identified six strategic groups within the US banking industry on the basis of portfolio specialisation (whether they concentrate on real estate loans, time deposits or US securities etc.). Porter argues that:

> Strategic groups are present for a wide variety of reasons, such as firms' differing initial strengths and weaknesses, differing times of entry into the business, and historical accidents (1980, p. 130).

Firms within a strategic group tend to have similar characteristics. For example, within the car market, some manufacturers (such as Ford and General Motors) compete over many market segments, others (such as Porsche and Ferrari) offer high-price and high-quality sports cars, whilst Hyundai and KIA compete in the low-price, utility segment.

The identification of strategic groups has implications for the treatment of entry. Entry barriers are greater for those firms which wish to wrestle market share from Ford than for those which wish to offer a single product line, by, say, entering the 'value for money' strategic group. Ford not only has advantages conferred by economies of scale and scope, but also the benefits of an established major distribution network and of having undertaken heavy promotional activity. Firms already established in a market and wishing to relocate to a different strategic group face *mobility barriers*, which can be defined in the same way as the barriers to entry to a market as a whole. It is conceivable that entry to the market is easy, but entry to a particular strategic group within the market is hard. These high mobility barriers could enable the firms within this strategic group to earn high profits which persist over time. Analysis of profits and their persistence at the overall level of the market could present a misleading picture.

The typical cross-section study of neoclassical economics becomes even less appropriate if individual firms cannot be aggregated meaningfully to strategic groups. Transaction cost economics suggests this may well be the case as each firm will have a different history which makes its current path unique. To gain understanding requires much more attention to specific firms, for instance by means of case studies. Some economists are recognising that large inter-industry studies may yield little in the way of general principles (for instance, Reid, 1987). However, this approach is still uncommon outside the study of multinational firms and the broader management literature (such as Waterman and Peters, 1982).

■ *2.19* Conclusion

The SCP approach involves the logical application of neoclassical models to draw deductions about the performance of markets. It has the merit of being derived from a well-established body of positive economics and suits economists' preferences for dealing with the objective rather than the subjective. Despite its attractiveness and its widespread use, the SCP approach is criticised on several counts. The most fundamental relates to its reliance on neoclassical theory. Since it is the case that equilibrium states and perfect information are never found in practice, analysing markets as though these abstract conditions apply can be misleading. This is an important consideration if policy recommendations are to be derived.

This does not imply that the SCP approach is without value. Some markets may be sufficiently stable for the SCP approach to generate useful results. The slower the pace of technology, the more constant are people's tastes, and the more mature the market, the more likely it is that the SCP approach will not be misleading. It is therefore more suitable, for example, for analysing the car market at the end of the twentieth century than at the beginning. Despite this, greater insights would seem to come from a rejection of this approach. The Austrian view with its wider concept of competition generally yields conclusions and policy prescriptions that are better suited to the uncertain and changing environment within which most firms operate. Moreover, the growing interest in transaction cost economics is beginning to direct the focus of study from the market as a whole to the individual firm. An important way forward would be to develop a synthesis that recognises the unique features of the individual firm, and links this to aspects of the market.

■ *Chapter 3* ■

Market Concentration

Many economic sins have been laid at the doorstep of market concentration (J. V. Koch, 1980, p. 209).

■ 3.1 Introduction

Implementation of the neoclassical structure–conduct–performance (SCP) approach requires a means to identify different market structures. Traditionally, a central role has been accorded to measures of market concentration which focus upon the number and size distribution of firms within a market.

Economists' fascination with this concept seems misplaced. There are ambiguities in the interpretation of market concentration measures, practical problems in their construction, and significant theoretical deficiencies. At best, market concentration provides a limited guide to the structure of a market. Given the widespread use of these measures, it is important that these limitations are recognised and minimised – for instance, by adjusting measures for the impact of international trade. But the argument can be taken further. If competition is viewed as a process, concentration measures become redundant.

■ 3.2 Market concentration and structure

The structure of a market can be described by considering (either jointly or separately) the number of firms, product differentiation, entry conditions, and the degree to which firms are vertically integrated. The most frequently used measure is *market concentration*. It shows the extent to which production of a particular good or service is confined to a few large firms. The fewer the number of firms and/or the more disparate their sizes, the more concentrated (and – the implication is – the less competitive) the market.

The attraction of market concentration is easily understood. Differences in the number and size distribution of firms are key factors distinguishing the theoretical models of perfect competition, oligopoly, monopoly and monopolistic competition. Market concentration is easily estimated since published data on the number and size distribution of firms are generally available. For other structural variables published information is rare and the selection of quantifiable proxies may require subjective judgement.

Market concentration is theoretically attractive. Interest is not with the structure of a market *per se*, but with the deductions that can be made about performance. Concentration can shed light on the degree of market power. The extent to which a firm has market power may be revealed by the margin between price and marginal cost (**Section 2.3**). Such relationships frequently form the basis of analysis in the new industrial organisation literature. The contention is that price–cost margins are positively related to the Herfindahl–Hirschman index of market concentration (Appendix 1). Likewise, Stigler (1964) shows that the higher the Herfindahl–Hirschman index the greater are the opportunities for operating a cartel effectively, because members will find it easier to detect secret price-cutting.

3.3 Alternative measures of market concentration

Information on the structural characteristics of a market may be obtained from a *concentration curve*. Firms are ranked in size order from the largest to the smallest and then plotted against their cumulative output. For market *A* (**Figure 3.1**) the concentration curve shows that the largest firm supplies around 60 per cent of the market and the largest three firms around 90 per cent of the market. Market *B* contains a larger number of firms and is less concentrated (its curve always lying below that for market *A*). Compared with *B*, *C* has more firms but is more concentrated up to the four-firm level.

Measures of market concentration seek to transform the information on the number and size distribution of firms presented by the

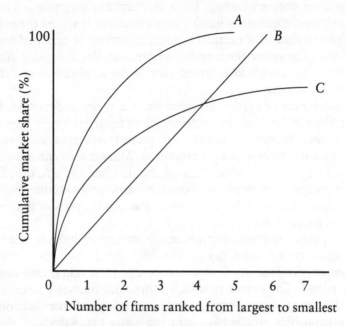

Figure 3.1   *Comparison of concentration curves*

concentration curve into a single value. They vary in sophistication. Some are *absolute measures* which combine the number of firms present and their size disparities. With one exception (the concentration ratio) these consider all the firms in a market, that is they are *summary measures*. *Relative concentration measures*, in contrast, focus on the disparities in the sizes of firms operating in a particular market, and effectively ignore differences in the number of firms present. Here it is argued that the more unequal the size distribution of firms, the more concentrated and less competitive the market.

There are four main absolute measures:

☐ *Concentration ratio*

This measures the cumulative market share of the largest X firms (ranked in descending order of size):

$$CR_x = \sum_{i=1}^{x} S_i \qquad\qquad (3.1)$$

where: CR_x = the X firm concentration ratio
S_i = the percentage market share of the ith firm

A value close to zero would indicate that the largest X firms supply only a small share of the market; 100 per cent could indicate a single supplier. The concentration ratio is popular because of its limited data requirements.

☐ *Herfindahl–Hirschman index* (HHI) (Hirschman, 1964)

This is calculated by summing the squares of the market shares (output of the firm divided by total output) of all firms in the market:

$$HHI = \sum_{i=1}^{n} S_i^2 \qquad (3.2)$$

where: S_i^2 = the square of the market share of the ith firm, measured as that firms output divided by total output
n = the number of firms in the market

This index would be close to zero when there are a large number of equal-sized firms; and 1 under monopoly. The Herfindahl–Hirschman index can be expressed as a *number equivalent* measure of concentration. Say the HHI gives a value of 0.2. Taking the reciprocal shows that this value would obtain if the market were made up of five equal-sized firms.

In the USA, the Department of Justice uses a variant of the HHI, squaring the percentage share of the market in deriving indices for its merger guidelines (**Section 8.6**). The market is regarded as unconcentrated when this measure gives a value below 1000 and as highly concentrated above 1800.

☐ *Hannah and Kay index* (Hannah and Kay, 1977)

The Herfindahl–Hirschman index can be regarded as a special case of the Hannah and Kay index. Market shares are raised to the power α, the choice of which is left to the investigator. Hannah and Kay suggest that a in the range 0.6 to 2.5 gives the 'most sensible' results. The measure is typically calculated in a form that presents the answer as a number equivalent measure directly:

$$HK = \left(\sum_{i=1}^{n} S_i^\alpha \right)^{1/(1-\alpha)} \qquad (3.3)$$

☐ *Entropy index* (Jacquemin and de Jong, 1977)

Market shares are weighted by the logarithm of the market share:

$$E = \sum_{i=1}^{n} S_i \log(1/S_i) \tag{3.4}$$

A value of zero for the entropy index would indicate that there is only one firm in the market. Higher values are harder to understand intuitively. The maximum value that can be taken by the entropy index in the case of firms with equal market shares would be the log value of the number of firms in the market. The advantage of this measure is that it can be decomposed to show how different sub-groups contribute to the overall level of concentration. This may be useful for investigating markets containing strategic groups (**Section 2.18**).

There are two main examples of relative concentration measures:

☐ *Variance of the logarithms of firm size* (Hart and Prais, 1956)

$$V = \frac{1}{N}\sum_{i=1}^{n} (\log S_i)^2 - \frac{1}{N^2} \left(\sum_{i=1}^{n} \log S_i \right)^2 \tag{3.5}$$

As with the entropy index, this can be decomposed and its value would be zero if all firms were identical in size.

Figure 3.2 *Derivation of the Gini coefficient from the Lorenz curve*

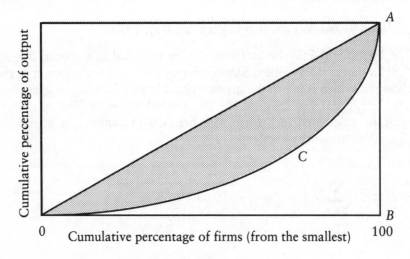

Cumulative percentage of output

0   Cumulative percentage of firms (from the smallest)   100

☐ *Gini coefficient*

Figure 3.2 shows a Lorenz curve for a particular industry. Here the firms are ranked by size and cumulated from smallest to largest as a percentage of the number of firms in the market. This is plotted against the cumulative percentage of output. The greater the deviation of this curve from the diagonal line, the greater the inequality in firm sizes. The Gini coefficient summarises this information into a single measure. Referring to **Figure 3.2** it is the shaded area 0*AC* divided by the triangle 0*AB*. The Gini coefficient can vary between zero, when all firms are of equal size (and hence when the Lorenz curve is the same as the line of absolute equality, 0*A*, in **Figure 3.2**) and 1, when a single firm produces the total market output.

■ *3.4* Theoretical considerations

According to neoclassical theory, the greater the number of firms and the more uniform they are in size, the greater the degree of competition likely to be present. Any measure of concentration should seek to capture these two elements – the number of firms and their size distribution. On these grounds, the relative concentration measures are less satisfactory because no account is taken of the number of firms. Consider the variance of logarithms. The main assumption is that the greater the similarity in firm size, the greater the competition. The drawback is that whenever all firms are the same size the summary measure will always take the value of zero. Theoretically, economic performance would be expected to differ if there were two, as opposed to 200, equal-sized firms in the market. This problem is avoided with measures such as the entropy index, where the maximum value depends on the number of firms in the market. The higher the numerical value of the index, the greater the expected level of competition.

The commonly used concentration ratio is also flawed because it takes only partial account of these two elements. It ignores the relative size variation across the *X* largest firms. As a result, the same concentration ratio could describe a market where there are *X* similarly sized firms or a situation close to monopoly where one firm dominates. It also neglects all except the largest *X* firms. Consequently two markets with identical shares held by the largest *X* firms have identical concentration ratios, even though one market contains more firms in total and is likely to be more competitive.

The Herfindahl–Hirschman index (HHI) is theoretically elegant. It includes all firms, and squaring their respective market shares gives greater weight to large firms. For these reasons (and its relative ease of calculation), the HHI is extensively used. Sleuwaegen *et al.* support the US Department of Justice's switch to a variant of the HHI from the four-firm concentration ratio after 1982:

> The upper H [HHI] index threshold delineates better than before a region of industries characterised by high H index, as well as high C_k [CR_x] values, related under either collusive or non-collusive behaviour to possible allocative inefficiencies (1989, p. 639).

But there is still ambiguity over the HHI's interpretation. The number equivalent measures do not correspond to a unique size distribution of firms. It is simply the value that would obtain if the market were comprised of that number of equal-sized firms. In practice, many different size distributions (and hence markets with very differing levels of competitiveness) could give the same value for the HHI. This defect also mars the Hannah and Kay measure. Furthermore, although this reformulation of the HHI identifies the arbitrary nature of raising firm size to the power two, it gives little theoretical guidance in the choice of the power.

There are many different bases upon which to identify size differences between firms. These include sales, number of employees, capital employed and value added. These bases suffer from a number of drawbacks. In the case of sales revenue, firms involved in retail distribution and those involved in assembly operations will appear larger than firms at an earlier stage of production or those which are more vertically integrated. In the cases of either labour or capital employed, a bias is introduced if there is a systematic positive relationship between size of firm and capital intensity. If small firms are relatively more labour-intensive, employment measures will overstate their importance. A further disadvantage of capital employed is the variety of accounting conventions firms can use to value their assets. For these reasons, value added – which is measured by subtracting the cost of inputs from sales revenue – may give more satisfactory results.

■ 3.5 Hannah and Kay axioms

Hannah and Kay (1977, pp. 52–5) suggest a number of other generally desirable features of a concentration measure. The most important of their seven axioms are:

1. the concentration curve ranking criterion;

2. the sales transfer principle;
3. the entry condition;
4. the merger condition.

Referring back to **Figure 3.1**, concentration measures should rank market *A* as more concentrated than market *B*, whose concentration curve is always lower. This is satisfied by all the measures except the variance of logarithms, which 'misbehaves' in some particular cases. Where concentration curves intersect (as with markets *B* and *C*) then the ranking of the two markets will vary between measures depending on the weightings given to different parts of the concentration curve. For instance, taking a three-firm concentration ratio will show *C* to be more concentrated, the five-firm concentration ratio will show the reverse. In contrast, by giving greater weight to the large firms, the HHI and Hannah and Kay index will generally show *C* to be more concentrated than *B*.

The sales transfer principle argues that concentration should increase if customers switch from smaller to larger firms, and vice versa. The concentration ratio will meet this requirement only if the transfer is between the largest *X* firms and those outside this grouping. If the transfer is within the largest *X* firms, or within the group of smaller firms, then the concentration ratio will be unchanged.

The entry of new firms, below the average size of existing firms, should reduce concentration (assuming the relative market shares of existing firms remain unaltered). The concentration ratio is the measure most likely to violate this axiom, although the Gini and variance of logarithms measures may also fail on this criterion. In the case of the concentration ratio the problem is that the share of the largest *X* firms is unlikely to be affected by the entry of small firms.

Hannah and Kay argue that mergers should cause an increase in concentration. Again the concentration ratio, Gini and variance of logarithms measures do not always satisfy this axiom. The concentration ratio is unaltered if the merged firms are not among the largest *X* (unless the merger brings the new firm into the top *X*). However, the concentration ratio does increase if the merger is between firms within the largest *X*, or between a firm in the largest *X* and one outside this group. The entropy index may also fail to meet this criterion.

These axioms have received support from many economists, despite some qualifications over the merger condition. (Whereas Hannah and Kay postulate that mergers should increase concentration, implying reduced competition, some argue that it is theoretically possible for mergers between firms of an intermediate size to lead to increased rivalry.) Only the HHI and Hannah and Kay indices satisfy all of these axioms. At the other end of the spectrum, the variance of logarithms performs particularly badly on these criteria.

3.6 Further comparisons of market concentration measures

The strengths and weaknesses of the various concentration measures can be illustrated by considering their performance in various hypothetical situations. The characteristics of the seven markets in **Table 3.1** have been carefully chosen to test sensitivity to changes in the number of firms or their size inequality, and to the effects of mergers.

Markets *A*, *B* and *C* contain firms of equal size but differ in the numbers of firms. The level of concentration in market *C* would be expected to be lower than in *B*, which in turn would be expected to be less concentrated than in *A*. Most measures suggest this is the case. The exceptions are the Gini coefficient and the variance of logarithms which give the value zero in all three markets. This points up a major defect of the relative concentration measures, that, in focusing on the size inequal-

Table 3.1   *Comparison of summary measures of concentration*

Market	A	B	C	D	E	F	G
Firm 1	33.3%	20.0%	10.0%	33.3%	40.0%	40.0%	38.0%
Firm 2	33.3%	20.0%	10.0%	33.3%	30.0%	30.0%	28.0%
Firm 3	33.3%	20.0%	10.0%	31.4%	25.0%	15.0%	13.0%
Firm 4	–	20.0%	10.0%	1.0%	5.0%	10.0%	10.0%
Firm 5	–	20.0%	10.0%	1.0%	–	5.0%	5.0%
Other firms	–	–	5@10%	–	–	–	6@1.0%
Concentration ratio:							
3-firm (CR3)	100.0	60.0	30.0	98.0	95.0	85.0	79.0
4-firm (CR4)	100.0	80.0	40.0	99.0	100.0	95.0	89.0
Herfindahl–Hirschman	0.330	0.200	0.100	0.321	0.315	0.285	0.253
Hannah and Kay, $\alpha=2$	3.00	5.00	10.00	3.16	3.18	3.51	3.95
Entropy[1]	1.10	1.61	2.30	1.19	1.22	1.39	1.65
Variance of logarithms[1]	0	0	0	2.920	0.654	0.562	2.030
Gini coefficient	0	0	0	0.420	0.275	0.360	0.638

[1]. Natural logarithms were used to calculate the entropy and variance of logarithms measures.

ity between firms, they fail to take account of the number of equal-sized firms.

Markets *A* and *D* are very similar. The difference is that instead of three equal-sized firms, there are an extra two firms in market *D* each with a 1 per cent share of the market, with a corresponding adjustment to the third largest firm. Theoretically the effect of this change on market concentration would be expected to be negligible. This is shown by the absolute concentration measures. However, the relative measures indicate substantial changes in the market and, in fact, an increase in concentration. This is because the addition of the two tiny firms has introduced a large degree of inequality. The relative measures are therefore highly sensitive to how a market is defined and to the availability of reliable statistics. This is an important drawback because data on small firms are often difficult to collect. However, omission of small firms does not seriously affect those summary measures of concentration where firms are weighted on the basis of their market share.

Markets *E*, *F* and *G* contain a wider range of firm sizes and differ principally in the number of firms. Theoretically, market *G* would be expected to be the least concentrated, followed by *F* and then *E*. This is suggested by the absolute measures, but the relative measures again yield perverse results. For instance, market *G* differs from market *F* principally in the addition of six firms, each with 1 per cent of the market. But this has a marked effect on the values of the Gini coefficient and the variance of logarithms, which both suggest that market *G* is more concentrated.

This illustration has demonstrated that the relative measures of market concentration have severe limitations, performing satisfactorily only where the number of firms remains constant. It has also indicated several deficiencies in the widely used concentration ratio. In fact it is the entropy, HHI and Hannah and Kay indices that conform most consistently with prior expectations. However this discussion can be taken only so far. As Donsimoni *et al.* note:

> In short, there is no such thing as an 'optimal' index of concentration, both because different industries behave differently as well as because no obvious widely accepted normative judgements exist to guarantee its optimality (1984, p. 428).

The most suitable index for any empirical investigation is the one that best relates to the particular aspect of firm behaviour under investigation.

■ *3.7* Concentration measures in practice

A major limitation of measures of concentration is their extensive data requirements. Often the task is simplified by taking data from government statistical sources. (The agencies charged with the enforcement of competition policy (Chapter 8) are exceptions in that they tend to construct their own market data from information provided by firms.) For the concentration ratio, X is usually taken to be 3, 4 or 5 although in the USA concentration ratios are also published for $X=8$, $X=20$ and $X=50$ (see, for instance, United States Department of Commerce, Bureau of the Census, 1977).

Unfortunately the government data invariably relate to industries, rather then markets. The concentration ratio, for instance, now becomes:

$$CR_x = \sum_{i=1}^{x} P_i \qquad (3.6)$$

where: CR_x = the X firm concentration ratio
  P_i = the percentage share of production of the ith firm

The identity of firms grouped as an industry may differ from those grouped as a market (**Section 2.10**). The problems can be illustrated by considering the UK Standard Industrial Classification 1992 (SIC 92) (Mears, 1992). SIC 92 breaks the economy into broad sections which may then be split into subsection, division (two-digit), group (three-digit), class (four-digit) and subclass (five-digit). **Table 3.2** shows the classification of the manufacture of soft furnishings. In total there are 17 sections, 14 subsections, 60 divisions, 222 groups, 503 classes and 142 subclasses.

The UK SIC 92 classification is readily comparable with that adopted elsewhere. It follows exactly the European Community's NACE Rev. 1 (Commission of the European Communities, 1990b) to the four-digit level (**Table 3.2**). It is also identical in content and coding at the division level (two-digit) to the 1989 revision of the International Standard Industrial Classification (ISIC Rev. 3) (United Nations, 1989). At the three- and four- digit levels code numbers may differ or classes may have to be combined, but it is possible to convert directly from ISIC Rev. 3 to SIC 92 or NACE Rev. 1. For instance, the manufacture of made-up textile articles, except apparel, is assigned to Class 17.40 under both SIC 92 and NACE Rev. 1 and to 1721 by ISIC Rev. 3.

Table 3.2 *Comparison between the SIC 92 and SIC 80 classification of soft furnishings*

		SIC 92		SIC 80
Digit level	Aggre-gation	Heading	Aggre-gation	Heading
1	Section D	Manufacturing	Division 4	Other manufacturing industries
	Sub-section DB	Manufacture of textiles and textile products		
2	Division 17	Manufacture of textiles	Class 45	Footwear and clothing industries
3	Group 17.4	Manufacture of made-up textile articles, except apparel	Group 455	Household textiles and other made-up textiles
4	Class 17.40	Manufacture of made-up textile articles, except apparel	Activity 4555	Soft furnishings
5	Subclass 17.40/1	Manufacture of soft furnishings		

The UK's Central Statistical Office states that relevant factors in classifying industries:

> include the nature of the processor or of the work done, the principal raw material used, the type or intended use of the goods processed or handled, and the type of service rendered (1979, p. 2).

This is typical of the way in which firms are categorised, and pays little heed to the economist's theoretical idea of the market, being firmly grounded in supply-based considerations. The more disaggregated the data, the easier it is to gain an approximation to the market. Recognising this, most economists use data at the three- or four-digit levels. For instance, Utton and Morgan argue that they:

> have chosen to work at the more narrowly defined product level ... it has the great advantage in most instances of coming much closer to the concept of a market and thus is more likely to throw light on the issue of market power which is of direct relevance to competition policy (1983, p. 2).

However, even at this level (four-digit) the data are generally insufficiently disaggregated to eradicate this problem. Groupings at the highest level of disaggregation may still combine several markets. For instance, NACE Rev. 1 groups all motor vehicles within Class 34.10. An investigation by the Monopolies and Mergers Commission (1979) found that insulated electric wires and cables split into at least five separate markets: mains cable, supertension cable, general wiring cable, winding wires and strips, and telecommunications cable. The UK classification in use at the time (SIC 68) coded them all to 362. (Even in the USA, where the 'seven-digit' level of disaggregation splits firms into around 12 000 categories, problems of relating industry-based data to markets is encountered.)

Data are collected for 'establishments', which are then classified according to their principal activity. In other words, where a firm's products span more than one industrial classification, this complication will be hidden in the statistics. The establishment will be classified to a particular industry, even though this may account for only a proportion of its total output. This creates a further point of divergence from the concept of the market. Industries where this problem is significant can be identified by constructing measures of specialisation and exclusiveness. *Specialisation* measures the proportion of the output of a grouping of firms that can be genuinely attributed to that grouping. *Exclusiveness* shows the extent to which firms classified to a particular grouping represent the total output of those products.

The UK Standard Industrial Classification was first developed in 1948 and has been updated in 1958, 1968, 1980 and 1992. As Robinson points out:

> Industries as such have no identity. They are simply a classification of firms which may for the moment be convenient. A change of techniques and of organisation may require a new classification and a new industry (1958, p. 8).

The resulting changes in definition increase the difficulties of empirical research spanning more that one version of the SIC. **Table 3.2,** showing how soft furnishings are classified according to both SIC 80 and SIC 92, illustrates this. Even where data are available on the same classification basis, there may still be difficulties because of differences in the level of detail collected. The more aggregated the data, the less concentrated, *ceteris paribus*, the market. The results of the 1968 Census of Production cannot be directly compared with the 1972 Census results. Although both used SIC 68 (Central Statistical Office, 1968), the 1968 information was available in more disaggregated form.

3.8 The effects of international trade on concentration

A further problem with the use of government Census statistics to measure concentration is that they relate to the production of domestic firms only, and at the national level. This raises two problems. First, many regional markets exist, particularly for low-value, bulky products and for services. The absence of regional classifications creates a particular problem for large countries, as Weiss and Pascoe (1986) illustrate for the USA. Adjustment for regional markets changed the concentration ratio for the cement industry from 24 per cent to 71 per cent. Secondly, markets which transcend national boundaries are becoming increasingly important, which – unless taken into account – may lead to misleading conclusions. For instance, in a market where imports provide a major source of supply, domestic concentration ratios may suggest the market to be much less competitive than it really is. As Bacon and Eltis argue:

> Foreign competition sets an upper limit to profit margins in an economy where imports compete with home producers over the entire range of output (1976, p. 24).

In open economies (such as the UK and other members of the EC) the link between recorded concentration and market power must inevitably be weakened if foreign competition is ignored.

Cannon (1978) was the first to make adjustments for international trade in empirical work. He found that including international trade at the product group level (four-digit) had only a minor impact, moderating concentration ratios in the UK by an average 1.1 percentage points for 1963 and by 2.9 percentage points for 1968. Utton and Morgan show (1983, p. 10) that it is more appropriate to adjust concentration ratios for international trade using the formula:

$$C_x = \frac{(Q_x - X_x)}{Q - X + M} \cdot 100 \tag{3.7}$$

where: C_x = the trade adjusted concentration ratio (for X firms)
Q_x = sales at home and abroad by the X largest domestic producers
X_x = exports by the X largest domestic producers
Q = total sales
X = total exports
M = total imports

Exports are deducted from domestic output because they have no effect on domestic competition. Conversely, imports are an extra source of supply for domestic consumers. The effect of these two adjustments to the calculation is to reduce the value of the concentration measure, suggesting a more competitive market.

Equation (3.7) takes account of the fact that the export propensity of large firms is greater than that of small firms. Although successful with a pilot study, lack of data forced Utton and Morgan to revert to the assumption made in previous studies that the largest domestic producers were responsible for the same share of exports as their share of domestic production (the *neutral export assumption*), employing the formula:

$$C_x = \frac{Q_x}{Q+M} \cdot 100 \qquad (3.8)$$

It has subsequently been shown that equation (3.8) is wrong under the neutral export assumption. Where lack of data precludes adjustment for the different export propensities of larger firms, equation (3.9) is correct (Clarke, 1985, p. 38):

$$C_x = \frac{Q_x}{Q + \dfrac{MQ}{Q-X}} \cdot 100 \qquad (3.9)$$

These modifications markedly improve the concentration ratio as an indicator of the state of competition in a market. However, the trade-adjusted figures tend to overstate the competitiveness of the market where a foreign supplier is one of the X largest firms, or where there are import controls. The concentration measure also fails to take account of 'own imports' from overseas branches of domestically based producers. This will also tend to understate the degree of concentration in a market. In the motor vehicle industry, say, it is difficult to see how Ford and General Motors find their market power in the UK reduced by the cars they import. The likely effect of 'own imports' was considered by Utton and Morgan. Assuming leading producers were responsible for 10 per cent of all imports – a level they viewed as 'probably too great for most products' (1983, p. 15) – they concluded that trade adjustment would still show a notable decrease in average concentration.

■ *3.9* Trends in concentration

Trends in recorded concentration may be used to indicate changes in competitiveness: evidence of increasing concentration was used to advocate a strengthening of UK competition policy (Department of Prices and Consumer Protection, 1978). Aggregate concentration measures may be used to portray informationabout the number and size distribution of firms in the manufacturing sector as a whole. Here concentration ratios are typically used. In the USA and the UK, aggregate concentration has increased in the immediate postwar period, but has been fairly stable since 1963 in the USA and 1968 in the UK (**Table 3.3**).

Nissan and Caveny (1993) use a wider variety of measures to assess trends in US concentration, although their study is confined to changes in the sales and assets of the top 25 firms relative to those of the *Fortune 500* (Chapter 2). Whilst the Gini coefficient showed no trend, the other measures attested to an increase in concentration between 1967 and 1990, and especially during the 1980s. For instance, using sales data, the HHI rose from 0.0081 in 1967 to 0.0118 in 1990, and the entropy index declined from 0.5594 to 0.4814.

Of greater interest is the situation at the market level. According to Clarke and Davies (1983), inferences about trends at the market level can be drawn from aggregate concentration. Using the Herfindahl–Hirschman index, they showed that aggregate concentration in the UK manufacturing sector increased by 47 per cent in the period 1963–8, essentially as a result of greater concentration at the industry level (three-digit). The other explanatory factor was that diversification between industries had increased. The more diversified firms' activities were within the manufacturing sector, the higher the level of aggregate concentration. (But it is worth pointing out that the more industrial firms diversify outside the manufacturing sector, the more misleading the measures of aggregate concentration in manufacturing become.)

Table 3.4 presents UK data at the market level and reveals great diversity in the trends and levels of concentration. Whereas the motor vehicle and tobacco industries are highly concentrated, clothing, printing and publishing, and plastics processing are examples of markets which appear highly competitive since the five largest firms control less than a fifth of the market. Iron and steel production has become progressively more concentrated; the reverse is true of motor vehicle parts, office machinery and data processing equipment, and telecommunications equipment. The decline in concentration in the motor vehicle industry in 1989 reflects the establishment of Japanese car plants in the UK.

Table 3.3   *Comparison of aggregate concentration levels in manufacturing, 100-firm concentration ratios*

Year	USA[1]	UK[2]	EC[3]
1947	23		
1949		22	
1953		27	
1954	30		
1958	30	32	
1963	33	37	
1967	33		
1968		41	
1970		41	
1972	33	41	
1975		42	24
1977	33	41	24
1980		41	25
1982	33	41	26
1984		39	
1986		39	
1988		39	
1989		38	

Sources: White (1981); Department of Trade and Industry, *Census of Production*, Business Monitor PA1002 (various years); Commission of the European Communities (1985).

[1] Shares of value added.

Adjustment for international trade alters the picture considerably. Utton and Morgan's results (1983) show that since the earliest year studied (1958) international trade has progressively lowered the average concentration ratio in the UK. By 1977, trade had reduced the domestic concentration ratio of 64.8 by ten percentage points. Using the amended formula of equation (3.9) (which leads to slightly lower concentration levels than equation (3.8)) the Department of Trade and Industry (1986) suggest that the impact of foreign trade on market concentration continued to increase in the period up to 1983. Unadjusted five-firm

Table 3.4 *Trends in seller concentration in selected UK manufacturing industries, 1980–9, five-firm concentration ratios calculated by net output*

Industry (3-digit SIC 1980)	1980	1985	1989
Iron and steel	73	83	96
Pharmaceutical products	43	41	48
Hand tools and finished metal goods	14	11	10
Mining machinery, construction and mechanical handling equipment	18	14	14
Manufacture of office machinery and data processing equipment	70	64	58
Telecommunications equipment	49	46	38
Motor vehicles and engines	91	93	87
Motor vehicle parts	40	33	26
Bread, biscuits and flour confectionery	65	54	50
Tobacco	100	99	99
Hosiery and other knitted goods	32	29	29
Clothing, hats and gloves	12	16	17
Printing and publishing	21	19	19
Rubber products	59	47	49
Processing of plastics	12	10	10

Source: Department of Trade and Industry, *Census of Production,* Business Monitor PA1002 (various years).

concentration ratios for 1983 averaged 50.1 per cent; with trade adjustment, the figure falls to 35.9 per cent (**Table 3.5**).

In individual markets, the inclusion of international trade leads in some cases to a dramatic reduction in the concentration ratio. Marfels (1988) shows the effects of adjustment for international trade in automobiles (**Table 3.6**). Adjustment reduces concentration levels – as measured by the HHI as well as by the concentration ratio – quite dramatically, with the exception of Japan in the 1980s.

■ *3.10* Criticism of the use of concentration

The reliance upon measures of market concentration to indicate market structure – and, hence, of the degree of market power – can be criticised

Table 3.5   *Average five-firm concentration ratios for the UK, with and without adjustment for international trade*

Concent-ration	1970[1]	1973	1977	1979	1979[2]	1981	1983
Unadjusted	49.0	50.9	48.9	48.5	51.4	50.9	50.1
Adjusted	41.3	40.9	38.1	36.5	39.3	37.6	35.9

Source: Derived from Department of Trade and Industry (1986).

[1] Years 1970–9 based on SIC 1968
[2] Years 1979–83 based on SIC 1980

from a number of viewpoints. Using market concentration in isolation to capture market structure and then as a basis for deductions about conduct and performance can lead to mistaken conclusions. One deficiency is that market concentration fails to account for linkages between firms. Shared directorships, for example, could have a marked influence on the behaviour of apparently independent firms. Similarly, concentration measures may mislead where one of the smaller firms is part of a larger concern, or where there are joint marketing and production agreements between firms. A further deficiency is that market concentration alone cannot identify oligopoly, where behavioural characteristics are essential. For instance, where there are six firms in a market, they constitute an oligopoly if – and only if – there is recognition of mutual interdependence.

An empirical investigation may show that the four-firm concentration ratio is, say, 80 per cent in 1980 and remains unchanged ten years later. Taken at face value, this implies no change in competition and that competitive forces are weak. However, the measures of market concentration ignore the identity of firms, and may fail to show that the four largest producers in 1980 have been replaced by four different firms by 1990. This is an important limitation, since studies of trends in concentration over time traditionally form a major plank in the formulation of policies designed to promote competition in the economy.

The logic for the concern with concentration is that, in a highly concentrated market, firms can earn abnormal profits by raising prices above costs. An alternative interpretation – still within the neoclassical paradigm – is that competitive pressures operate to force the emergence of a size distribution of firms such that costs are minimised. The causation is not from structure to performance but in the opposite direction. Baumol (1982) argues this result from the viewpoint of

Table 3.6 *Levels of concentration in the automobile market before and after adjustment for international trade*

	4-firm concentration ratio		Herfindahl–Hirschman index (HHI)		Numbers equivalent HHI	
	Unadj.	Adjusted	Unadj.	Adjusted	Unadj.	Adjusted
United States:						
1970	100.0	91.0	0.341	0.270	2.9	3.7
1980	97.4	80.0	0.461	0.271	2.2	3.7
1986	97.2	78.4	0.383	0.235	2.6	4.3
Great Britain:						
1970	100.0	89.2	0.338	0.260	3.0	3.8
1980	100.0	67.0	0.333	0.157	3.0	6.4
1986	96.0	66.7	0.308	0.147	3.3	6.8
W. Germany:						
1970	94.5	73.7	0.345	0.182	2.9	5.5
1980	89.8	59.8	0.274	0.157	3.6	6.3
1986	88.7	65.3	0.259	0.142	3.9	7.1
Japan:						
1970	87.9	78.2	0.277	0.252	3.6	4.0
1980	87.8	88.9	0.249	0.288	4.0	3.5
1986	86.0	89.7	0.236	0.309	4.2	3.2

Source: Marfels (1988).

contestability, whilst Demsetz (1974b) reached similar conclusions arguing that efficiency dictates market concentration (**Section 2.6**).

Other arguments also suggest that high concentration need not imply poor performance. Detrimental performance can be positively established only if an increase in market concentration results in changes to the price–cost margin and nothing else. This reduces performance – as measured in terms of satisfaction of current wants – without any compensating benefits. But if increased market concentration leads to increased expenditure on research and development activity, society may benefit in the future through improved products or reduced production

costs. Taking this perspective, the impact of the increase in market concentration on economic performance becomes more difficult to evaluate.

This reveals a limitation of the neoclassical SCP approach. The
theoretical validity of using measures of market concentration as an
indicator of performance is based on the analysis of markets that are in
equilibrium and where 'competition' refers to the model of perfect
competition. Where economic agents have to adapt to a constantly
changing world in which they face uncertainty and have incomplete
information, the extent to which market structures approximate perfect
competition or monopoly is a poor indicator of the process of
competition. Here, the level of market concentration reveals nothing
more than how the competitive process has worked out in previous time
periods. The number and size distribution of firms at any point in time
represents a snapshot of a market in the process of adjusting towards
equilibrium. However, before this can be reached, unanticipated
changes will cause movements towards a different equilibrium.
Consequently, new institutional economists (especially those of the
Austrian School) regard market concentration as of little importance, a
view which receives support from the Commission of the European
Communities:

> the conventional wisdom that the structure of a market determines
> the forms and intensity of competition scarcely seems to apply in the
> present conditions in the Community market. The competitive
> situation is largely determined by external factors and firms' ability to
> cope with them (1985, p. 212).

■ 3.11 Conclusion

Market concentration is widely used and performs a central role in identifying differences in market structure within the SCP approach. Despite
their popularity, market concentration measures are theoretically suspect. They have theoretical limitations and (given the problems likely to
be associated with their calculation in practice) it seems pointless to ago-
nise over the choice between market concentration measures. If a
relationship exists between a concentration measure and the performance of an industry, then it is likely to show up whether studies use
concentration ratios, the Herfindahl–Hirschman index or some other
construct. From the viewpoint of the new institutional economists, their
calculation often represents misplaced effort as information on the

structure of a market at a given point in time is too insubstantial to convey the complexities of a changing environment.

This does not deny that market concentration measures may provide useful information on the characteristics of a market. Rather it argues for more consideration in their use. Small changes in concentration are unlikely to be meaningful, but a concentration ratio of 80 per cent presents a very different industry from one with a concentration ratio of 20 per cent. Taken with other information, this can give insights into the likely competitive nature of the industry.

■ *Chapter 4* ■

The Advertising Debate

> Like romance, advertising is an activity to which most people have been exposed and about which little is known. (H. Demsetz, 1974a, p. 67).

■ *4.1* Introduction

Firms spend a great deal of money on promotional activity, in which advertising plays a prominent role. Many economists view this as a waste of resources – one firm's expenditure neutralising that of rival firms – while for others it plays an important part in the operation of the market economy.

Firms in the UK spend broadly the same on advertising as they do on research and development: roughly 1 per cent of GDP. There are, however, marked variations in the level of advertising between countries and between industries. The traditional view of advertising is that it persuades people to buy a firm's product, so increasing the firm's market power. Advertising not only distorts consumer choice, but uses resources which could have been used elsewhere. Society's welfare is reduced; firms enhance their profits at the expense of consumers. Increasingly, this view is being questioned. Advertising may perform a valuable role, enabling consumers to make better informed choices and promoting the operation of the competitive process.

Table 4.1 *Media distribution of advertising expenditures, 1990 (percentage)*

	Newspapers and magazines	Television	Radio	Other
France	56.1	24.8	6.6	12.5
Germany	74.0	15.8	5.1	5.1
Japan	43.2	36.7	5.6	14.5
UK	63.4	30.5	2.2	3.9
USA	54.8	33.3	10.7	1.2

Source: Calculated from data in Waterson (1992).

■ 4.2 What is advertising?

Colley defines *advertising* as:

> mass paid communication, the ultimate purpose of which is to impart information, develop attitudes and induce action beneficial to the advertiser (1961, p. 51).

Advertising is normally used when the potential audience is large. It can take many forms: media advertisements (**Table 4.1**), direct mail, leaflets, or sponsorship. The content of an advertisement can vary considerably. It can simply display the name of the product or it may compare the product with that of rivals. It may provide detailed information about the product's attributes, or may simply enhance its image.

Advertising is one of many forms of *promotional activity*. Instead of advertising, a firm might promote sales by employing more sales representatives, by altering the product's packaging, or by widening wholesale and retail margins. For instance, one study (Backman, 1967) found that advertising expenditure on breakfast cereals in the USA equalled 14.9 per cent of revenue compared with only 2.2 per cent for crackers and cookies; the latter were more heavily promoted by sales representatives (7.9 per cent against 2.0 per cent). Avon also relies heavily on sales representatives, spending in the USA in the 1960s only 2.7 per cent on advertising whereas the average advertising–sales ratio for the cosmetics industry was 15 per cent.

Advertising can be either a substitute for, or a complement to, other forms of promotional activity. This complicates the economic analysis of its effects since it is difficult to disentangle them from those of other promotional activities. Indeed, some economists refer to 'advertising' when they are really discussing promotional activity in general. For example, Dorfman and Steiner say:

> we mean by advertising any expenditure which influences the shape or position of a firm's demand curve and which enters the firm's cost function (1954, p. 826).

More often than not economists ignore the fact that different promotional activities overlap. Mostly, this reflects the problems associated with collecting data on forms of promotional activity other than advertising. Given that the effects of advertising and other promotional activity are similar, empirical work which considers only advertising will give misleading results.

■ 4.3 Why advertise?

Advertising (and promotional activity in general) is impossible to explain within the context of models which assume perfect information. It would be irrational for a firm to incur the costs associated with product promotion if consumers were already aware of its existence, quality, price and terms of sale. Only where consumers have imperfect information is there any point in advertising or other forms of promotional activity. Where existing consumers are partially aware of the product and its attributes, then advertising and other types of selling costs can – by informing and/or persuading – generate a higher level of sales. Furthermore, advertising could be used to inform new consumers about a product, to remind ex-consumers or to hamper the entry of new firms into the market.

Many industrial economics texts do not ignore advertising, but their treatment is invariably unsatisfactory and schizophrenic. The neoclassical assumption of perfect information is dropped selectively on behalf of consumers so that firms have an incentive to advertise, but an asymmetry is held, with firms themselves being fully aware of the quantity of advertising needed to maximise their profits. As Kay notes:

> Such perverse treatment of the knowledge condition requires selective suspension of disbelief on the part of the analyst, and it is essential to have no sense of the absurd (1984, p. 39).

The Austrian approach, by incorporating bounded/procedural rationality (Section 1.3), imperfect information and the view of competition as a process, provides a much more sympathetic framework.

Table 4.2 *Advertising as a percentage of GDP in selected countries*

	1981	1985	1990
Austria	0.61	0.70	0.95
Belgium	0.43	0.49	0.60
Finland	1.27	1.03	1.03
France	0.49	0.57	0.78
Germany	0.82	0.83	0.85
Italy	0.42	§0.49	0.62
Japan	0.74	0.78	0.89
Netherlands	0.81	0.83	0.96
Spain	0.76	0.86	1.56
Sweden	0.62	0.70	0.80
UK	1.02	1.11	1.20
USA	1.28	1.41	1.36

Source: Waterson (1992), Advertising Association (1992).

■ 4.4 How much advertising?

Advertising expenditure in industrialised countries generally accounts for between 0.4 and 1.5 per cent of GDP (**Table 4.2**). **Table 4.3** shows substantial variations in the level of advertising expenditure relative to sales revenue (*advertising intensity*) between industries. This picture is common across countries, with the same industries tending to display high advertising intensities. Consumer goods are more heavily advertised than industrial products. For instance, in the UK in 1980 manufacturers of consumer goods spent twice as much on advertising (relative to sales) as manufacturers of industrial products. Within the consumer goods sector, advertising intensity is generally higher for non-durable goods. These findings lend support to the view that inter-country differences (**Table 4.2**) in overall expenditures on advertising reflect variations in the relative importance in the economy of different goods (Leff and Farley, 1980).

A profit-maximising firm engages in advertising up to the point at which the expected marginal benefit from advertising equals the expected marginal cost of advertising. If advertising were banned, firms would use other methods of communicating with customers, but clearly their preference for advertising implies that it must be less expensive.

Table 4.3   *Advertising intensities by product groups for the UK, 1991*

Product category	Advertising–sales ratio
Cold treatments	20.27
Indigestion remedies	18.64
Shampoos	14.75
Cereals	9.78
Toothpaste	8.11
Coffee	6.42
Air fresheners	5.55
Potato crisps and other potato products	3.42
Watches	2.96
New motor cars	2.06
Books	1.81
Beer	0.93
Washing machines and dryers	0.68
Training shoes	0.61
Cigarettes	0.55
Wine	0.47
Personal stereos	0.22
Spectacles	0.15
Hairdressing	0.01

Source: Advertising Association (1993).

Explanations for variations in the levels of advertising between industries therefore turn on differences in product and market characteristics that affect the efficiency and cost-effectiveness of advertising.

Advertising is more suitable for promoting consumer goods than industrial products because it involves mass communication. The markets for consumer products are generally larger and geographically scattered. Industrial buyers are likely to be smaller in number and require more detailed information than can be provided by an advertisement. Salesmen may yield greater benefits in these circumstances.

Consumer durable goods have a longer life, are often more complex products, and tend to involve a greater outlay than consumer non-durables. An error of judgement in purchasing a durable good has a greater effect on the consumer's welfare. Consequently, consumers require more information than can be communicated effectively via advertising. The more complex the product, the greater the use consumers make of alternative information sources such as consumer publications. This is consistent with procedural rationality (**Section 1.3**). Consumers have evolved 'rules' that influence their purchasing behaviour: seek out information for durable goods, do not bother for non-durable goods. With durable goods, advertising is also likely to be less effective in promoting sales than competition on the basis of price. Empirical evidence supports these contentions. In an international study, Keown *et al.* (1989) found that the median advertising–sales ratio for 142 durable products was 3.81, compared to 5.18 for 217 non-durables.

The importance of product type can be illustrated by introducing the concept of *search* (Stigler, 1961). When knowledge is imperfect, consumers can improve their decisions by searching for information on product characteristics, product availability and alternative prices. Search can take several forms – visiting or telephoning sales outlets, surveys of available literature, and verbal enquiries. However, the incremental benefit received by the consumer is likely to decline as the amount of search increases. This can be illustrated by considering a consumer wishing to purchase a car. Assume he has already decided upon the make and model, but wishes to buy the car at the 'best' price. The greater the number of dealers already contacted (search), the less likely it is that contacting an additional dealer will locate a better offer and, even if a better offer is found, it is likely to be only marginally better. In other words, both the prospect of making savings from identifying a lower price, and their size, will fall with the number of dealers contacted. Recognising also that the collection of information is costly, search is worthwhile only up to the point where the expected marginal benefits equal the expected marginal costs.

The optimal levels of search for durable and non-durable goods are compared in **Figure 4.1**. For ease of exposition, it is assumed that the marginal costs of search (CC) are constant and the same for both types of good. The marginal benefit functions differ (DD for the durable good, NN for the non-durable) since the potential discounts on the durable goods are likely to be much larger in absolute terms. Given the higher unit price and the larger expected savings from identifying a lower-priced source, the optimal level of search for the durable good will be higher ($0Y$ compared to $0X$). Where consumers are expected to search extensively for lower prices then the producer's interests are served by keeping prices low. Not only is advertising less effective, but reduced advertising expenditure may allow the producer to be more competitive on price.

The optimal amount of search may also be lower for goods that are purchased frequently, or which account for a relatively low proportion

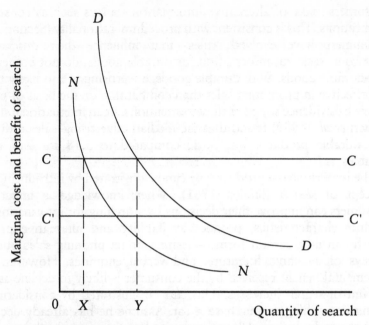

Figure 4.1   *The optimal level of search*

of a consumer's total expenditure. For inexpensive goods, efforts to use sources of information other than advertising are unwarranted – and, in the case of frequently purchased goods, the consequences of a mistaken purchase are relatively short-lived. Therefore, in both cases, it is often rational for the consumer to make a decision between products with unknown characteristics on the basis of advertising messages. Keown *et al.* (1989) provide the supporting evidence that high-priced items have lower advertising–sales ratios. However, their evidence is ambiguous on the relationship between advertising and frequency of purchase.

Nelson (1974b) takes the analysis further. *Search goods* are those consumer goods whose qualities can be evaluated effectively before purchase (such as books or compact discs). The qualities of *experience goods* can only be evaluated effectively after purchase (such as car servicing, shampoo and photographic film). Whilst advertising has a role in informing consumers about the features of search goods, it can only signal the existence of experience goods. Higher levels of advertising are likely in the latter case since advertising may be the only source of information available to the consumer. Davis *et al.* (1991) offer support for this hypothesis. Their analysis of over 300 products advertised in the UK in 1989 shows an average advertising intensity of around 0.4 per cent for search goods compared with 4.0 per cent for experience goods.

Higher levels of advertising for experience goods should also be positively associated with product quality. This behaviour can be explained from the perspective of the new institutional economics. Individuals or groups evolve procedures (or 'rules') to simplify complexity. They will repeat their purchases if an experience good proves to be of high quality. This will encourage firms offering good quality products to advertise more heavily because of the prospect of earning larger returns on their advertising outlays. High advertising may be interpreted by consumers as evidence of product quality and a firm's intention to remain in the market (at least long enough to recoup its advertising expenditure).

The more volatile is the market (for whatever reason), the greater the level of advertising. Where there is a rapid turnover of customers (as in the baby food market) there will be heavy advertising to inform the new consumers (Telser, 1964) (although customer turnover above some critical level actually reduces the returns to advertising, making it less attractive). Furthermore, where product characteristics change rapidly, there will be a need to advertise to increase consumers' awareness. Advertising levels will also be relatively high where the entry of new firms is rapid. New entrants must counteract the influence of past advertising by existing firms: heavy advertising is required to inform consumers of the attributes of their own products.

■ 4.5 Advertising and market structure

An alternative approach to explaining why advertising levels vary between markets considers differences in market structure. For instance, Dorfman and Steiner (1954) show that for a profit-maximising monopolist, the optimal level of advertising intensity depends on the ratio between advertising and price elasticities. (This is derived in Appendix 2.) The greater the consumers' responsiveness to advertising messages and the lower their responsiveness to changes in the product price, the higher will be the optimal level of advertising relative to sales.

In markets characterised by oligopoly, it is often argued that advertising and other forms of promotional activity play a more important role than price competition. If this is the case then advertising intensity should vary with the level of concentration (Cable, 1972) as shown schematically in **Figure 4.2** – often referred to as the *inverted U hypothesis*. Cable finds advertising intensity to be at its maximum when concentration measured by the HHI equals 0.40, which is characteristic of an industry of many small firms dominated by two large firms.

The explanation for high advertising intensity in oligopoly is that changes in prices are quickly noticed by rival firms, which may rapidly

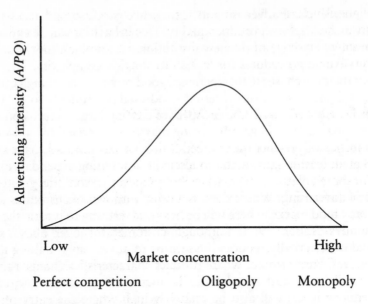

Figure 4.2   *Advertising intensity and market concentration*

match the price change with an adverse impact on the initiating firm's profits. Changes in advertising expenditure are less likely to be immediately countered. Rivals may not react to an increase in advertising because it presents a less obvious threat to their market share. If rivals do react, it may take some time for them to implement and to receive the benefits of their own advertising campaign. Advertising has the further advantage over price changes that it can more easily be reversed. Although Else (1966) disagrees, suggesting that competitive pressures act as a ratchet, making it difficult to reduce advertising levels, it is relatively easy to withdraw an unsuccessful advertising campaign. Price cuts cannot be so readily reversed without causing complaints from customers.

Cowling (1972) – in an extension to Dorfman and Steiner's analysis – shows the optimal advertising intensity of an oligopolist to depend on the way in which rivals react. For instance, the optimal amount of advertising is lower in cases where rivals respond to an increase in advertising by holding prices constant and mounting their own campaigns. If the oligopolists collude, then the optimal amount of advertising is also lower. In fact, it is likely that advertising intensity for a colluding oligopoly would be the same as predicted by the Dorfman–Steiner condition for a profit-maximising monopolist. Referring back to **Figure 4.2**, the effect of collusion would be to reduce the height of the curve over the oligopoly range. Gisser (1991) suggests another modification to the relationship. He finds support for the inverted U hypothesis where industries face a low price elasticity of demand (between 0 and –2). However, when demand is very price-elastic, he argues that advertising intensity continues to increase with concentration.

■ 4.6 The costs of advertising

Firms can choose to vary the number of times a particular advertisement is repeated, or they can decide to alter the combination of advertising media used. How the cost of achieving a sale varies with these changes is another factor affecting the optimal level of advertising. If advertising costs per unit of output fall, this will put firms with a small market share at a disadvantage unless they are multi-product firms able to capitalise on advertising a common brand name.

The presence of an *advertising threshold* could be one reason why unit advertising costs decrease. Threshold effects relate to the observation that (in any given period) a certain absolute amount of advertising has to be undertaken before any increase in sales is noted. For instance, Albion and Farris (1981) suggest that two or three advertising messages are required before much notice is taken by consumers. Once past this threshold, advertising costs per unit of output will fall if the repetition of an advertisement generates a more than proportionate increase in sales. Chamberlin suggests a psychological reason why this might occur:

> Control of the buyer's consciousness must be gained, and while it is being gained additional expenditure yields increasing returns (1962, p. 133).

However, others have tended to disagree, suggesting that each time a message is repeated, the number of new contacts made diminishes. This is the situation found by empirical studies: Simon's (1970) is typical in noting diminishing returns (and, therefore, increasing unit costs) from successive mailings in a survey of mail order advertising. Consequently most economists would agree with the pattern of response to a repeated advertisement postulated by Lambin (1976). Levels of advertising below 0*T* (**Figure 4.3**) yield no increase in sales. Once advertising exceeds this threshold level, sales are affected, but diminishing returns immediately set in and the addition to sales falls with each repeat of the advertisement.

Increased expenditure can be coupled with a change in the type of advertising in order to ensure the most effective package. Where there

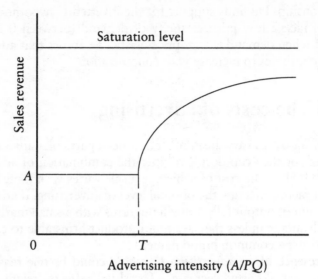

Figure 4.3   *Responsiveness of sales to level of advertising*

are economies of scale, this will result in a reduction in the cost of advertising per unit of sales. *A priori*, scale economies could be the result of pecuniary savings (for instance with larger advertising programmes attracting media discounts) or they may reflect the fact that as expenditure on advertising increases it is possible to organise it more effectively (technical economies). Technical economies may occur where the most efficient media are those such as national television which require a large outlay or where the most effective advertising programme uses several media in combination.

There is little evidence on the existence of pecuniary economies. After an extensive review, Schmalensee (1972) concluded that discounts are of little importance in television advertising. There is rather more evidence on the existence of technical economies – Brown (1978) and Peles (1971) both reported their existence in the beer and cigarette industries.

■ 4.7 The 'advertising as persuasion' view

Advertising will not only bring benefits to the firm in the form of increased sales, it will also have an impact on the environment within which the firm operates and the prices charged to consumers. The traditional view – advanced, among others, by Bain (1968) and Comanor and Wilson (1974) – is that advertising works by persuasion, and results in increases in both market power and prices (the process is summarised in **Figure 4.4**).

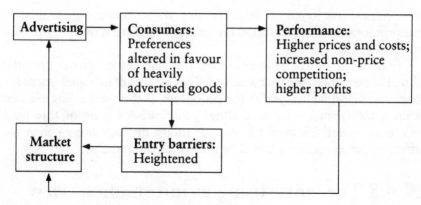

Figure 4.4 *The 'advertising as persuasion' view*

The *advertising as persuasion* view implicitly assumes that advertising distorts consumers' preferences. This may cause consumers to make wrong choices, selecting advertised goods instead of those which would give them greater satisfaction or buying a product in the mistaken belief that it is better than its rivals'. By altering consumers' preferences to favour the advertised product, demand for the product becomes less sensitive to price changes. Advertising also has the effect of reducing the cross-elasticity of demand between the advertised product and its close substitutes. This makes consumers less responsive if rival firms reduce prices or increase their promotional activity. More formally, it can be shown that for a profit-maximising firm the Lerner index (**Section 2.3**) is related to own price elasticity of demand (derived in Appendix 4):

$$\frac{P - MC}{P} = -\frac{1}{\varepsilon} \qquad (4.1)$$

where: P = price
MC = marginal cost
e = price elasticity (invariably negative)

Consequently a lower absolute value of own price elasticity must be associated with a higher profit-maximising price.

Advertising can create first-mover advantages which confer entry barriers of the 'Bain type' (**Section 2.7**). Since customers display a greater attachment to the products of existing firms, there will be fewer people switching between brands, and hence likely to try a new product. To overcome brand loyalty an entrant must either advertise more heavily or offer substantial price discounts. In either case, the entrant's profitability is adversely affected. Moreover, advertising is a sunk cost to the extent that it is product-, rather than firm-, specific. The more the new entrant has to engage in advertising whose benefits are limited to the promotion of the product in question, the less attractive entry to that market will be.

Existing firms will be able to exercise their market power once the threat of new entry has been reduced. This will result in higher prices for consumers and higher profits for producers. If the market has become more concentrated – because either economies of scale or threshold effects in advertising confer a cost advantage on large firms – then the effect on prices and profits will be particularly marked.

■ 4.8 The 'advertising as information' view

This alternative view, adopted by Stigler (1961), Telser (1964) and Nelson (1974b, 1978), stresses the role of advertising in providing information. In an environment where knowledge is imperfect and uncertainty abounds, advertising plays an important part in reducing consumers' ignorance. As in the 'advertising as persuasion' view, it is recognised that advertising influences consumers' behaviour, but it is not regarded as having adverse consequences for consumers' welfare. For consumers to make the 'best' choices they need to be fully aware of all possible alternatives. Stigler's analysis shows that, for any product, there is an optimal amount of search – or, in other words, an optimal amount of knowledge. Although all decisions will be made on the basis of incomplete information, advertising reduces this incompleteness by effectively reducing transaction costs through lowering the costs of search (e.g. to C'C' in **Figure 4.1**). Consumers benefit by being able to choose those products that match more closely their preferences.

Austrian theorists would have some sympathy with Stigler's approach, but they would argue that an optimal level of search cannot be determined, because this requires knowledge that economic agents cannot possess. However, they would agree that advertising provides information and plays an important and beneficial role in the economy. As Littlechild reasons:

> Consumers do not always know what products are available, and even if they know of their existence they are not always aware of their properties. And consumers cannot, of course, seek further information about a product or property of whose existence they are unaware (1986a, p. 34).

Advertising helps the competitive process: by supplementing other sources of information, it facilitates entrepreneurial action by economic agents.

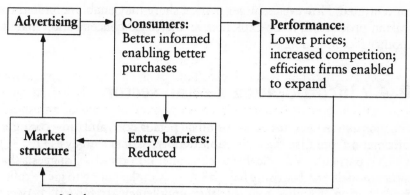

Market concentration may increase or decrease

Figure 4.5 *The 'advertising as information' view*

Taking the view of advertising as information, rather different conclusions emerge as to the effects of advertising on market structures and prices (summarised in **Figure 4.5**). By providing information on product characteristics, advertising makes demand more price and cross-price elastic. Nelson, for instance, argues:

> But this does not imply more inelastic demand curves with advertising than without ... One of the major sources of inelasticity of demand is the very lack of information that advertising provides: that the brand is advertised as such together with some specific information about the brand. It is not surprising, therefore, that advertising increases demand elasticities (1975, p. 225).

Advertising (and other forms of promotional activity) can make consumers more responsive to price changes and price differentials, increasing their concern to buy the 'right' alternative. With demand more price-elastic, it follows that the profit-maximising price will be lower. If consumers are more responsive to price signals, firms will be under more pressure to offer attractive prices. Prices will also be lower because of the increased competition brought about by a reduction in entry barriers. Entry is facilitated because advertising offers an effective means whereby new firms can make potential customers aware of their existence and of the attributes of their products.

The overall effect on concentration is ambiguous. Lower prices and increased competitive pressures imply that any firm has less market power. Despite this, firms offering products that best meet consumer requirements will expand and make profits at the expense of their less efficient rivals. As a result, the market may actually become more concentrated. However, a larger market share may enable economies of scale in production to be exploited, so increased concentration may be another factor leading to lower prices.

■ 4.9 Incorporating a retail sector

The alternative views of 'advertising as persuasion' and 'advertising as information' polarise the discussion unduly. Steiner's analysis (1978b), which is particularly applicable to consumer non-durables, suggests that earlier models of advertising have been too simple, failing to give explicit consideration to the role of the middlemen (retailers) between manufacturer and consumer. Steiner argues that – in the absence of manufacturers' advertising – different brands of a particular good will be very close substitutes. Retailers' choice of which brand to stock will be based on the different prices offered by rival manufacturers. With many options available, the market penetration of any one brand (and manufacturers' market power) will be low. Competition between retailers will be limited, so their profit margins (and the prices charged to consumers) will be high. The costs of distribution at the retail stage will be relatively high, because – in the absence of product information from the manufacturer – the retailer may have to provide such information to consumers.

As manufacturers begin to advertise, they increase their power relative to retailers and gain additional sales without cutting prices. They can achieve this because customers now expect to find advertised brands on retailers' shelves, so the retailer who fails to stock such items risks losing customers to rivals. Manufacturers may exercise their power to secure a reduction in their discounts to retailers. This is superficially in agreement with the view of 'advertising as persuasion'. Increased manufacturers' advertising results in higher prices charged to retailers. For consumers, though, the prices of advertised brands may actually fall (consistent with the 'advertising as information' view). This will be due in part to the more rapid turnover of advertised products (permitting lower retail margins) but also to a reduction in the costs of distribution. Because consumers are better informed about the products on sale, retailers are required to provide less information. Also with advertised brands widely available, retailers are under pressure to attract customers by cutting prices since consumers use the price of advertised goods to choose between retailers. Steiner's analysis receives support from Reekie's study of 1000 product lines:

The product groups which received very high advertising support by their respective manufacturers were quite obviously those on which the retailer levied the smallest margins (1982, p. 137).

Further support comes from Liebermann and Ayal (1992) in their study of an Israeli firm's sales of three non-durable products over the period 1977–83 (see also **Table 4.4**).

According to Steiner, the ultimate effects of advertising will depend on how the market develops. One of the outcomes he envisages is a market dominated by advertised brands. Here the price to the consumer may be no lower than in the unadvertised case. The reason for this is that manufacturers raise their wholesale price as a result both of their increased market power and the increased costs of promotional activity. Entry barriers will be enhanced because a new brand must be heavily advertised to gain a foothold.

In the other outcomes envisaged by Steiner, 'advertising as persuasion' best describes the effects at the manufacturer level, whilst at the retailer level the predictions are more consistent with a view of 'advertising as information'. A market dominated by retailers' private labels ('own brands') is rare in practice, but there are many examples of his alternative scenario where advertised and 'own brands' co-exist. Here consumer prices will be below pre-advertising prices since, at the manufacturer level, competition from attractively priced 'own brands' constrains manufacturers' power, while manufacturers' advertising constrains that of the retailer.

4.10 Advertising and market concentration

To assess the competing views of advertising, attention must be paid to the empirical evidence. Although there have been a large number of studies of the effects of advertising on market concentration, profits and prices (mostly designed to test the 'advertising as persuasion' view), results have been inconclusive.

The view of 'advertising as persuasion' suggests a positive relationship between the level of advertising and market concentration. In contrast, either a positive or a negative relationship would be consistent with the view of 'advertising as information'. Empirical results have been mixed. For example, Guth (1971) and Mann and Meehan (1971) found strong positive relationships, but Telser (1964), Doyle (1968) and Reekie (1975) found few significant relationships. More notable is the absence of any strong negative relationships which would have been weighed against the persuasive view of advertising. An exception is Lynk (1981), who noted that the introduction of television provided a new and economical way for new entrants to reach consumers, allowing them to achieve market share at the expense of incumbents.

Deficiencies in the measures of concentration used may provide one explanation of the varied findings (see Chapter 3). Another explanation may be that the relationship between advertising and concentration is two-way: the level of advertising influences market concentration, but, at the same time, the degree of market concentration influences the level of advertising (this latter point is illustrated in **Figure 4.2**). Simultaneous equation methods might distinguish between the two effects, but most studies use single equation regression models. Differences in the industry mix used in the studies may also explain different empirical results: if advertising intensity varies with the level of concentration (**Figure 4.2**), empirical results will depend on the degree to which the sample contains highly concentrated industries.

4.11 Advertising and market share instability

Another test of the two hypotheses is to investigate an association between advertising intensity and the stability of the market shares of the leading firms. The 'advertising as persuasion' view predicts low price and cross-elasticities, which would imply greater stability of market shares. Moreover, differential responses by incumbents to the entry of new firms, might create instability in the shares of the principal firms in the market. If high advertising intensity creates entry barriers, market shares should be more stable. An inverse relationship could also be argued on the grounds that, if advertising increases concentration, this facilitates collusion, resulting in more stable market shares.

The first to test these ideas was Telser (1964), who found that high advertising intensity was associated with less stable market shares. Eckard (1987) used Census data for the USA between 1963 and 1982 to investigate the stability of the shares of the four largest firms in 228 four-digit industries. His results are consistent with the view that advertising fosters competition, in that high advertising intensity did not promote greater stability of market share. His subsequent study of the 1971 ban on television and radio advertising of cigarettes in the USA (Eckard, 1991) found the market shares of firms and brands to be more stable in the period following the ban. Concentration, which had been declining, was now stable or increasing. He also noted that the entry of new brands virtually ceased for four years. Eckard concludes:

> On balance these results are inconsistent with the market power theory of advertising. The evidence suggests that, whatever other impacts the television ban has had, its unintended side-effect on cigarette industry competition has likely been negative (1991, p. 132).

This is typical of much the work in this area. Caves and Porter (1978) and Meisel (1981) are among the few that offer support – albeit weak – for the 'advertising as persuasion' view.

■ *4.12* Advertising and profits

Empirical tests of the relationship between advertising and profits can seek only to provide evidence against the 'advertising as persuasion' view. Again this is because both a positive and negative relationship are consistent with an informative role for advertising, but a positive relationship only is consistent with the persuasive view of advertising.

Studies of advertising and profits encounter two major problems. The first concerns the treatment of advertising expenditure. Some studies have treated advertising as contributing to a stock of goodwill which depreciates over time. Here the relationship between advertising and current profit can disappear: Bloch (1974), for example, using a 5 per cent rate of depreciation of goodwill, failed to find any significant results. This may be because the stock of goodwill adds to the amount of capital employed. This deflates measures of profitability which use capital employed as the denominator. If advertising is regarded as a current expense whose effects are dissipated within a fairly short period, then there appears to be a strong positive relationship with profits. This seems the most appropriate treatment given empirical evidence which suggests that the main effects of advertising are generally felt within a few months. For instance, the effects of an advertising campaign on the sale of well-established, low-priced, frequently purchased goods are likely to be dissipated within six to nine months (Clarke, 1976; Holstius, 1990).

The second problem with empirical studies concerns the direction of causation in the relationships found. Is it that high advertising has led to increased profitability or is the high advertising simply a consequence of high profits? Albion and Farris, after reviewing over 50 studies, conclude that most do find a positive relationship, although:

We do not know whether the correlation between industry profits and industry advertising means that profitable industries advertise more, advertising increases industry profits, or both (1981, p. 177).

■ *4.13* Advertising and entry barriers

Several studies have shown that high advertising intensity either reduces or has no impact on barriers to entry. In their study of generic pharmaceuticals in the USA between 1984 and 1988, Grabowski and Vernon (1992) found that high advertising–sales ratios did not act as an effective barrier to entry. Kessides (1991) provides evidence that advertising has facilitated entry into the US manufacturing sector. He takes this as rejection of the 'advertising as persuasion' view, but support for the 'advertising as information' view. Behaviour in the market for optician services in the UK since advertising was permitted in 1985 is also consistent with the latter view. Many new opticians have set up, including Lenscrafters of the USA and Vision Express. Advertising intensity has been greater amongst the new entrants, for whom advertising is a way of facilitating entry. However, to secure a rapid and effective entry, new entrants have complemented advertising with other forms of promotional activity such as leafleting, free gifts and free trial periods for contact lenses.

Some studies see advertising as a factor inhibiting entry. These include the study by Rizzo and Zeckhauser (1990) of physician services in the USA. Rosenbaum and Lamort (1992) suggest that US manufacturing industries with high advertising–sales ratios have significantly lower entry rates. Geroski and Murfin (1991) paint a more complex picture of advertising and entry: falling concentration and rising import penetration in the UK car industry after 1968 was accompanied by a marked increase in advertising intensity. Advertising initially fostered competition by easing entry to the market, but continued advertising made it harder for later entrants. They argue that:

> advertising facilitates entry to the extent that an entrant can account for a large share of total industry advertising, but that advertising inhibits entry because the acquisition of a large advertising share is costly (1991, p. 799).

An entrant's success is influenced by how much it advertises relative to the incumbents. In an expanded market, where all are advertising heavily, it is more expensive to gain the advertising share required for successful entry.

■ *4.14* Advertising and prices

Investigating the relationship between advertising and prices would seem to offer the best chance of assessing the relative strengths of the two hypotheses. Support for the 'advertising as persuasion' view would come from the identification of a positive relationship, while a negative relationship would be consistent with the view of 'advertising as information'.

There are three aspects to this relationship and the results of a number of empirical studies are summarised in **Table 4.4**. It should be borne in mind that these studies are incomplete because they ignore the effects of advertising on transaction costs (for example, consumer search costs). Strictly speaking, the relevant price is that paid by consumers plus the associated transaction costs. Reduced transaction costs are as important as lower product prices in improving consumers' welfare.

Several studies have focused on the links between advertising and price elasticity of demand. For manufacturers selling to distributors, advertising was associated with a lower price elasticity of demand (the effect suggested by the 'advertising as persuasion' view) whereas, at the retail stage, advertising was associated with a higher price elasticity (consistent with an 'advertising as information' view). These results seem to offer empirical support to the Steiner model.

A second approach is to consider whether advertised brands are associated with relatively higher prices (for instance, Connor and Petersen, 1992). Advertised brands always appear to command a price premium over unadvertised rivals. Unless they confer additional satisfaction on consumers, this would support the 'advertising as persuasion' view. Yet, by themselves, studies of relative prices are insufficient to determine the effect of advertising upon economic welfare. Ignoring potential effects on search costs, what is important is how the price of the advertised brand compares with the price at which it would be sold if there was no advertising.

Studies of the effect of advertising on the absolute level of market prices also face the difficulty of finding relevant comparisons and taking into account sufficient information. For instance, Rizzo and Zeckhauser (1992) examined the impact of advertising by physicians in the USA. On first sight, it appears that advertising significantly lowers the price of physician services. More detailed investigation reveals that physicians may advertise in order to obtain more desirable patients. They argue that advertising actually leads to higher prices, higher quality services and fewer patient visits.

Some support is given to the view of 'advertising as information': for instance, Steiner (1973) showed that toy advertising introduced in the

Table 4.4 *Summary of the empirical evidence on the relationship between advertising and prices*

Advertising and:	Price elasticity	Relative prices	Absolute prices
At the manufacturer level	*Negative* Comanor and Wilson (1974), Lambin (1976)	*Positive* Buzzell and Farris (1977), Farris and Reibstein (1979)	*Positive* Liebermann and Ayal (1992)
At the retail level	*Positive* Wittink (1977), Eskin (1975)	*Positive* Burnett (1979), Reekie (1979), Connor and Petersen (1992)	*Negative* Benham (1972), Maurizi (1972), Maurizi et al. (1981), Cady (1976), Steiner (1973), Cox et al. (1982), Office of Fair Trading (1982), Kwoka (1984), Paterson (1984), Liebermann and Ayal (1992) *Positive* Rizzo and Zeckhauser[1] (1992)

[1.] Higher prices associated with higher quality

USA in the late 1950s and in France in the mid-1970s led to lower prices. Retailers' margins on toys sold in Canada at Christmas 1972 averaged 20.2 per cent for heavily televised toys but 46.1 per cent for those toys not promoted by television advertising. Lower prices were also noted following the lifting of the ban on advertising by the legal profession in the USA in 1977 (Cox *et al.*, 1982). Prices of uncontested divorces, wills and other simple procedures fell by a half in some cases. Paterson (1984) found that those lawyers who advertised their fees always charged considerably less.

Benham's study (1972) of the prices of eyeglasses (spectacles) compared average retail prices in states of the USA which permitted advertising with those where it is banned. In the former states, eyeglasses were significantly cheaper (averaging $26 against $33). Benham's results –

Table 4.5 *Prices of the cheapest prescribed standard spectacles by country*

Advertising allowed	$	Advertising banned	$
UK	19.80	Ireland	34.50
Belgium	20.10	New Zealand	44.50
Japan	22.10		
USA	23.40		
W. Germany	23.50		
France	26.10		

Source: *The Economist*, 15 March 1986.

which were confirmed by Maurizi *et al.* (1981) and Kwoka (1984) – also appear to apply to other countries (Office of Fair Trading, 1982). In 1985 opticians in the UK were allowed to advertise as part of a package of deregulation measures. Prices fell by about 20–25 per cent in the following year (*The Economist*, 15 March 1986). Further comparisons are given in **Table 4.5**.

Benham also provides a counter to the often advanced argument that advertising 'must be paid for', so the extra costs will imply higher prices. In those US states which prohibited advertising, the typical retailer of eyeglasses was a sole trader with a localised catchment determined by the high costs of consumer search. Concentration levels were low. By reducing search costs, advertising enabled consumers to find lower-priced outlets more easily. With consumers' willingness to travel to low-priced outlets, such opticians could gain customers from a wider area. This permitted economies of scale. Over time larger outlets, group practices and discount chains began to develop, raising the level of concentration. This has also been noted in the UK. In 1985 independents took a 54 per cent share of the market, but this had declined to 25 per cent by 1991. Two new entrants (the Boots Opticians and Specsavers chains) had acquired market shares of 15 and 10 per cent respectively (Fulop and Warren, 1992). Advertising 'must be paid for', but the extra costs can be more than offset by the advantages of scale economies, allowing lower net prices to be offered to consumers.

■ 4.15 Conclusion

Economists do not dispute that advertising has important effects on resource allocation. Rather the controversy concerns whether its effects are generally favourable. Those who adopt an 'advertising as persuasion' view argue that it leads to higher prices and increased market power. Others stress the informative role of advertising, seeing it as a means of reducing search costs and making consumers more responsive to differences in prices.

The empirical evidence is mixed. In part, this is due to the complexities of performing valid tests, but it also perhaps suggests that the theoretical focus of attention has been too narrow in expecting that one view of advertising will be correct in every case. Rather than consider whether advertising generally has particular effects, it may be more pertinent to ask in what particular circumstances these occur. The markets where advertising seems to have adverse effects are those for low-priced, non-durable goods. Here, it is irrational for consumers to search heavily and so decisions may be made simply on the basis of advertising. However Steiner's model suggests that even here advertising will not invariably have adverse consequences for the consumer. Advertising may also generate higher levels of concentration. Again, this in itself is not indicative of a reduction in welfare. The reasons for such a change need to be carefully considered. Higher levels of seller concentration may not be accompanied by increased market power but by lower prices for consumers. In fact, the few studies that have analysed the impact of advertising on retail prices have generally found the effects of advertising to be beneficial.

■ *Chapter 5* ■

Monopolies – Good or Bad?

The evidence that monopoly is important is negligible, and the evidence that it is a quite minor influence on the workings of the economy is large (G. J. Stigler, 1982, p. 24).

■ 5.1 Introduction

Market (or monopoly) power is generally condemned by neoclassical economists on the grounds that it leads to a misuse of resources and a reduction in economic welfare. Such concerns have led to the establishment of bodies (for instance, the Monopolies and Mergers Commission in the UK) whose aim is to identify the presence of market power, and then to regulate or to eliminate any monopoly abuse. The task of such bodies is by no means straightforward. Market power is not always easily identified. Moreover, economists have different views on the factors giving rise to market power and disagree over the circumstances in which monopolies operate against the public interest.

■ 5.2 Monopolies and market power

It is implicit within the structure–conduct–performance approach (SCP) (Chapter 2) that monopoly leads to poor performance and is detrimental to economic welfare. In this context, a monopoly is defined as a single seller, but this characteristic, by itself, has few implications for welfare. What is important is the extent to which a monopolist possesses market power.

To a neoclassical economist, a firm has market power when it has discretion to choose the price it charges for its product, and has the potential to earn long-run abnormal profits. As shown by Cowling and Waterson (1976) and Clarke and Davies (1982) the extent to which price exceeds marginal cost (the Lerner index of market power, **Section 2.3**) can be related to the level of market concentration (see Appendix 1). Such power is therefore absent in perfect competition, where firms have to respond to the price set by the market. The potential for market power is greatest in monopoly, but can also be a feature of oligopoly. This point is implicitly recognised in competition policy. For instance, in the UK a firm (or several firms operating jointly) holding a 25 per cent market share can be referred for investigation by the Monopolies and Mergers Commission.

Yet, identification of market power is not so clear-cut. Data on the number and size distribution of firms are insufficient: barriers to entry are necessary for the monopolist (or oligopolists) to exercise market power. Consider the case of a single seller; without entry barriers such a firm has no market power because the threat of potential competition effectively replaces the market discipline imposed by actual rivals and, in the long run, the single seller will be able to earn only normal profits.

▌ 5.3 The impact of market power on economic welfare

Figure 5.1 depicts the traditional neoclassical case against monopoly (the *market power hypothesis*). Under perfect competition, price and output would be at $0P_c$ and $0Q_c$ respectively. The demand curve shows that for units up to $0Q_c$ consumers would be willing to pay more than the price actually charged. According to Marshall's measure of *consumer surplus*, the benefit to consumers is gauged by the vertical difference between the demand curve and the price line. Total consumer surplus is equal to areas 1, 2 and 3, while the total cost of producing output $0Q_c$ is shown by areas 4 and 5.

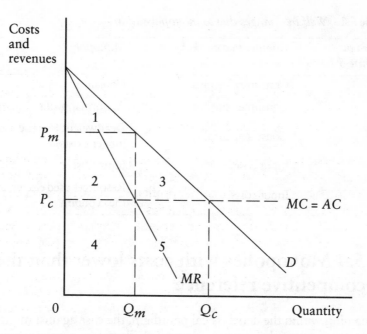

Figure 5.1 *Reduction in economic welfare due to monopolisation*

Faced with the same demand and cost conditions, the monopolist protected by entry barriers is able to raise price (to the benefit of its own profitability) by reducing output. The profit-maximising monopolist would equate marginal revenue with marginal cost and charge $0P_m$ for the lower output $0Q_m$. Consumer surplus would be reduced to area 1. With units $0Q_c$–$0Q_m$ no longer produced, the associated consumer surplus (area 3) disappears. This benefit is completely lost to society. It is alternatively described as an *allocative* or *deadweight loss*. By contrast, area 2 represents a transfer of benefit from consumers to producers. What was formerly consumer surplus is now abnormal profit for the monopolist. In reducing production below the competitive level, resources have been released and production costs are now represented by area 4. Area 5 is not a loss to the economy as a whole because these resources are released to produce output (equivalent in value to area 5) in their next best alternative use. These changes in welfare are summarised in **Table 5.1**.

Although the analysis has been simplified by assuming constant costs, the essential conclusion is unaffected: monopolisation reduces economic welfare, resulting in a net loss of area 3. The extent of the welfare reduction depends on the price elasticity of demand for the product and on the difference between monopoly and competitive prices.

Table 5.1   *Welfare changes due to monopolisation*

Area in Figure 5.1	Competitive market	Monopoly
1	Consumer surplus	Consumer surplus
2	Consumer surplus	Abnormal profit
3	Consumer surplus	Deadweight loss (i.e. no longer exists)
4	Input costs	Input costs
5	Input costs	Resources used elsewhere in the economy

5.4 Monopolies with costs lower than the competitive reference

Remaining within the neoclassical paradigm, the case against monopoly is not always straightforward. **Figure 5.2** illustrates a situation where costs are lower in monopoly (MC_m) than under perfect competition (MC_c). Under perfect competition, price is $0P_c$ and output $0Q_c$. A monopolist protected by entry barriers charges a higher price of $0P_m$ and produces output $0Q_m$ causing a deadweight welfare loss. The monopolist again makes abnormal profits, but here they arise not so much from the fact that the monopolist's price is higher, but that its costs are lower than the competitive norm. These resource savings in the monopoly sector permit increased output elsewhere, and if this productive gain outweighs the deadweight welfare loss, there will be an overall improvement in society's welfare.

Williamson (1968) noted that this improvement in welfare may occur even where cost savings are quite small. This is confirmed by Needham (1978, p. 246) who showed that a monopoly price 20 per cent above the competitive level requires a cost reduction of only 4 per cent (when the absolute value of price elasticity of demand is equal to 2) for the productive efficiency gains to offset the allocative loss.

Economists of the Chicago School would not be surprised to find monopolists with costs lower than the competitive reference. Demsetz's *efficiency hypothesis* (1973, 1974b) contends that if some firms have a cost advantage over rivals then market concentration will increase, since the competitive advantage this confers results in the efficient firms growing over time at the expense of others (**Sections 2.6** and **3.10**) Profitability rises along with measures of concentration, but the

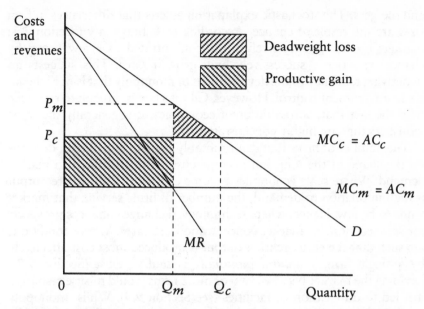

Figure 5.2 *The effects on welfare of a monopoly with costs lower than in perfect competition*

causation runs from lower costs to higher profits and greater market concentration.

It is not easy to accommodate the idea of lower costs in monopoly within the neoclassical paradigm. The explanation cannot turn on unexploited scale economies because that would imply a market in disequilibrium. Instead the monopolist may have lower costs from access to superior technology, which is unavailable to firms operating in a competitive environment. Yet the neoclassical approach does not explain how such innovation can occur (see Chapter 6). Setting aside this complication, if monopolists did achieve lower costs, policy recommendations would no longer be clear-cut. Monopolies might or might not reduce welfare. It would depend on whether – and the extent to which – their costs are higher or lower than in a competitive industry.

5.5 Reasons for the development of monopoly

The means by which a firm acquires its dominant market position is relevant to its effects on welfare. Three explanations for the development of a monopoly are commonly cited: stochastic factors, cost conditions and mergers. The stochastic explanation asserts that differences in firm sizes are the result of chance. According to Gibrat's law (**Section 2.3**) markets become progressively more concentrated as a few firms (by chance) experience successively high growth rates. This suggests an underlying tendency to the development of monopoly that is not amenable to government control. However, Gibrat's law is difficult to reconcile with the fact that, across different economies, it is generally the same industries that are highly concentrated.

The number of firms that can profitably operate in a market depends on the shape of the long-run average cost curve compared to market demand. Where scale economies become exhausted only where output is high in relation to demand, the number of firms serving that market tends to be few. Hence, where technological change enhances prospects for scale economies, market concentration increases. Where conditions are such that the entire market output is produced most cost-effectively by a single firm, a *natural monopoly* is said to exist (**Section 9.2**). Dividing the market between two or more firms would misuse resources if it led to duplication of facilities (see **Section 9.9**). Whilst monopoly may be advocated on the grounds of low cost, the potential exists for the monopolist to reduce economic welfare as it pursues the maximisation of profits.

Horizontal mergers within the same industry may also cause greater concentration. The motive for merger may be greater market power, or the desire to rationalise production or distribution methods, to economise on transaction and management costs and, generally, to make more efficient use of resources. In all of these cases, the development of monopoly not only gives the opportunity for increased market power, but it may also bring the prospect of improvements in the use of resources. Recognition of these beneficial effects questions the traditional neoclassical argument against monopoly.

■ 5.6 Harberger's welfare loss estimates

Taking the traditional neoclassical view that monopoly reduces welfare through the exercise of market power, a number of empirical studies have sought to gauge the extent of the welfare loss. Harberger's study (1954) was the first. He calculated that the welfare – or deadweight – loss in any particular market (area 3 in **Figure 5.1**) could be measured by using the formula (derived in Appendix 3):

$$W = \frac{1}{2}(\frac{\Delta P}{P})^2 PQ\varepsilon \qquad (5.1)$$

where: W = welfare loss
         P = price
         Q = quantity
         Δ = change in
         e = price elasticity of demand

Having estimated the welfare loss from monopoly by market, the welfare loss for the economy as a whole could be derived by summation across markets.

While information on sales revenue (PQ) is often readily available from production censuses and published company accounts, the difference between competitive and monopoly price levels can only be estimated. Harberger assumed that the rate of return that firms in competitive markets would earn in long-run equilibrium is equivalent to the average rate of return in manufacturing industry. Individual industry rates were then compared with this average to estimate the price differentials due to market power. In addition, Harberger assumed unit price elasticity of demand (e) for all industries.

His cross-section studies using data aggregated at the industry level indicate that the activities of the manufacturing sector of the USA in the 1920s resulted in a reduction of welfare equivalent to 0.1 per cent of GNP. At this time, manufacturing industries accounted for only about 25 per cent of the USA's output. If market power were present to a similar extent in other sectors, then the estimate of total welfare loss in the economy would be a mere 0.4 per cent. This must call into question the validity of policies designed to combat market power, and supports Stigler's comment (1956) that economists would be better employed fighting fires and termites.

■ 5.7 Criticisms of the Harberger approach

Harberger's study is the subject of a number of criticisms. Wahlroos (1984) points to a failure to adjust for 'risk' premiums: in equilibrium, rates of return are affected by the variability of earnings of each industry. In consequence, Harberger's estimate overstates the actual welfare loss by a third. Most other critics suggest that Harberger's estimate is a considerable understatement. For instance, unit price elasticity of demand implies marginal revenue equal to zero. Marginal costs are unlikely to be zero so this is inconsistent with profit maximisation. It is also dubious to suggest that the average rate of return in manufacturing industry reflects the competitive rate of return (normal profits). In fact, Harberger's data suggest that the manufacturing sector was not in long-run equilibrium, since it was earning a higher rate of return than other sectors of the economy. This would cause the price differential due to monopoly – and, in turn, the welfare loss – to be underestimated.

Harberger's use of rates of return and price differences to reflect market power can be disputed. First, the high level of aggregation introduces a distortion. Monopolistic markets with high rates of return become less visible when aggregated with markets earning lower rates of return. Secondly, once a firm is isolated from competitive forces the pressure to maximise profits is reduced. Market power may be reflected by inflated costs rather than by inflated profits and, even where owners and top management do seek to maximise profits, they may be frustrated by lower-level managers and operatives pursuing other objectives. This is captured by Leibenstein's concept of *X-inefficiency* (1966). Similarly, Williamson (1963) shows how managerial discretion can lead to inflated costs where there is a difference between the objectives of owners and managers. Finally, Cyert and March (1963) point to *organisational slack* which allows salaries and wages to rise above market levels. All in all, if costs are not kept to a minimum then the observed difference between competitive and monopoly prices will understate market power, and again give a low estimate of welfare loss.

These criticisms would be less valid if it is assumed that firms' objectives are to maximise long-run, rather than short-run, profits. It is unlikely that a monopolist would maximise the discounted value of a profit stream by maximising profits in each time period. A high price in a given time period may attract new entrants and erode the monopolist's market share, together with prospects of continued high profits. Instead of determining output by equating current marginal cost and marginal revenue, a firm with market power may set a lower price to preclude – or, perhaps, slow down – entry. This *limit-pricing* strategy (**Section 2.7**) would produce price and output levels closer to the competitive reference, and make Harberger's assumption of unit price elasticity more plausible.

▌ 5.8 Cowling and Mueller and the calculation of welfare loss

Methods similar to Harberger's have been used, among others, by Schwartzman (1960), Bell (1968), Worcester (1973), and Siegfried and Tiemann (1974), to give similarly low estimates of welfare losses. By contrast the different approach taken by Cowling and Mueller (1978) suggests that welfare loss may be substantially higher.

While Cowling and Mueller also adhered strictly to the neoclassical tradition, their work is more soundly based theoretically than Harberger's. Drawing from oligopoly theory, they first estimated welfare losses at the level of the firm before aggregating. From data on the price–cost margin, price elasticity of demand was estimated for each firm studied, and, thereby, the competitive rate of return and the level of monopoly profit. Their method – shown in detail in Appendix 4 – gave the deadweight welfare loss as half the amount of monopoly profit (area 3 in **Figure 5.1** is half area 2):

$$W = \frac{\pi}{2} \qquad (5.2)$$

where: π represents monopoly profits

According to Cowling and Mueller, the deadweight loss does not represent the total reduction in welfare. Expenditures are incurred to build up or to maintain a monopoly position: expenditures – for instance, on excessive advertising or product differentiation – which are unrelated to production costs. These inflate reported costs above those of a competitive firm. Cowling and Mueller's second measure of welfare loss includes the indirect effects of advertising (A). Compared with perfect competition, it leads to yet a further reduction in output and increase in price. The formula for welfare loss then becomes:

$$W = \frac{(\pi + A)}{2} \qquad (5.3)$$

If advertising expenditure is also regarded as undesirable, the welfare loss increases to:

$$W = A + \frac{(\pi + A)}{2} \qquad (5.4)$$

Yet a fourth measure adds after-tax monopoly profits (π'):

$$W = \pi' + A + \frac{(\pi + A)}{2} \qquad (5.5)$$

The reasoning here is that any return above a competitive level acts as an incentive to other firms to enter the market to capture the abnormal profit for themselves. But to break down the entry barriers protecting the incumbent monopolist requires extra expenditure that can also be regarded as reducing society's welfare. Cowling and Mueller assume

Table 5.2   *Cowling and Mueller's estimates of welfare loss due to monopoly*

Measure	Welfare loss (% of gross corporate product)	
	USA	UK
(5.2) $\pi/2$	3.96	3.86
(5.3) $(\pi + A)/2$	6.52	4.36
(5.4) $A + [(\pi + A)/2]$	12.27	5.39
(5.5) $\pi' + A + [(\pi + A)/2]$	13.14	7.20

Source: Derived from Cowling and Mueller (1978).

that these expenditures are equal to after-tax abnormal profits, arguing that it would be rational for rivals to expend this amount if they could be certain of capturing the monopoly profits:

> Obviously this estimate is but a first approximation. It is an underestimate, if the firm has incurred expenditures in acquisition and maintenance of its monopoly position, which are included in current costs. It is an overstatement if actual and potential competitors can successfully collude to avoid these wasteful outlays (1978, p. 734).

Cowling and Mueller's empirical results for the USA (1963–6) and the UK (1968–9) are summarised in **Table 5.2**. Only the first measure can be directly compared with Harberger's in that it purports to measure just the deadweight welfare loss. Cowling and Mueller's estimate is much higher because of the different techniques used: when they reworked their calculations for the USA using an approach similar to Harberger's the allocative loss fell to 0.4 per cent.

While Cowling and Mueller's approach is theoretically more sophisticated, it again rests on neoclassical analysis. Implicit in this is the assumption that monopolies are never beneficial. Although there is substance to their argument that there are costs beyond those which are incurred in production and distribution, it does not necessarily follow that these are a waste to society. For instance, advertising may provide valuable information (see Chapter 4).

5.9 Masson and Shaanan and the calculation of welfare loss

A more recent calculation of welfare loss by Masson and Shaanan (1984) drew upon limit-price theory (**Section 2.7**). This approach (very different from that used by Harberger, but with similarities to the Cowling and Mueller study) involved hypothetical calculations of prices which would have prevailed had existing firms acted together as a profit-maximising monopolist facing no potential competition.

To measure the strength of competition required calculation of the deviation between the actual price charged and the collusive, profit-maximising price. It was assumed that entry depends on the extent to which actual price–cost margins exceed the limit-price and that, when existing firms operate in a market where entry is not blockaded, their joint profit-maximising price–cost margin is above limit-price. This enabled the collusive profit-maximising price to be inferred from simultaneous equations. A comparison of the hypothetical outcomes with empirical observations indicated the impact of actual and potential competition, as well as the resultant welfare losses.

Masson and Shaanan's overall estimate of welfare loss in the USA for 1950–66 was 2.9 per cent. If competition (either actual or potential) in the economy had been totally absent, then this welfare loss would have been 11.6 per cent. Assuming, as in the Cowling and Mueller approach, that all advertising and after-tax profits also reduce welfare, then this estimated loss rises to 19 per cent.

■ *5.10* Summary of welfare loss estimates

Table 5.3 summarises the various estimates of welfare loss for several economies. Most of these studies use a Harberger-type approach deriving low estimates of welfare reduction. Gisser (1986) is an exception; his low welfare loss estimates are based on a Cournot model of oligopoly. Those that indicate much higher ranges generally use methods similar to Cowling and Mueller.

The general inference to be drawn is that the presence of monopoly results in a small deadweight loss. However, where firms' costs are increased as a result of monopolisation, X-inefficiency or extra expenditure incurred to defend the monopoly position, then welfare losses may rise considerably.

One qualification to these results concerns the level of aggregation. Total welfare loss is simply the sum of the welfare losses in each market. The more closely the data classification corresponds to the concept of a market, the more accurate the results. Highly aggregated data tend to understate welfare losses because of the averaging effect on estimated price–cost margins. Cowling and Mueller, whose work was at the firm level, illustrated this point by comparing the deadweight losses for the USA calculated at different levels of aggregation. At the four-digit level

Table 5.3 *Summary of empirical studies on the welfare effects of monopoly*

Author	Period	Country	Welfare loss
Harberger (1954)	1924–8	USA	0.1
Schwartzman (1960)	1954	USA	0.1
Kamerschen (1966)	1956–61	USA	5.4–7.6
Bell (1968)	1954	USA	0.02–0.04
Shepherd (1970)	1960–9	USA	2.0–3.0
Worcester (1973)	1956–69	USA	0.2–0.7
Siegfried and Tiemann (1974)	1963	USA	0.07
Cowling and Mueller (1978)	1963–6	USA	4.0–13.1
Masson and Shaanan (1984)	1950–66	USA	2.9
Wahlroos (1984)	1962–75	USA	0.04–0.90
Gisser (1986)	1977	USA	0.1–1.8
Jones and Laudadio (1978)	1965–7	Canada	3.7
Cowling and Mueller (1978)	1968–9	UK	3.9–7.2
Wahlroos (1984)	1970–9	Finland	0.2–0.6
Jenny and Weber (1983)	1967–70	France	0.13–8.85
	1971–4	France	0.21
Pezzoli (1985)	1982–3	Italy	0.4–9.4
Funahashi (1982)	1980	Japan	0.02–3.00
Oh (1986)	1983	Korea	1.16–6.75
Ong'olo (1987)	1977	Kenya	0.26–4.40

of the Standard Industrial Classification (**Section 3.7**) the estimated welfare loss was 83 per cent of that estimated at the firm level (1978, p. 741). At the two-digit level of aggregation this figure fell to 78 per cent. However, even where studies are based on firms, aggregation errors may occur if the firms operate in more than one market and their power varies between these different markets.

Aggregation may give a misleading impression of welfare losses by market. Many studies show welfare losses at the level of the industry. For instance, Siegfried and Tiemann (1974) found large losses in the motor vehicle, petroleum refining and plastics industries. However (as noted in **Section 2.10**), industries rarely contain the same group of firms as markets. Using a Cowling and Mueller-type approach causes similar difficulties since the studies concentrate on large firms, which are invariably multi-product, operating in several markets. These points have particular significance for policy. Certain markets might impose large welfare losses, but escape the attention of the authorities.

▌ 5.11 The relationship between market ▌ structure and profit

An alternative method of evaluating market power is to investigate empirical relationships between market concentration (a proxy measure of market power) and the levels of profit. Effective collusion increases both firm and market profitability and the argument is that firms collude more readily in concentrated markets. With few firms, interdependence is high, and firms are more likely to anticipate effective collusion. Entry barriers are relevant because firms will regard collusion as worthwhile only where there are barriers preventing the rapid erosion of collusive profits. The traditional SCP approach would therefore anticipate a positive statistical relationship between concentration and profitability (Bain, 1951), or between concentration, barriers to entry and profitability (for instance, Bain, 1956, 1968; Mann, 1966).

These hypotheses were given some support by early empirical work: for instance, Weiss (1974) reported over 50 studies supporting the market power hypothesis. The first of these (Bain, 1951) concluded that only a weak positive relationship existed between market concentration and rate of return on equity, a result generally confirmed by the later studies. Research in the USA since the early 1970s has generally reported the disappearance of this relationship (for instance, Domowitz *et al.*, 1986). However, Salinger (1990) using Census data for the period 1972–84 concluded that a significant but weak relationship continued to exist during the 1970s, and strengthened after 1981 suggesting the business cycle as an explanation. Salinger's study also used import-adjusted concentration ratios (**Section 3.8**) which improved the correlation with profits. In contrast, work in the UK has given little support to the market power hypothesis: many studies have failed to find a positive relationship between concentration and profitability (for instance, Hart and Clarke, 1980; Clarke, 1984).

Demsetz's efficiency hypothesis suggests a different interpretation of any positive relationship: high profits in concentrated markets could simply be indicative of greater efficiency. Demsetz proposes a method of testing this:

if efficiency is associated with concentration, there should be a positive association between concentration and the difference between the rate of return earned by large firms and that earned by small firms (1973, p. 5).

This can be contrasted with the market power hypothesis which makes no case for any systematic variation between the rates of return of small and large firms in industries with high levels of concentration. Demsetz successfully tested his hypothesis using US data on four-digit Census industries for five years selected from the period 1958–70. Subsequent work by Demsetz (1974b) provided additional support for the efficiency hypothesis.

Peltzman (1977) – like Demsetz, an economist of the Chicago School – has developed a test of the efficiency hypothesis that is more sophisticated. Firms which make cost-reducing innovations will grow over time, so that rising concentration is associated with falling production costs. This expectation was confirmed by his empirical study of the USA for the period 1947–67. Peltzman's work has been criticised by Scherer (1979, 1980) for giving insufficient attention to the characteristics of those markets where increases in concentration had occurred. Scherer argued that increased concentration has not been associated with process innovations, but with product developments in consumer goods markets. Peltzman (1979) countered that his simple point was that more efficient firms grow faster than others, whatever the reason for the efficiency advantage. Lustgarten (1979) and Salinger (1990), who used simplified versions of Peltzman's model for the USA for the periods 1954–72 and 1972–84 respectively, supported his results.

Several other studies support the efficiency hypothesis. These include Carter (1978), Gale and Branch (1982) and Ravenscraft (1983), who showed (for the USA) that profitability is linked more to high market share (conferred by superior products or lower costs) than to levels of market concentration. More recently, Eckard (1990) found that concentration changes in US manufacturing industries were positively correlated with relative labour productivity growth advantages of large firms. Using Canadian data, Dickson (1991) concluded that – whilst collusion effects may be present – the observed relationship between concentration and profitability is largely due to efficiency. In contrast, work for the UK by Clarke, Davies and Waterson (1984) gave little empirical support to the efficiency hypothesis. Moreover, re-analysis of Demsetz's original data for 1963 by Amato and Wilder (1988) failed to uphold his conclusions. They argued that Demsetz's findings are dependent on a high level of data aggregation.

5.12 Other tests of the market power/ efficiency hypotheses

To shed further light on the debate as to whether monopoly indicates market power or superior efficiency, some economists have considered the relationship between concentration and a firm's beta. *Beta* measures the variability of earnings of any share relative to the variability of earnings of the stock market as a whole. A number of studies (for instance, Sullivan, 1978; Lee *et al.*, 1990) have found *beta* to be negatively related to concentration. This has traditionally been accepted as consistent with a market power interpretation, but Binder (1992) argues otherwise. If one of the largest firms in the market grows because of increased efficiency, then the market becomes more concentrated, but product price falls. A lower product price reduces the value of *beta*, producing a negative correlation with concentration. On its own, evidence of high concentration, but low *beta*, is insufficient to distinguish between the market power and efficiency hypotheses.

The ambiguity of the tests, and the practical problems of using profit measures, have caused several economists to turn attention to the relationship between concentration and price. Notable amongst these is Weiss (1989). He regards tests using price as superior because there is little risk that differences in accounting practices introduce data errors. Moreover, theory would expect market power to increase price, whereas greater efficiency would generally be associated with lower price. He argues that a positive relationship between concentration and price can be interpreted unambiguously as evidence of market power.

One of the studies by Weiss considers Portland cement. This is a good case for analysis because the product is homogeneous and traded in the USA in a number of regional markets. Weiss was able to use data for seven years during the period 1948–80 to compare concentration levels against price across a sample of 24 major metropolitan markets. Price was positively related to concentration although there was no evidence of a critical concentration ratio (a level of concentration at which price suddenly increases). Weiss also reports on the many studies of concentration–price relationships that have focused on the banking industry. These include Berger and Hannan (1989), who compared the interest rate offered on retail deposits against three-firm concentration ratios and the Herfindahl–Hirschman index. They investigated 470 banks operating in 195 local markets and concluded that banks in the most concentrated markets offered deposit rates that were 25–100 basis points less than those paid by banks in the least concentrated markets. These results are typical. Research into the relationship between concentration and price has generally provided support for the market power hypothesis. Selling prices are higher, and buying prices lower in concentrated markets, although the effect is usually small.

Although Weiss is confident enough to conclude: 'I believe that the evidence that concentration is correlated with price is overwhelming' (1989, p. 283), it would be rash to take the results as unqualified evidence that monopoly implies market power. For example, Jackson (1992) has reworked Berger and Hannan's study. He confirms their overall result, but shows that subdividing the data reveals an inconsistent and more complex picture. Those markets where concentration was low (three-firm concentration ratio less than 50) continued to conform to the market power hypothesis. However, in markets of medium concentration (ratio between 50 and 67) no significant relationship was found, whilst in those markets where concentration is high (ratio over 67) the relationship between concentration and price was strong, significant and negative, contrary to expectation. Benham (1972) also provides evidence which questions Weiss's conclusion. Although Benham did not explicitly investigate price and concentration in the market for eyeglasses (**Section 4.14**), he presents sufficient information to deduce that the relationship was negative.

■ *5.13* The persistence of abnormal profits

Empirical studies of market power commonly use a cross-section approach and make the implicit assumption that markets are at, or near to, equilibrium. The expectation is that any positive relationship between concentration and profits will continue through to future time periods. In other words, if such findings are attributed to market power, then it is argued that established firms are effectively isolated from potential competitors by entry barriers and that their high profits will persist. This is the essence of the traditional concern with market power, as the report of the White House Task Force on Antitrust Policy says:

> Above-average profits in a particular industry signal the need and provide the incentive for additional resources and expanded output in the industry, which in due time should return profits to a normal level. It is the persistence of high profits over extended time periods and over whole industries rather than in individual firms that suggest artificial restraints on output and the absence of fully effective competition (1969, I-8-9).

However, at any point in time some firms, markets or industries may not be in (or even close to) equilibrium. A positive association between market concentration and profitability may reflect disequilibrium and so be inadmissible as evidence that high profits are a consequence of market power. Only if the relationship is sustained through time is the case made.

Brozen (1970) tested for this persistence of profits by repeating Bain's pioneering study (1951) of the relationship between concentration and profits for subsequent time periods. His results show an increase in profits in manufacturing in the USA between the two periods 1936–40 and 1953–7. There was a slight reduction in the profitability of those industries that were highly concentrated in 1935, against a marked increase in profitability of the industries with an eight-firm concentration ratio below 70 at the start of the period. In fact, the difference in profitability between high- and low-concentration industries virtually disappeared; this finding was confirmed by Brozen's later work (1980) and by Qualls (1974). Even in industries categorised as having 'high entry barriers', above average rates of return were eroded over relatively short time periods.

Other early support was provided by Stigler's study in the USA where he found that:

> the rates of return have no persistent tendency to remain in a fixed industrial pattern. It is true that, if we know the rates of return in a given year, we can predict the hierarchy of rates of return with considerable confidence in the next year; the coefficients of successive annual rates of return are usually 0.7 to 0.9. But within a period of about six years the correlation has vanished (1963, p. 5).

Keating's (1991) analysis of US data for the period 1973–81 found the pattern of rates of return in a given industry to be volatile, displaying no inter-temporal stability. High-return industries fell dramatically in rank over time whilst those with low returns initially rose significantly, if more slowly. There has been evidence that profits do not persist even in highly concentrated industries. Coate (1988) investigated US four-digit industries with four-firm concentration ratios over 50 between 1958 and 1982. He noted that profits decayed to equilibrium levels within ten years.

Such evidence challenges traditional thinking. If above (or below) average profits do not persist, barriers to entry must be generally unimportant, and market power only a passing phenomenon. Together with the work of Demsetz and Peltzman, this evidence casts serious doubts upon the view that market power is a problem. Instead it begins to suggest that high rates of profits could be consistent with an efficient use of resources.

However, the case is still by no means proven. Salinger, for instance, found little reduction in profitability when testing the Brozen hypothesis using US data for the period 1972–82. In combination with his earlier findings on concentration and profits, this leads him to draw a rather different conclusion:

> although the data are consistent with the hypothesis that market power is the reward for successful innovation, the market power that does result tends to be long-lived (1990, p. 313).

To Salinger, both efficiency and market power effects exist simultaneously. Innovation leads to increased concentration which gives rise to market power.

One possible explanation for the apparent inconsistencies between studies relates to the level at which profits persist. Rather than being a market phenomenon, it could be a function of factors specific to particular firms or groups of firms (Section 2.18). The presence of high mobility barriers could enable firms in particular strategic groups to earn high levels of profitability over extended time intervals. The firm may also have acquired a competitive advantage by previous actions. By supplying products attractive to customers, the firm may have built up a strong brand image and substantial goodwill. Such advantages operate at the level of the firm as opposed to the market and, if they prove difficult to emulate, will make individual firms successful over long periods of time. Mueller argues:

> The management of Kellogg's does not reach into a bag of products each year and just happen to be lucky enough to come up with cornflakes and the other highly profitable products that it sells every time. Even if luck was partly involved in Kellogg's original development of these products, its continued dominance of the cereals market over the last 100 years is not simply a matter of a continual 'luck of the draw' (1991, p. 7).

Consequently, empirical tests using firm-level data (for instance Cubbin and Geroski, 1987b; Geroski and Jacquemin, 1988) are more likely to find evidence of persistence of profits. However, such data have their own limitations (Section 2.11). For instance, persistent high 'profits' could simply be a consequence of a firm's under-recording of intangibles in its asset base. Moreover, results remain open to interpretation: persistent profits may not be due to market power protected by entry barriers but to a general superior efficiency. The source of this efficiency lies within the individual firm and not only allows it to attain above average profitability, but enables it to adapt to changes in its market and environment such that this profitability is sustained.

■ 5.14 The effect of entry

The persistence of profits can be undermined on three counts: by exogenous changes in cost and demand conditions, by competition within the market, and by entry from outside the market. Empirical evidence reveals that entry is considerable. For instance, Geroski (1991a) shows that in the UK over the period 1974–9 an average of around 50 new firms per year entered each of the 87 three-digit manufacturing industries examined. Studies also reveal that rates of entry vary between markets and over time. Entry provides another promising area for research, although empirical work is, as yet, unable to go far in distinguishing between the market power and efficiency hypotheses.

Abnormal profits should encourage new firms to enter a market. The evidence for this is mixed. In studies of manufacturing industries, Jeong and Masson (1991) note that high profits stimulate entry in Korea, and Schwalbach (1991) concludes that entry in Germany is motivated by positive profits and the expectation of a growth in demand. In contrast, Dunne and Roberts (1991) show that high price–cost margins are negatively related to entry in the USA. Traditional theory would take the absence of new entry as evidence that entry barriers facilitate the exercise of market power by incumbents. However, this finding could also arise because the incumbent firms possess efficiency advantages that new entrants are unable to emulate.

More direct evidence relating to the market power hypothesis is provided by studies that have focused upon the existence and height of entry barriers. Bain (1956) pioneered this research, finding that high barriers to entry led to high profits. Amongst more recent studies, Geroski (1991b) found barriers sufficiently high for incumbents to maintain prices 15–20 per cent above costs without net entry occurring. Likewise, Andersen and Rynning (1991) showed that high entry barriers were essential to the profitability of concentrated markets.

A corollary of these findings is the expectation that high rates of entry into a market imply an absence of market power. Theory predicts that substantial entry would act as a force to reduce profits to normal levels. This view receives support from Jeong and Masson (1991), who found that entry to the Korean manufacturing sector caused profits to decline. Others have not found such a link between entry and profits (for instance, Geroski, 1991b; Mueller, 1991). Bresnahan and Reiss (1991) in their study of local geographical markets for five retail and professional services reported that, whilst the entry of the second or third firm into an erstwhile monopoly or duopoly did significantly affect conduct, this was not the case with the addition of a sixth or subsequent firm.

The absence of a negative relationship between the rate of entry and profitability may be explained by considering the costs that entrants must overcome in order to survive and become competitive in new markets. Where new, small firms gain entry, it is typical for them to displace an existing small firm and for themselves, in turn, to be rapidly displaced:

> The average entrant is, it seems, basically a tourist and not an immigrant, enjoying a life that is often nasty, brutish and above all short (Geroski, 1991c, p. 283).

The influence of such entrants on the profitability of dominant incumbents will be minor at best:

> The leading firms in most industries stand calmly in the center, as if in the eye of the tornado, while myriad smaller challengers whirl in and out along the periphery (Mueller, 1991, p. 12).

Food retailing in the UK provides an example. It appears that prospective entrants systematically overestimate the profitability of shops serving a local market. This leads to the entry of many small, new firms often taking over existing outlets, whose owners have realised that not even normal profits are to be had. This substantial turnover of firms offers little competition to the handful of dominant food retailers (notably Sainsbury, Tesco, Safeway). The entry of the major German food retailer, Aldi, in the early 1990s may prove more effective. However, Geroski (1991a) notes that even where a new entrant is the subsidiary of an existing firm it can take up to ten years to become competitive in a new market (a finding similar to that of Biggadike, 1976).

If the market comprises several strategic groups (Section 2.18), this may provide another reason why high entry rates and high profits coexist. Some strategic groups provide an easier means of access to the market than others. Even after entry, the newcomer may still find itself unable to compete effectively with firms in other strategic groups because of high barriers to mobility within the market. For instance, the US brewing industry between 1950 and 1980 comprised two strategic groups: national producers and regional producers (Tremblay, 1985).

There was no entry to or exit from the national group of four producers, which advertised more widely and more intensively than the regionals. This suggests that a new firm would find it easier to enter as a regional brewer, but once established, transition to the national group might prove difficult:

> The high risk of a new national advertising campaign and the high sunk cost needed to go national may have been great enough to keep regionals out of the successful national strategic group (Tremblay, 1985, p. 194).

Those strategic groups to which entry is very difficult may offer the prospect of higher profits. This suggests that market power may not be a market-wide phenomenon; rather it may be a feature of a certain niche or segment of the market. Even here, the welfare inferences are still ambiguous: high profits could be consistent with the dominant incumbents' possession of either market power or efficiency advantages.

The thrust of the contestable markets hypothesis (**Section 2.6**) is that it is potential rather than actual entry that it is the important constraint on market power. Again the empirical evidence is mixed. Schwalbach (1991) argues that cigarette and asbestos industries in Germany are contestable in that they are highly concentrated, but exhibited no entry during the study period despite low entry barriers (although he was unable to establish whether profits were at normal levels). Weiss (1989) adopts a very different approach in testing for contestability. He considers that a market cannot be contestable if price rises systematically with concentration. He concludes that the evidence does not provide support for the contestability hypothesis:

> I also believe that contestable markets is a largely empty box and that until someone provides us with clear evidence that it exists somewhere, it should play no role in public policy (1989, p. 283).

■ 5.15 An alternative view of market power

The findings of the previous sections would cause no surprise to economists outside the neoclassical mainstream. For instance, if transaction costs are considered, even the evidence of market power found in the studies of price and concentration may be undermined. The price at which a good is sold may not give a complete picture of the costs of purchase incurred by the consumer if transport costs and the costs of information are excluded. If this is the case, then little can be inferred from a positive relationship between the price and concentration. If higher price is associated, say, with increased advertising that reduces the cost of search (**Section 4.4**), then it may be wrong to draw the conclusion that society's welfare has been adversely affected.

Transaction cost theory presents another slant on the efficiency hypothesis and the level at which profits persist (**Section 5.13**). It can be argued that firms may acquire specific assets, for instance, people who coalesce into a management team of above average efficiency. The members of the team may simply be paid the minimum required to keep them in their current jobs, but their exceptional team-work allows the firm to earn above average profits across the markets in which it operates. High profits are not a function of market structure, but of good performance by individual firms.

Austrian economists would go further. They are critical of those who ignore the competitive process and regard competition as a particular type of market structure. They would be sympathetic to attempts by the Chicago School to incorporate the effects of time into their models, accepting the conclusions of Brozen, Demsetz and Peltzman as essentially correct. They would also have sympathy with much of the recent research on entry. However, they would regard the calculation of welfare loss from monopoly power as misplaced effort which can lead only to erroneous policy recommendations.

Cowling and Mueller's conclusions (**Section 5.8**) are a case in point. In essence Cowling and Mueller adopt the view that all abnormal profit and expenditure in excess of that necessary to produce the product constitutes a welfare loss. This (and other) analysis is based upon comparison between the real world and static, equilibrium models which incorporate perfect information and ignore transaction costs. In effect, they take a snapshot of the economy and analyse the resulting array of markets – corresponding to the characteristics of the various neoclassical models – on the implicit assumption that all markets are in equilibrium (or less strongly that deviations from long-run equilibrium are random). However, these assumptions have not been empirically verified; in fact the opposite seems to be the case. Biased, but possibly plausible, pictures may result. As Schmalensee notes in testing the relationship between concentration and profits:

> The instability found here between two cyclically comparable years casts a good deal of doubt on the quality of evidence provided by inter-industry studies that use data for a single point in time (1987, pp. 420–1).

Austrian economists are well aware of this. Any similarity between 'empirical snapshots' and theoretical neoclassical models is superficial and illusory. It fails to recognise the competitive process which is continually changing market structures. It pays insufficient attention to the source of market power, and it misses the point that market power is generally transitory.

The view of competition as a continuing process remedies these defects. Monopolies may not arise from mergers or cost conditions, but simply as the result of successful product or process innovation. If a firm introduces a new product, its success or failure depends upon consumers' responses. If sufficient consumers are willing to pay the price asked, then the product will stay on the market. Alternatively, if a loss is made, the monopolist will withdraw the product. A firm which correctly assesses the market will prosper and gain a monopoly position until such time as others are able to enter. To go further and conclude that, where such firms have market power, resources are inefficiently utilised, is unsound.

This leads Littlechild to offer an alternative interpretation of the welfare loss calculations (see also Abbott and Brady, 1991). Instead of generating a welfare loss, Littlechild considers that an innovating monopolist: *'generates a social gain given by his own entrepreneurial profit plus the consumer surplus'* (1981, p. 358). Freezing a market economy at any point in time may reveal markets corresponding to that depicted in **Figure 5.1**, where a monopoly supplier produces output $0Q_m$ and charges a price of $0P_m$. Consider that this relates to the pioneer entrepreneur who first discovers an unexploited market opportunity for orange juice (**Section 2.16**). Austrians argue that the relevant alternative to monopolistic production is no orange juice at all, rather than the neoclassical alternative of production by many suppliers. Without the monopolist, orange juice would not have been produced, so area 3 cannot be taken as a measure of deadweight loss to society. Instead, society gains area 1 (consumer surplus created) and area 2 (abnormal or entrepreneurial profit) as a result of the pioneer's efforts, area 4 being the opportunity costs to society of the resources now used to produce juice. Society will gain further when other entrepreneurs enter this market. Entrepreneurial profit will be eroded and transferred to consumer surplus. As price and output move towards the competitive level, area 3 will also be added to society's welfare.

Pezzoli (1985) is one of the few economists to make any allowance for the beneficial effects of innovation in empirical work. He excludes from his calculation of welfare loss firms in those industries where research and development expenditure is high in relation to total sales (pharmaceuticals, electrical engineering and vehicles). This reduces his maximum estimate of welfare loss for the Italian economy in 1983 from 9.42 to 5.37 per cent. Pezzoli's method fails to capture the essence of Littlechild's argument. In principle, there is no reason why empirical studies could not reinterpret the areas in **Figure 5.1** to quantify the *beneficial* effects of monopoly on welfare.

Austrians argue that monopolies need not be regarded with alarm as long as it is possible for rivals to erode their market positions. The profits made by a successful innovator will attract competition from other firms in the future. Even a firm with 100 per cent of the market and protected by considerable entry barriers may not be able to exploit its monopoly position. If the prospects of abnormal profits are sufficiently attractive, other firms will have an incentive to break down the monopoly by developing lower-cost production processes or introducing superior products. However, profit prospects are not judged solely on the current profitability of established firms. Entry may occur where normal profits (or even losses) are being made. Each firm is unique and its entry decision depends on its profit expectations (dependent on its technology, know-how, management skills and so on, as well as on rivals' reactions).

When competition is regarded in this light, a firm with market power must be redefined as one which can slow down (or stop) the competitive process so as to sustain abnormal profits over longer periods of time. Although superficially similar to the neoclassical concept of barriers to entry, Austrians believe that competition is not impeded by barriers of the kind suggested by Bain (1956) or later neoclassical theorists (Spence, 1977; Dixit, 1982). Rather, barriers are viewed as impediments to the market process which cannot be overcome through time. They are not (as in neoclassical theory) an advantage possessed by a firm at a point in time. Consequently, product differentiation or absolute cost advantages are not regarded as entry barriers, because they can be eliminated by the development of new products and by changes in methods of production and distribution.

In general, the most effective barriers to entry are those imposed by the government and backed by the force of law; for instance, where governments grant legal monopolies, protect domestic markets by tariffs and other trade barriers, impose licensing requirements or grant exclusive rights to certain practices. The market for contact lens solutions in the UK provides an example (Monopolies and Mergers Commission, 1993b). Contact lens solutions cannot be supplied without a licence, which has proved difficult to acquire. Moreover, the licence requires products to be sold only through opticians and/or pharmacies. These restrictions have damaged competition by limiting entry and have allowed the dominant supplier (Allergan) and the dominant retailer

(Boots) to exploit market power through higher prices. Government-imposed barriers are generally very difficult to circumvent and imply that entry to such markets is essentially under the control of the government.

■ *5.16* Conclusion

Until the 1970s it was generally believed that the empirical evidence showing a positive (if weak) association between market concentration and profits was evidence that monopoly was harmful to economic welfare. However, studies which attempt to quantify this effect have often shown the reduction in welfare to be remarkably small (typically under 1 per cent of GNP). This by itself suggests that large-scale expenditure by governments to control monopoly abuses is unwarranted.

A persuasive minority suggests that monopoly may actually improve society's welfare. If the monopolist has lower costs, productive efficiency gains may outweigh the welfare losses caused by market power and empirical relationships between profit and concentration may be explained not by market power but by greater efficiency. From the perspective of transaction cost economics this superior efficiency is attributed to firm-specific factors conferring unique advantages to particular firms. Adopting the Austrian view of competition as a process reveals that monopolies are the temporary reward for beneficial – and hence profitable – innovation.

The debate on the welfare effects of monopoly has yet to be concluded. Certainly, universal condemnation of monopoly *per se* is inappropriate. The evidence suggests that monopolies are often beneficial to society. Where monopoly goes hand in hand with market power, what is at issue is the length of time over which this power can be sustained. It would appear that barriers are most effective (allowing market power to persist) where governments impose restrictions on the entry to markets. It seems that it is in these areas that unfettered monopolies will be most detrimental to welfare.

■ *Chapter 6* ■

Invention, Innovation and Diffusion

> The first premise of our undertaking should be noncontroversial: it is simply that economic change is important and interesting (R. R. Nelson and S. G. Winter, 1982, p. 3).

■ 6.1 Introduction

In the twentieth century, competition between firms has been largely on the basis of product improvements and cost advantages generated by developments in methods of production and organisation. However, textbooks often ignore the process of change, concentrating instead on the beneficial effects of price competition. This is a major omission, for as Schumpeter argues:

> But in capitalist reality as distinguished from its textbook picture, it is not that kind of [price] competition which counts but the competition from the new commodity, the new technology, the new source of supply, the new type of organisation … competition which commands a decisive cost or quality advantage and which strikes not at the margins of the profits and the outputs of existing firms but at their foundations and their very lives (1942, p. 84).

The lack of attention paid to new products and processes in most economic texts reflects the difficulty of incorporating the topic within the neoclassical approach. Adopting the assumptions of perfect information and using a form of analysis that is static is inappropriate to the discussion of change. Much of the work in this area has concentrated simply on identifying empirical relationships, typically between firm size or market structure and expenditures on research and development expenditure or the number of innovations. In contrast, economists who adopt an institutional approach have turned attention to qualitative studies of particular innovations, the relationships between innovations, and their impact upon the evolution of markets and industries.

■ 6.2 Change in the pharmaceutical market

For many goods and services, price competition is less important than competition based upon the introduction of new products and processes. This is vividly illustrated by the pharmaceutical market, which – although an extreme case – illustrates the general forces at work within markets. Here a firm's success largely depends upon its ability to launch new products: in 1976, Hoffman-La Roche, Hoechst and Bristol Myers each introduced over 40 new pharmaceutical products. As an illustration of the speed with which products change in this market Tischler and Denkewalter (1966) estimated that only 10 per cent of the prescriptions written in 1965 were for drugs that were available fifteen years earlier.

Figure 6.1 shows how the relative positions of the firms in the US pharmaceutical market have varied, with repeated changes in the market leaders in consequence of the introduction of drugs with superior pharmacological properties. As a result of developing successful new products (including the tranquillisers Librium and Valium) Hoffman-La Roche rose from tenth to second ranked firm in the USA (in terms of market share) in the ten years to 1972.

The fortunes of pharmaceutical firms are closely linked to the performance of specific products. Pfizer and Lederle held two-thirds of the UK market in broad spectrum antibiotics in the mid-1960s. Some ten years later, following the expiry of their patents and Beecham's introduction of ampicillin, they were no longer amongst the largest ten firms. In the 1980s, Glaxo's Zantac quickly gained supremacy over other anti-ulcer drugs. In the mid-1990s it faces competition from Astra's Losec, and generic forms of an earlier market leader, Tagamet, out of patent. In 1993, Marion Merrell Dow's Seldane held over 40 per cent of the world market for allergy treatments, but both Pfizer and Schering-Plough were introducing new drugs in the USA, whilst

Firm	1962 rank	1972 rank	Firm
Lily	1	1	Lily
Smith Kline	2	2	Hoffman-La Roche
American Home	3	3	American Home
Upjohn	4	4	Merck
Lederle	5	5	Bristol Myers
Merck	6	6	Abbott
Parke-Davies	7	7	Pfizer
Ciba-Geigy	8	8	Ciba-Geigy
Squibb	9	9	Upjohn
Hoffman-La Roche	10	10	Squibb
Abbott	11	11	Smith Kline
Pfizer	12	12	Johnson & Johnson
Bristol Myers	13	13	Schering-Plough
Warner-Lambert	14	14	Parke-Davies
Schering-Plough	15	15	Searle
Sterling	16	16	Lederle
Searle	17	17	Santoz-Wander
Robins	18	18	Robins
Santoz-Wander	19	19	Sterling
Burroughs Wellcome	20	20	Burroughs Wellcome
Johnson & Johnson	21	21	Warner-Lambert

Figure 6.1 *Ranking of firms in the US market for ethical pharmaceuticals (firms ranked by market share)*
Source: Derived from Cocks (1973).

Hoechst, Zeneca, Upjohn and Ciba were reported to be actively investigating new treatments (*Financial Times*, 29 April 1993).

One of the main reasons for the importance of product competition in the pharmaceutical industry is the strong patent protection offered in this field compared to other industries. As Hippel puts it:

> Pharmaceutical patents can be unusually strong because one may patent an actual molecule ... *and* its analogs. One need not make each analog claimed but can simply refer to lists of recognised functional equivalents for each component of the molecule at issue. For example, if a molecule has 10 important component parts, one patent application might claim x plus 10 recognised functional equivalents of x for each part. Obviously, by this means an inventor may claim millions of specific molecules without actually having to synthesize more than a few. Furthermore, demonstration that any of the analogs

so claimed does not display the medical properties claimed does not invalidate the patent (1988, p. 53).

Even with such protection pharmaceutical firms are still open to competition from the development of better products which are based on molecules without patent protection. Evidence suggests that new pharmaceutical products have an average life expectancy of only five years before they are rendered obsolete by products with improved pharmacological properties.

■ 6.3 The process of change

According to Schumpeter, there are three stages in the process of change: invention, innovation and diffusion. The first of these (*invention*) relates to the generation of a new idea and its subsequent development to a point where the conceptual and practical difficulties of its implementation have been overcome.

The second stage (*innovation*) occurs when the entrepreneur believes that it is worthwhile to commercialise the invention. Schumpeter (1934, p. 66) identifies five types of innovation:

1. the introduction of a new product or service, or an improvement in the quality of an existing product or service;
2. the introduction of a new method of production;
3. the development of a new market;
4. the exploitation of a new source of supply;
5. the reorganisation of methods of operation.

There is a tendency to focus narrowly upon the introduction of new products and processes which incorporate technological advances. Schumpeter's broader definition of innovation covers more of the ways in which the use of resources may be improved. This includes the adoption of improved organisational routines and the discovery of new markets. It incorporates the main methods by which economies evolve.

The entrepreneur cannot know in advance whether his innovation will succeed. If his expectations are correct then the innovation generates abnormal profits, as a result of either increasing revenue or reducing costs; but successful innovation prompts emulation by rivals anxious to improve their own profits. This is Schumpeter's third stage (*diffusion*). As a result of widespread imitation, the innovation becomes established as the basis for future invention and innovation. For instance, major technological developments such as that of the internal combustion engine or the microprocessor form the basis for further innovations in a particular sector.

The pace of innovation is not constant in a particular economy (or part of an economy). Innovations are highly dependent on the general process of change (for example, developments in technology) and, in turn, influence other areas of the economy. Institutional economists generally argue that an innovation cannot meaningfully be analysed singularly, but must be understood in terms of the evolution of the economy. The reasons for innovation and the connections between them are of particular interest.

■ 6.4 Why does change occur?

Models which incorporate the assumption of perfect information cannot explain inventions, nor change in general. This because perfect knowledge – an assumption which is at odds with an environment in which uncertainty and disequilibrium prevail – denies benefits to an innovating firm. Given the importance of these factors, they need to be discussed in some detail.

An early explanation of why invention occurs was provided by Taussig (1915). He identified spontaneous and induced invention. *Spontaneous invention* occurs simply because of human inquisitiveness, while *induced invention* is promoted by the prospect of financial reward. Schmookler (1966) argues that latent demand for a product stimulates its invention, whilst Hippel (1988) believes that innovating firms are separated from their non-innovating counterparts by asymmetries in profit expectations.

Accepting that changes are motivated by profits, then models based on perfect information can only explain the process of change if there are barriers to entry. These allow a firm to reap the benefits of its innovation – at least for a while – even when others are aware of the change. In fully contestable markets (**Section 2.6**), imitation of a new product or process would be instantaneous and widespread. Innovation would therefore be irrational since the extra costs incurred in research and development would bring no prospect of enhanced profits. The only exception would be the introduction of an innovation developed elsewhere, for example in a non-perfectly competitive capital goods industry. This case can explain the adoption of a new production process, but not the introduction of a new product.

Where agents have perfect information, any disequilibrium is fleeting. In practice, markets are likely to be in disequilibrium for some time. Equilibrium is restored only when diffusion has eliminated all innovatory profits; empirical studies suggest this may take several years. Furthermore, disequilibrium is likely to be the norm if ongoing innovation allows markets no opportunity to reach equilibrium before subsequent changes occur. As Schumpeter has argued:

> Now a theoretical construction which neglects this essential element of the case [disequilibrium] neglects all that is most typically capitalist about it; even if correct in logic as well as in fact, it is like *Hamlet* without the Danish prince (1942, p. 86).

Innovation takes place in an environment where uncertainty is endemic. This makes the assumption of perfect information invalid and the attainment of profit (or other) optimisation objectives impossible. Where change is continuous and unpredictable, even those economic agents who take steps to reduce their ignorance make mistakes. Some models have recognised that information is both imperfect and costly to acquire, and incorporate less ambitious objectives – such as the maximisation of the mathematical expectation of profit. Whilst this increases realism, it remains unsatisfactory because, in these models, entrepreneurs still do not make mistakes. It is only if past experience can be used to determine objective probabilities that the chance (risk) of achieving a particular outcome can be specified (**Section 1.3**). Furthermore these models continue to ignore the management costs involved in correctly interpreting and disseminating information within the firm and the complications resulting from changes in consumers' tastes.

An alternative approach is that of the new institutional economists (**Section 1.5**). For instance, Dosi and Orsenigo (1988) start from the premise that innovation takes place in a world which:

(a) is evolutionary and where change is never instantaneous;
(b) contains heterogeneous agents who make mistakes and learn over time;
(c) is irreversible, such that past history determines currently available options and selection mechanisms;
(d) is self-organising, with the system evolving in ways constrained both by economic factors (such as prices and competition) and institutional factors which influence decisions and expectations.

Information flows are far from perfect, and competition is regarded as a process occurring through time. Innovation is the major mechanism by which firms compete.

Within the new institutional economics, the Austrian and evolutionary approaches (**Section 1.5**) provide subtly different perspectives, but have much more in common with each other than with the neoclassical paradigm. From the Austrian stance, innovation is driven by entrepreneurs actively seeking to improve their positions; by successfully introducing new ideas ahead of other firms, a firm can enjoy abnormal profits which persist until the new idea has been widely adopted by rivals. In the evolutionary approach, decision-makers are less aware and less pro-active; rather they react to the environment and innovate if survival is threatened.

The Austrian and evolutionary approaches can be illustrated by reference to **Figure 6.2**. The upper half shows a number of autonomous firms in a small part of an economy. Most of these firms are classified to the same industry or belong to the same market. (The grouping of firms for the market differs from the grouping of firms for the industry, see **Section 2.10**.) Firms W, Y and Z face constraints imposed by the institutional environment, technology, prices of factors of production, and by the market structure in which they operate (which constrains the price they obtain for their products).

The way in which the economy in general (and this part of the economy in particular) evolves can be illustrated by taking any firm. The forces and constraints operating on Firm Y are detailed in the lower half of **Figure 6.2**. Firm Y has a current 'boundary' (the horizontal and vertical extent of the firm: the scale and scope of its activities together with the extent to which its operations are vertically integrated). It deploys its own technical and organisational know-how, built up over time. It also has its own culture ('the way we do things around here'), which has evolved over time. In addition, the firm has devised an incentive structure to reward/punish employees for operating in certain ways. In summary, Firm Y has both 'hard' and 'soft' characteristics. Some aspects (such as advertising expenditure and number of products) can be measured, while others (such as culture) can only be gauged against qualitative criteria.

A firm is 'successful' to a lesser or greater extent. How is this to be measured? It depends upon the selection mechanism for survival, determined by the institutional environment in which the firm operates. In a typical advanced market economy, the selection mechanism is financial. The earnings of the firm must be sufficient to cover the opportunity costs of all the factors employed. (However, if this performance has been achieved through behaviour regarded as 'unethical' in the particular institutional environment, this may not secure the long-term survival of the firm.)

The difference between the Austrian and evolutionary approaches can now be highlighted. In Austrian economics, *whatever* the firm's financial performance, the entrepreneur actively seeks improvement. In

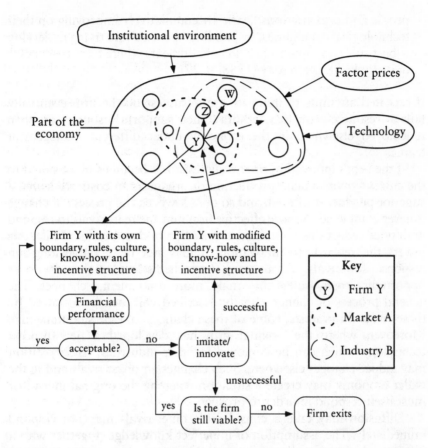

Figure 6.2 *Innovation from an Austrian/evolutionary perspective*

the evolutionary approach, if the firm's current performance is 'acceptable' (that is, if it covers the opportunity cost of the resources deployed) no change will be initiated. Only if current performance falls short of this will management seek improvement.

In both approaches, managers cannot know the best actions to take. They must conduct experiments to identify which actions lead to improved performance and must judge, for example, whether to imitate other firms or to innovate in more fundamental ways (through, for example, expenditures on research and development). This choice is influenced by other firms' behaviour. However, the firm may take 'wrong' paths, which leave it less well adapted to the current environment than its rivals. The resulting decline in its financial performance reinforces the drive towards change through imitation/innovation: the failure generates learning. According to Dosi and Orsenigo:

people and organisations 'learn' by cumulatively improving on their technological capabilities, by building 'theories' and trying to develop robust rules on 'how to live' in environments where tomorrow never quite looks like yesterday (1988, p. 27).

If repeated attempts to innovate are unsuccessful, the firm eventually fails as resource-providers withdraw their support. Resources are then redeployed elsewhere in the economy under different management teams.

If the firm's innovation proves successful, it becomes more suited to the current environment: production or organisation costs are lower, a superior product is offered, and so on. However, the process of change is never completed. A more effective firm may incite its rivals to respond with price reductions to mitigate the erosion of their profits. Whilst this lowers the rewards to innovation, it may not be a viable long-run response for rivals. Rivals may find themselves unable to cover opportunity costs, unless they make more fundamental changes. The general process of change already described will then be followed by these rivals (in practice, some of these changes may be simultaneous). Moreover, where the original firm has developed a new process technology which can be deployed in other industries, its innovation may induce changes elsewhere. Such changes amongst rivals and in the wider economy may create a situation whereby the original innovator must itself respond in order to prosper.

Diffusion may take a considerable time; rivals may not respond immediately. The assumption of imperfect knowledge (together with a differential response by entrepreneurs) ensures that innovators are rewarded by a period of abnormal profit before it is subsequently eroded by rivals. Entrepreneurs vary in their alertness to market developments, so different lengths of time pass before the superior attributes of the innovator's product or production process are recognised. Even if entrepreneurs simultaneously perceive new information, their responses may vary because of different attitudes and different perceptions of potential profit. In addition, rivals will be more alert to a product innovation than to a process innovation, which leaves the product unchanged.

■ 6.5 Invention and innovation

In popular usage, invention refers to advances in science and technology, but this is unnecessarily restricting. The term can be applied more broadly to the generation of any new idea. Invention does not just encompass the creation of a new product involving scientific advance (for example, the invention of synthetic penicillin) or process (like the invention of the float method of producing flat glass), it can also include developments which do not incorporate any scientific advance. The entrepreneur who (using existing technology) discovers a way of combining factor inputs to produce a new product is an inventor. An example is the invention of the credit card and the organisation required to make it effective.

Schumpeter's concept of innovation (**Section 6.3**) is useful because it suggests that – even without further scientific advance – much progress is possible simply from the utilisation of existing know-how to improve products and processes. Admittedly, scientific advance sets an upper limit to economic progress. As Freeman argues:

> No amount of improvement in education and quality of labour force, no greater efforts by the mass media, no economies of scale or structural changes, no improvements in management or in government administration could in themselves ultimately transcend the technical limitations of candle-power as a means of illumination, of wind as a source of energy, or iron as an engineering material, or horses as a means of transport (1974, p. 20).

Scientific advances are always inextricably linked with other types of invention. Society did not benefit from the discovery of iron, but from the invention of new products and processes using this discovery. Scientific inventions typically require complementary advances before their benefits to society can be realised.

Hippel (1988) investigated the sources of a sample of scientific innovations. Firms were categorised in terms of their functional relationship with the innovation. *Users* benefit from using the innovation. *Manufacturers* benefit from producing the innovation and selling it to others. *Suppliers* benefit from supplying the components or material necessary to produce the innovation. A firm can be in more than one category. The US firm, Boeing, is a manufacturer of aircraft and a user of machine tools. If it was involved in an innovative aircraft design, it would be categorised as a *manufacturer*. If it developed an innovative machine tool used in aircraft manufacture it would be classified as a *user*. Hippel found that innovations came from firms in each of these categories, but certain types of innovation tended to be associated with particular categories. Hippel believed these results were explained by differential profit expectations across the categories of firms:

innovations of a specific type are typically developed by firms that expect the most attractive return (1988, p.8).

For example, in the case of innovations in scientific instruments, *users* can expect the greatest benefits since they can employ the improved instrument to foster their competitiveness. Moreover, they are in the best position to keep this innovation secret from other firms and thereby sustain abnormal profits over a longer period than a *manufacturer* or *supplier* that must, of necessity, make it public to benefit.

Hippel's results depend on the presence of two conditions. First, it must be costly for a firm to change category. A *user* that innovates must not be able to become a manufacturer at zero (or trivial) cost. New institutional economists would argue that this is usually the case. For example, a *user* would not possess the marketing information and distributional infrastructure necessary for the effective commercialisation of the innovation. In contrast, the established *manufacturer* has these assets in place and, in addition, is able to exploit any economies of scope more effectively. A *priori*, a *manufacturer* is likely to anticipate a higher rate of return on an innovation capable of widespread adoption.

The existence of the second condition – that imperfections in the market preclude the sale of an invention at full value – is widely accepted by economists of all schools. It is only if the invention is specific to the production of one product that its full value may be realised. In other cases, selling the invention in the market is likely to be a poor option. It will be very difficult, if not impossible, to draw up a contract which prevents an invention, which is not specific to a particular product, being applied to areas not covered by the contract. To obtain the full rewards may necessitate exploiting the invention within the firm.

■ 6.6 The importance of innovation

The successful introduction of an invention will generally lead to an improvement in society's welfare. The main qualification to this statement is that, if more resources are devoted to the enhanced products and processes of the future, this implies less resources are available for the production of current goods and services. A trade-off therefore exists between current and future levels of welfare. Society is willing to forgo current welfare if it receives sufficient increases in future levels of welfare to compensate for this current loss. This balance is crucially dependent upon the rate at which society discounts future benefits: the lower the figure the greater should be research and development activity, and vice versa. However, whilst (ignoring the effects of taxation) the market rate of interest can be taken as a proxy for individuals' willingness to forgo marginal changes in current benefits in exchange for future benefits, economists have failed to determine at what rate society should discount future benefits (**Sections 7.3** and **7.8**).

Even so, innovation has been a major source of improvements in welfare. Economists were first aware of its quantitative importance in the 1950s in the context of economic growth. Solow (1957) found that the usual explanations for higher output (greater employment of labour and capital) accounted only for a relatively small proportion of increased output per man-hour in the USA during the period 1909–49. Instead, most of the gain in productivity was attributed to improvements in the quality of the labour force and to changes in production processes. Denison (1974) undertook a similar study. He was able to estimate the contribution to output of improvements in the quality of the labour force, but he found that changes in production methods were more important, being responsible for 48 per cent of the increase in output per worker for the USA over the period 1929–69. This result confirmed the findings of an earlier study of advanced economies (Denison, 1967). Both Denison and Solow underestimated the welfare benefits, because they ignored product innovation. Moreover, their work has been questioned because their analysis assumed that markets are in equilibrium. Despite these criticisms, Denison's and Solow's conclusions are similar to those of Nelson and Winter (1982) who use a more sophisticated, institutional approach.

6.7 The welfare effects of product innovation

Insights into how innovation enhances welfare can be obtained using neoclassical models to focus on the impact of different types of innovation at the level of the firm and market. Product innovation may be classified as either incremental or fundamental. *Incremental product innovation* involves the introduction of an improved product, which – compared with its predecessor – has at least one extra desirable characteristic or is better endowed with the same characteristics. Competition between car manufacturers, for example, has led to the development of such features as greater comfort, lower noise levels, better performance and greater fuel efficiency. The new product is more highly valued by consumers and, at an unchanged price, attracts sales away from rivals. For the innovating firm, this causes a rightward shift of its demand curve. In contrast, *fundamental product innovation* takes place when a new market is opened up and the innovator starts to satisfy

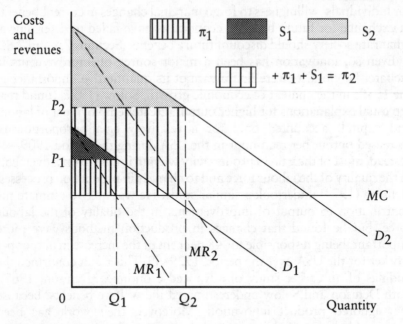

Figure 6.3 *Incremental product innovation under monopoly*

a latent demand. Examples of this are the market for business microcomputers discovered by Apple in the 1970s and home computers exploited by Sinclair a few years later.

Figure 6.3 illustrates an incremental product innovation by a monopoly. (As already noted, there is no rationale for product innovation to occur in a perfectly competitive market.) In this, and the following analyses, constant average costs are assumed for simplicity. It is also assumed that the marginal cost of the new product is the same as that of the product it displaces.

Before the improved product is introduced, price and output are $0P_1$ and $0Q_1$ respectively. After adopting the innovation, the demand curve shifts to the right, price rises to $0P_2$ and the new equilibrium output rises to $0Q_2$. Before the innovation, welfare is measured by areas $S_1 + \pi_1$ whereas after the innovation is adopted welfare equals areas $S_2 + \pi_2$. Abnormal profits have increased (π_2 rather than π_1). This must be the case, for otherwise the entrepreneur would have had no incentive to improve the product. Similarly, because the new profit-maximising output level must be higher after innovation, consumer surplus S_2 must be greater than S_1. Consequently there has been a net increase in welfare as represented by the equation:

$$\Delta W = (S_2 + \pi_2) - (S_1 + \pi_1) \tag{6.1}$$

Society will also benefit when a monopolist implements a fundamental product innovation. Because the market is not exploited before the innovation, the demand curve is latent. The net welfare gain following the introduction of the new product is the same as in the equation above but, in this case, the pre-innovation monopoly profits and consumer surplus are equal to zero.

6.8 The welfare effects of process and organisational innovation

Process innovation can take several forms. New techniques may be discovered which enable the firm to use less of at least one input. Alternatively, a method may be found which allows lower-cost inputs to be used. Welfare is improved with either type of process innovation. With the former, resources are released to produce other desired products, while with the latter an input with a relatively high opportunity cost is released to produce other goods. In both cases, firms adopting the innovation are able to reduce their costs.

Organisational innovation relates to the introduction of improved methods of administration, sequencing and control. For example, the Italian clothing firm, Benetton, discovered that it could respond more rapidly and more cheaply to changes in fashion by producing knitwear in a neutral colour to be dyed just before dispatch. Such organisational innovation will also enable a firm to reduce its costs. Hence its effects on welfare will be similar to those of a process innovation.

Figure 6.4 shows the case of a process innovation leading to cost reductions in a perfectly competitive industry producing consumer goods. It is assumed that the reduction in costs comes from an innovation in the capital goods industry, for instance, technical advances resulting in improved machinery (**Section 6.4**). This innovation is available to all firms in the industry. Using the original production process, price and output are $0P_1$ and $0Q_1$ respectively. After adopting the innovation, costs and price fall to $0P_2$ and the new equilibrium output rises to $0Q_2$. Before the innovation, welfare is measured by area S_1, whereas after the innovation is adopted consumer surplus increases, raising welfare to area S_2.

It should be noted that process innovations which reduce costs result in welfare gains even if the industry is a monopoly. **Figure 6.5** shows the pre- and post-innovation prices ($0P_1$ and $0P_2$) and output levels ($0Q_1$

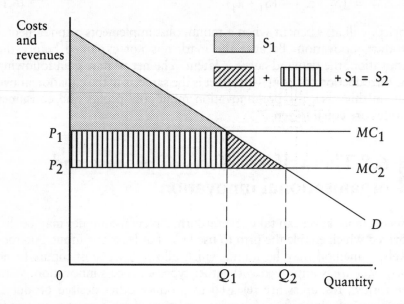

Figure 6.4 *Process innovation in a perfectly competitive market*

and $0Q_2$) of the monopolist. Using the same approach as in the earlier cases, the level of welfare before introducing the improved production method can be shown to be equal to the monopoly profit (π_1) plus the associated consumer surplus (S_1). After implementing the process innovation, welfare is equal to the new monopoly profit (π_2) plus the associated consumer surplus (S_2). Process innovation by a monopolist leads to an increase in welfare equal to:

$$\Delta W = (S_2 + \pi_2) - (S_1 + \pi_1) \tag{6.2}$$

6.9 An alternative view of the welfare effects of process innovation

The work of Nelson and Winter, within the evolutionary school of new institutional economists, reinforces the conclusions of the models discussed earlier, namely that innovation will enhance welfare. They offer a different perspective to that of neoclassical economics (**Sections 6.7** and **6.8**). Nelson and Winter (1982) suggest that calculation of the welfare effects of process innovation may be more complicated. Their model incorporates imperfect information, so that the costs of

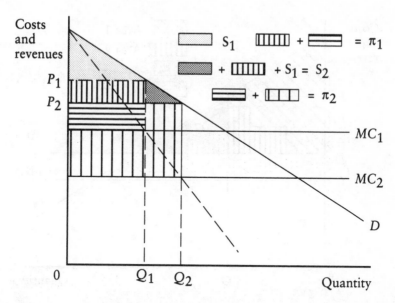

Figure 6.5 *Process innovation in a monopoly*

producing an identical product is likely to differ between firms. Since a firm's success depends on its costs relative to those of its rivals, there is an incentive to search for more efficient methods of production. This search may take the form of research and development (R&D), either to discover new production processes or to enable imitation of rivals' superior processes. In other words, firms can choose whether to be innovators or imitators. There is no guarantee that either type of search activity will be successful, but the expectation of success will be greater, the greater the expenditure devoted to search.

Nelson and Winter investigate two different scenarios of process innovation, called respectively the *science-based case* and the *cumulative technology case*. In the science-based case, it is assumed that developments elsewhere in the economy generate the potential for the industry to achieve enhanced productivity. (This is referred to as the *moving frontier*.) Here, a firm's chance of finding a lower-cost production process as a result of R&D is dependent upon the current level of R&D expenditure and the rate at which the moving frontier is advancing, but the level of R&D expenditures in previous years has no effect. In the cumulative technology case there is no external technological advance to tap. Instead, R&D success is determined by both current levels of expenditure and the success of R&D in previous years:

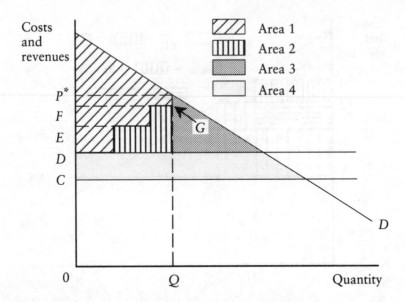

Figure 6.6   *Dynamic analysis of the welfare effects of innovation*

An innovative R&D success buys a firm not only a better technique, but a higher platform for the next period's search (Nelson and Winter, 1982, p. 283).

The welfare effects of innovation under both scenarios are illustrated in **Figure 6.6**. Nelson and Winter's approach is difficult to represent diagrammatically because of its dynamic nature. **Figure 6.6** should therefore be interpreted as showing a snapshot of the evolving situation.

With the science-based case, technological developments in the economy (the moving frontier) imply that firms can discover methods of production which can reduce costs to the level 0C. There are continual developments causing the level of 0C to fall over time. Consequently, firms are always chasing a moving target. However, if all firms achieve cost 0C, then (in a perfectly competitive market) price is also 0C and economic welfare is represented by areas 1 + 2 + 3 + 4. In practice, even the firm spending most on R&D is unlikely to discover ways of reducing costs as far as 0C, and instead has a cost level somewhat higher (say, at 0D, the current 'best practice' level). Firms expending less on searching for lower-cost techniques have higher costs (say, equal to 0E and 0F). Combining these findings, the boundary DG represents the various average cost levels in the market as a whole. Given the total output from all firms currently in the market, price is 0P*. Actual welfare is equal to area 1, which falls short of the maximum potential gain in welfare (1 + 2 + 3 + 4) for three reasons:

1. excess production costs caused by departures from current 'best practice' – area 2;
2. the loss of consumer surplus which would be obtained if the current 'best practice' were adopted in a competitive market – area 3;
3. excess production costs because current 'best practice' departs from the lowest cost technique which, in principle, is available – area 4.

Figure 6.6 can also show the welfare implications of Nelson and Winter's cumulative technology case. Here, all advances are generated within the industry, so area 4 is inapplicable.

An interesting aspect of Nelson and Winter's work is the conclusion that a more competitive market may lead to less rapid innovation and a higher level of price. An increase in the number of firms results in greater output, squeezing profits by depressing price to a level closer to costs. Whilst this reduces the apparent reduction in welfare loss attributable to areas 2 and 3, it may result in an overall reduction in society's welfare through time. Reducing the incentives to innovate may reduce R&D expenditures and consequently slow down the rate at which costs fall over time. Although increased competition initially provides consumers with the benefits of lower prices, this may not compensate for the absence of lower costs and even lower prices in the future.

The departures from the maximum welfare gain illustrated above can be regarded as more apparent than real. In other words, they could be interpreted as a necessary consequence of the process of change. Without the incentive of lower costs – and hence the possibility of enhanced profits – there would be no reason for the firm to innovate or to imitate. Further, the size of this apparent welfare loss will fall over time as more firms adopt (or improve on) the current level of best practice. Qualifying this comment, it should be remembered that over time both 0C and 0D will be moving downwards, so the maximum potential welfare gain will be continually altering.

■ *6.10* Innovation and employment

Although innovation leads to benefits for society, it does not necessarily follow that every member of society gains. Since welfare has increased overall, in principle the gainers could compensate the losers. However, while the benefits are generally spread thinly over consumers as a whole, the losses may be concentrated on just a few. The latter may well resist

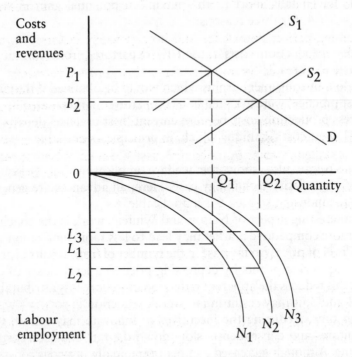

Figure 6.7   *The impact of a process innovation on factor employment in a perfectly competitive industry*

such a change. Analysis of the effects of innovation on the employment of factors of production will identify groups likely to suffer a loss of welfare as a result of change.

Figure 6.7 shows the impact of a process innovation in a perfectly competitive industry. Demand and supply curves for the product are shown in the upper part of the diagram. Initially the market price and output are $0P_1$ and $0Q_1$ respectively. The corresponding derived demand curve for labour (N_1) is shown below the horizontal axis. (It might equally well have shown the derived demand for capital.) Before the process innovation, $0L_1$ units of labour are required to produce quantity $0Q_1$. The process innovation, by reducing marginal cost, shifts both the demand for labour schedule and the market supply curve to N_2 and S_2 respectively. If the effect of the new production method leaves the capital–labour ratio unchanged then the demand for both factors of production increases. In this example, labour demand will increase from $0L_1$ to $0L_2$, with a similar increase in the demand for capital. Alternatively, if the change results in a higher capital–labour ratio, then the demand for labour will fall. This is shown by the post-innovation demand for labour curve N_3 in **Figure 6.7**, with employment falling to $0L_3$.

Assuming perfect knowledge and homogeneous factors of production, the reduction in welfare suffered by displaced factors will be transitory as they will be rapidly re-absorbed into the economy. With imperfect knowledge, it may take time for displaced factors to find alternative employment. Also, the expanding industries may require different labour skills. Technological unemployment can arise if the growing sector requires skills highly specific to the new technology but displaced labour is skilled in more traditional trades. When skills become redundant, the value of human capital is reduced. Social problems may also arise, particularly if the industries adopting labour-saving innovations are regionally concentrated.

■ 6.11 The diffusion of innovation

In neoclassical economics, the perfect knowledge assumption implies that complete diffusion occurs instantaneously. In practice, the adoption of an innovation by rival firms may take several years. Mansfield (1985) noted that it took about twelve to eighteen months for rivals to become aware of new developments. His earlier work (Mansfield, 1968) measured the length of time it took for 60 per cent of relevant rivals to adopt the innovation. This time-interval varied widely from around one year (packaging beer in tin cans), to twenty years (the continuous annealing of tin-plated steel). Diffusion was faster the more profitable the new process, and slower the more capital required to adopt the process, but the average diffusion time was in excess of ten years.

Where an innovation is implemented by a *manufacturer* or *supplier* (using Hippel's categorisation (1988), see **Section 6.5**), the firm will take active measures to speed diffusion, since this will enhance innovatory profits. This is not the case with an innovation by a *user*. Here the longer the innovation is kept secret the higher the profits to the innovator. But even in these cases diffusion occurs as secrets cannot be kept forever (Antonio Stradivarius was an exception). Other firms have an incentive to discover their rivals' developments. Such knowledge is spread when employees of the innovating firm acquire jobs with a rival. However, Hippel also found that innovations were diffused through informal know-how trading between engineers in the innovating firm and those elsewhere, including those in rival firms. This had the effect of reducing abnormal profits. This process can be explained from an institutional perspective, recognising the importance of the 'institution' of professional engineers. An engineer has allegiance to his firm, but also to his fellow professionals. Faced with a problem, he may turn to professional contacts for advice, even though these may be employed by rival firms. As an example, Engineer A may be given the task of developing a process improvement to counter one introduced by Engineer B's firm. Engineer A has previously given help to B, who is therefore under some obligation to return the favour. This may take the form of passing on important know-how relating to his firm's earlier process innovation. This informal networking reduces innovatory profits and speeds diffusion (and may trigger further innovations).

The diffusion process typically follows the pattern illustrated by **Figure 6.8**. Although most studies have considered the diffusion of a process innovation, it seems reasonable to assume that the diffusion of a product innovation would follow a similar path. The top diagram in **Figure 6.8** shows the proportion of firms which have introduced the innovation at different points in time and is typically an S-shaped curve. The bottom diagram presents the information in a different way by showing the rate at which firms take up the innovation. This gives a bell-shaped curve.

One explanation of the S-shaped diffusion curve is that (following innovation) all relevant firms are aware of the innovation, but differences in the vintage of each firm's capital stock lead to differences in the optimal time to imitate. Stoneman (1983) suggests that the largest firms tend to be the first to adopt a process innovation developed in the capital goods industry. This is because their larger market share means that the rate of return on innovation is more attractive. It is not worthwhile for firms below a certain size to introduce the innovation until it becomes less expensive. If firm sizes approximate a normal distribution, then the diffusion process will be as shown in **Figure 6.8**.

Another explanation is provided by likening the diffusion process to the spread of epidemics, such as whooping cough or flu. For a disease to spread, it is necessary for people without immunity to be exposed to those with the infection. Initially, few people have the disease so the rate of infection is slow, even with a large population of uninfected individuals. As the number infected grows, the epidemic spreads more rapidly until the rate of infection reaches a maximum. Beyond this the spread of the epidemic slows because, although there are many infected people, fewer people are left to catch the disease. The spread of information may be analogous to the spread of disease. Entrepreneurs need to find out about innovations before they can implement them, and this is difficult when only a few firms have adopted them. Conversely, the rate of adoption will slow when the process has already been implemented by most of the relevant firms.

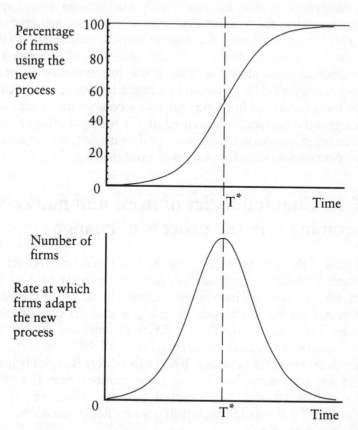

Figure 6.8   *The time path of diffusion of a process innovation*

The introduction of a new product or production process generates a welfare gain, which increases as diffusion proceeds. Referring to the previous analysis of the welfare effects of innovation, the perfectly competitive model (**Figure 6.4**) may now be interpreted as showing the situation after the diffusion has taken place and the market returned to equilibrium. In the monopoly case, the analysis of **Figure 6.3** understates the extent to which changes occur. If a monopolist introduces a new and successful product which earns abnormal profits, this acts as a spur to other firms (both new and existing) to imitate. Unless there are restrictions imposed by government, rivals are able to introduce an effective substitute for the innovator's product. Patents may slow down the diffusion process, but they cannot prevent it if the potential rewards are sufficiently attractive. Imitation alters the structure of the market as the monopolist's position is broken down. Output increases, depressing the market price. The more extensive the imitation, the smaller abnormal profits become. Eventually imitation becomes so widespread that price reaches the 'competitive' level where abnormal profits are zero. This increases the area of consumer surplus, enhancing welfare.

A similar situation arises with the diffusion of a process (or organisational) innovation. A monopolist implementing a process innovation (**Figure 6.5**) is rewarded by a higher level of profits, and there will be some initial fall in market price as a consequence of the lower costs. Again the prospect of enhanced profits will lead others to adopt the same techniques to enter the monopolist's market, further reducing market price and eroding the monopoly position.

6.12 Characteristics of firms and markets prominent in the process of change

Discussion of the process of change needs to be extended to consider the characteristics which distinguish those firms and markets that have good records for invention and innovation. Research in this area has generally concentrated on the importance of firm size and the type of market structure. The level of innovation is difficult to measure. For instance, patent counts suffer because of heterogeneity and the complication that many patents are never exploited. R&D expenditure is typically used as a proxy for innovation, but this (an input measure) may not be well correlated with innovation (an output measure). Moreover, there is some evidence that small firms, which have no R&D specialists, under-record their expenditures.

Jewkes, Sawers and Stillerman (1969) provided evidence on the characteristics of firms active at the invention stage. Of 70 important, early-twentieth-century, scientific inventions only 24 originated in the research departments of large firms: most of the rest originated from research institutes, universities and individuals. Similarly, Hamberg (1966) found that, of 27 important scientific inventions in the period 1946–55, only seven were made by large firms.

Although this might suggest that large firms are relatively bad at generating scientific invention, two points must be noted. As Freeman argues when referring to Jewkes, Sawers and Stillerman: 'If [the] list is broken down, the share of corporate R and D is weak before 1930, but dominant since' (1974, p. 208). Secondly, since society does not benefit until innovation occurs, it is arguable that the source of inventions is of less importance than the source of innovations. Even Jewkes, Sawers and Stillerman, when referring to invention, conceded that:

this is, after all, the less important part of the story of technical progress and that the real determinants of the rate of advance will be the scale and the speed of the efforts made to perfect new commodities and devices and to contrive ways of producing them cheaply and in quantity (1969, p. 152).

The so-called *Schumpeterian hypothesis* is the most widely tested innovation hypothesis. This is conventionally interpreted in two ways; monopoly or large absolute firm size are conducive to innovation. However, it is difficult to discern Schumpeter's own views since his ideas on the relationships between competition, size and innovation change significantly between *The Theory of Economic Development* (1934, first published in German in 1912) and *Capitalism, Socialism and Democracy* (1942).

The large absolute size variant of the hypothesis stems from a belief that innovation generates only a temporary advantage. Where protection from imitation is absent, rewards are largely determined by the rapidity with which the innovator can exploit his initial advantage. This depends on the innovator's organisational ability, especially in marketing and production. It is argued that small firms lack the ability to exploit rapidly their innovations and (in consequence) earn a lower rate of return. Nelson and Winter's theoretical work (1982) provides support for such a link between large firms and innovative activity. A given process innovation generates greater returns in the case of a large firm, because the costs of the innovation are spread over a larger total output. Hence (compared to small firms) large firms can generate higher returns to the innovation. Another factor favouring large firms is the chance nature of returns to R&D. Since a small firm can afford only a small expenditure on R&D, it may experience prolonged periods during which it fails to develop a successful innovation. This places innovating small firms at a disadvantage because (compared to large firms and those following an imitation policy) their techniques are often more dated and (consequently) costs are relatively higher.

Kamien and Schwartz, surveying the empirical evidence, found partial support for the contention that large firm size is conducive to innovation:

Relative R&D activity, measured either by input or output intensity, appears to increase with firm size up to a point, then level off or decline beyond it (1975, p. 32).

This result is supported by Freeman (1974), whose investigation of a number of economies found R&D programmes to be mainly conducted by large firms with over 5000 employees, while probably 95 per cent of small firms were without a specialised R&D programme. However, amongst the larger firms, he also noted that research activity tended to diminish when the firm exceeded a certain size. In contrast, Pavitt *et al.* (1987) conducted a survey of over 4000 important innovations in the UK during the period 1945–83 and found that smaller firms (employing less that 1000) were responsible for a much larger share of innovations than indicated by their share of R&D expenditures. This suggests that the relationship between firm size and innovative activity may be 'U-shaped'. This relationship was also found in investigations of R&D intensity and firm size by Cremer and Sirbu (1978) for France and Bound *et al.* (1984) for the USA, but when Levin *et al.* (1987) adjusted the US data for *technological opportunity* (that is, industry effects), doubtful observations and business unit size, the relationship vanished. As Cohen and Levin conclude:

> The most notable feature of this considerable body of empirical evidence on the relationship between firm size and innovation is its inconclusiveness (1989, p. 1069).

It has often been suggested that Schumpeter regarded monopoly as a market structure favouring innovation. This contention may be misplaced: it stems from his criticism of perfect competition, that the:

> introduction of new methods of production and new commodities is hardly conceivable with perfect – and perfectly prompt – competition from the start (1942, p. 105).

However, this rejection of perfect competition should not be taken as automatic support for monopoly as the market structure which best promotes innovation.

Many studies have investigated the relationship between market concentration and R&D expenditure. Most studies have found a positive, but very weak relationship. For instance, from a survey of the empirical evidence, Kamien and Schwartz (1982) found that the positive correlation between R&D intensity and concentration was considerably reduced when technological opportunity is taken into account. Geroski (1990), using price–cost margins to proxy profits for the periods 1970–4 and 1975–9, showed that monopoly is not conducive to innovation, since both small firms and new entrants act to stimulate innovation. In their review of the evidence, Cohen and Levin state:

these results leave little support for the view that [*ex ante*] industrial concentration is an independent, significant, and important determinant of innovative behaviour and performance (1989, p. 1078).

Most tests of both the large absolute size and monopoly variants of the Schumpeterian hypothesis fail to consider that the direction of causation may be reversed, with innovation leading to the increase in firm size and/or levels of market concentration *ex post*. Moreover, the tests usually adopt a neoclassical approach which is at variance with Schumpeter's evolutionary perspective. From an institutional perspective, the aggregation of firms (as if they were homogeneous) is suspect. Firms classified according either to a particular industry or market are heterogeneous in the technologies they employ and the efficiency of their operation. Whilst averages can be calculated, they do not present a meaningful picture of the industry. Furthermore, whatever the period chosen the firms are unlikely to be in equilibrium in the neoclassical sense.

Nelson and Winter's work on the analysis of process innovation is closer to Schumpeter's approach and gives rather more support to the monopoly variant of his hypothesis:

> not only may a relatively concentrated industry provide a better shelter for R&D than a more fragmented industry structure, but that production and technical advance may also be more efficient in such a setting (1982, p. 350).

They find that not only does high concentration generate innovation, but also that innovation itself leads to increased concentration in markets that were initially competitive. Their work also suggests (in the cumulative technology case) that greater competition slows down innovation. This occurs because the lower profit margins consequent on the lower price in a more competitive market reduce the incentive to innovate.

Another aspect of their work suggests that concentrated markets may not always favour innovation. This would be the case where an 'entrenched monopoly' – an established large firm, unwilling to innovate, but able to imitate rapidly – creates a dynamic barrier to entry against small innovators. For there to be a serious welfare implication here, two further conditions must be met. First, international competition must be absent. Secondly, there must be no competition from firms developing innovations which use radically different technology (against such firms, the imitation skills of the established dominant firm would be ineffective).

Table 6.1 *Business research and development expenditures by industry as a percentage of value-added for selected industries, 1988*

Industrial sector	UK	France	Germany[1]	Japan	USA
Textiles and footwear	0.3	0.4	0.6	1.3	n.a.
Wood and furniture	0.1	0.1	1.0	0.6	0.4[2]
Paper and printing	0.2	0.3	0.3	0.8	n.a.
Chemicals	6.6	8.9	8.6	10.6	5.5
Pharmaceuticals	22.4	28.9	14.9	12.9	15.3
Petroleum refining	3.4	2.3	6.9	6.1	7.7
Rubber and plastics	0.7	4.2	2.2	3.6	3.2[2]
Stone, clay and glass	0.6	1.4	1.8	3.9	0.9[2]
Ferrous metals	1.3	2.3	1.6	3.9	0.8
Non-ferrous metals	1.4	2.3	1.8	7.9	2.2
Metal products	0.8	0.7	2.2	1.2	1.4
Non-electrical machinery	1.9	2.1	4.9	3.2	1.9
Computers	15.7	7.9[2]	7.9	13.7[2]	n.a.
Electrical machinery	3.2	2.6	8.7	4.4	1.1
Electronics	22.2	30.5	15.1	17.6	24.9
Shipbuilding	0.1	1.0	2.0	20.0[2,3]	n.a.
Motor vehicles	6.7	8.8	7.7	9.5	11.0[2]
Aerospace	18.6	44.3	39.6	0.5[3]	43.2
Instruments	5.4	4.7	5.8	14.6	7.7
Total manufacturing	4.7	6.0	5.6	6.1	7.3

Source: Cabinet Office (1992).

[1.] Data from Germany relate to 1987.

[2.] Data not available for 1988, nearest year used instead.

[3.] The majority of Japanese aerospace R&D is reported under shipbuilding.

Nelson and Winter's results stem from some fairly implausible assumptions. For instance, they rule out the possibility of entry, so competition is limited to that between firms initially in the industry. Also, it must be borne in mind that Nelson and Winter equate 'monopoly' with four, initially equal-sized firms in a market (referred to as 'tight oligopoly') and 'competition' with sixteen such firms. Despite this, Nelson and Winter's work is instructive in showing how innovation may influence (and be influenced by) market structure, ease of imitation and the rapidity of technological change. Innovation is more effective than imitation in enhancing a firm's profits in industries where rapid technical progress is taking place.In contrast, imitation is the more successful strategy in industries where underlying scientific advance is relatively slow and imitation easy.

Nelson and Winter's conclusions as to the variables that influence the pace of change are consistent with empirical findings. **Table 6.1** shows large variations in R&D intensities between industries across countries, with high levels of R&D expenditure in those industries where scientific advance is rapid (such as electronics and aerospace) and low levels in mature, slowly-advancing, industries (such as wood and furniture, stone, clay and glass).

■ *6.13* Conclusion

Economic theory has to explain a world in which change is endemic. In this context, the neoclassical approach based on the assumption of perfect knowledge is limited, because it treats innovation as an exogenous shock to which firms have to respond. A more fruitful approach is to regard research and development and innovation as activities undertaken to further a firm's objectives. With this approach, entrepreneurs expend resources on invention and innovation if they believe, *ex ante*, that this will result in abnormal profits that will persist at least until the costs of the development have been recouped. Whether a firm competes by introducing new products and processes, by discovering new markets or on price will be determined by the relative attractiveness of these options. Firms pursuing innovation strategies are more likely to be large firms (perhaps monopolies) in areas where scientific and other advances are rapid. However, the features leading to success in innovation are the same as those which generally lead to success overall – in short, effective entrepreneurship.

■ *Chapter 7* ■

The Foundations of Industry Policy

> When we come to industry policy ... It is true to say that academic economists still attend conferences in the hope that they might acquire a clearer view of what it really consists of and of course, in fairness, what rationale if any lies behind it (D. Swann, 1983, p. 3).

■ *7.1* Introduction

When economists turn their attention from theoretical work towards problems of public policy they often become schizophrenic. In theoretical work careful attention is paid to the logical derivation of conclusions from initial assumptions. These same theoretical models then become the foundation for policy prescriptions, sometimes with little thought as to their real-world relevance.

Nowhere is the contrast between meticulously derived theory and loosely derived policy prescriptions greater than in the area of industry policy. Economists often argue that governments should intervene in industry when markets fail to provide an efficient utilisation of resources. Unfortunately discussion of the circumstances in which market failure occurs is often inadequately developed. Furthermore, in practice, governments often intervene for reasons that have (at best) only a hazy connection with market failure.

The case for industry policy be must be carefully made: objectives should be clearly specified, theoretical justification spelled out, and the resource implications carefully analysed. In a changing and uncertain environment, it is impossible to measure objectively the success of a policy; nor can the costs of the policy for other areas of the economy be readily identified. Alleged cures for market failure need to be well thought out: otherwise they may do more harm than the problem they aim to treat.

■ 7.2 What is industry policy?

Most government action has some effect on the industrial sector of the economy. In many instances, this is simply a consequence of policy elsewhere – for example, import controls to help the balance of payments, prices and incomes policies to counter inflation and increases in interest rates to control the money supply or to halt an exchange rate depreciation. In other instances, government action has a more deliberate effect on the operation of industry, but would generally still not be considered as 'industry policy'. This is because the main objective is to influence some other aspect of the economy, as is often the case with expenditure on infrastructure and on education.

Industry policy usually relates to those policies whose main direct effect is upon individual firms and industries, or on industry as a whole. As Lindbeck defines the term:

> By industry policy is meant political actions designed to affect either *the general mechanisms* of production and resource allocation or *the actual* allocation of resources among sectors of production by means other than general monetary and fiscal policies which are designed to influence various macro-economic aggregates (1981, p. 391).

To the European Commission:

> Industrial policy concerns the effective and coherent implementation of all those policies which impinge on the structural adjustment of industry with a view to promoting competitiveness (Commission of the European Communities (CEC), 1992a, p. 42).

Policies covered by these definitions include competition policy intended to affect markets with certain characteristics or firms pursuing certain types of behaviour; regional policy to influence the spatial location of industry; innovation policy to influence the technology used by firms; and trade policies designed to protect specific firms and industries.

In practice, industry policy is predominantly directed at the industrial or secondary sector of the economy, but there is no reason why the types of policies advocated (and the theoretical arguments that justify them) cannot be applied to the primary and tertiary sectors of the economy. This is likely to become more prominent with the continued development of the service sector in advanced economies and the growing interdependence of the industrial and service sectors (Chapter 10).

■ 7.3 The theoretical case for industry policy

Economists normally argue that intervention in industry is justified if it results in a net increase in economic welfare. Most change benefits some people, and adversely affects others. As long as those who gain could, in principle, compensate those who lose, whilst still deriving benefit from the change, welfare is enhanced (this is the *potential Pareto improvement criterion*). Although a theoretically sound objective, changes in economic welfare are difficult to quantify (**Section 6.1**). Proxies – such as improved employment, increased output or a more favourable balance of trade – must be rejected because they are often poorly related to economic welfare. For instance, measures to increase employment or output could lead to the production of a quantity, quality and mix of goods and services which reduces society's welfare.

The time dimension adds a further complication, because there is a trade-off between current and future levels of welfare. Assuming full employment, more resources devoted to the production of goods and services in the present implies fewer resources devoted to investment aimed at enhancing future production. Society will be willing to forgo current welfare if it is compensated by a sufficient increase in future welfare. The rate of compensation depends on the rate at which society discounts future benefits (the *social time preference rate*); the lower the rate of discount the greater the quantity of resources that should be devoted to investment and to research and development (R&D) activity. While the market rate of interest can be used to derive an individual's willingness to forgo marginal changes in current benefits in exchange for future benefits, this may not apply to society as a whole.

It is argued that government intervention can improve welfare in cases where markets fail to provide an efficient utilisation of resources. Five circumstances are cited where markets produce levels of output that are not optimal from the viewpoint of society:

1. monopoly;
2. public goods, such as defence;
3. externalities, such as pollution or congestion;
4. common property rights;
5. differences between private and social time preference rates.

If these circumstances are to provide the rationale and justification for industry policy, the conditions in which they occur need to be carefully specified. Discussion is often incomplete, missing the crucial point that market failure cannot occur under the assumptions of perfect information and zero transaction costs (Coase, 1937, 1960), as they will be corrected automatically and costlessly by informed economic agents.

The transaction cost approach (see **Sections 1.5** and **2.17**) presents a way of recapturing market failure. This approach rejects the neoclassical assumption that economic agents can assimilate and interpret unlimited amounts of information (maximisation rationality, **Section 1.3**). Combining bounded rationality with imperfect information means that individuals differ in the amount (and type) of information they possess. As a result, uncertainty prevails and individuals perceive the future in different ways. This creates opportunities for some individuals to take advantage of 'favourable' developments, some to make mistakes, some to engage in deceitful and untrustworthy behaviour. The transaction cost approach recognises that agents seek the most cost-effective method of achieving a particular objective. Consequently, their decisions include a consideration of such costs as those of acquiring information, of making, monitoring and enforcing contracts, and of policing legal rights. In such an environment – where information flows are imperfect and (partly because of this) transactions between parties incur costs – market failure again becomes a theoretical possibility. The five types of market failure then merit further discussion.

■ 7.4 Market failure arising from monopoly

Neoclassical analysis traditionally shows that monopoly leads to an inferior allocation of resources by restricting output below the competitive level. An optimal allocation of current resources requires output to be increased until the marginal benefit derived by consumers (indicated by the demand curve) equals the marginal cost of production. It is argued that this level of output will not be attained because the monopolist maximises profit by equating marginal cost with marginal revenue. The result is a reduction in consumer surplus and a deadweight loss of welfare to society (**Section 5.3** and **Figure 5.1**).

Coase's analysis shows that this is not an equilibrium outcome. It is unstable because the potential exists for an improvement in the welfare of both the monopolist and consumers. Given the neoclassical assumptions of perfect information (and, implicitly, zero transaction costs, they could share the extra benefits of an increase in output without incurring any costs. For instance, the monopolist might agree to supply his product to customers at marginal cost in exchange for a lump-sum payment equal to his former 'profit-maximising' level of profit (area 2 in **Figure 5.3**) plus half the deadweight loss (area 3). In this case, the erstwhile deadweight welfare loss is distributed equally between producer and consumers. In practice, the distribution of area 3 depends upon the respective bargaining abilities of the monopolist and consumers. Coase is pointing out that the logical consequence of the neoclassical assumptions is that the monopolist's price and output are exactly the same as those resulting under perfect competition.

Such a conclusion is critically dependent on the absence of transaction costs. In practice, the costs incurred by a producer in identifying customers and striking bargains with them individually may be punitive. Instead, the monopolist may find that the best way to 'maximise' profits is just to charge all consumers a single, common price. This is, of course, a return to setting price with reference to marginal cost and marginal revenue (although the assumption of imperfect information means that the monopolist will find it difficult – or even impossible – to identify marginal costs and revenues precisely).

■ 7.5 Public goods

A *public good* has two characteristics. First, non-rivalry in consumption ensures that consumption by one individual does not reduce the quantity available to others. Secondly, it is impossible to exclude from consumption individuals who have not paid for the product. Defence is the classic example.

An individual's demand curve shows how highly he values each extra unit of the good. With non-rivalry in consumption, individual demand curves are summed vertically to show the marginal benefit derived by society from any given level of output. In **Figure 7.1**, marginal social benefit (MSB) is the sum of individual demands D_A and D_B. The socially optimal level of output, $0Q_{opt}$, is where marginal social benefit equals the marginal social cost of production (MSC). The cost of the public good is divided between consumers according to how highly they value it. Individual A pays $0P_a$, while individual B pays $0P_b$. Neoclassical analysis suggests that market forces would produce a sub-optimal level

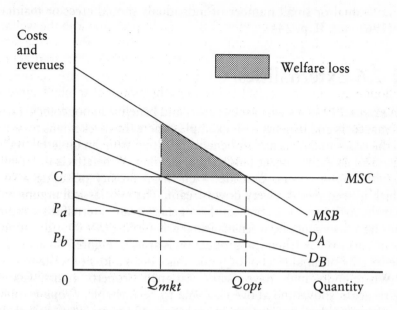

Figure 7.1   *The public good argument for market failure*

of output because it would be in an individual's interest to understate his valuation of the good in order to reduce his contribution towards the costs of provision. This is the *free-rider* problem. For instance, if either individual argues that the public good is worthless to him then the market would underprovide. Output level $0Q_{mkt}$ (reflecting just the valuations of individual A) might result.

The analysis of the previous section is applicable here. With perfect information and zero transaction costs, the welfare loss would not occur. All parties would recognise that they can improve their positions by moving to the overall output $0Q_{opt}$. Furthermore, no individual would be able to hide his valuation of the public good in order to free-ride. In such circumstances, mutually beneficial exchange will occur between individuals, raising output to the socially optimal level. Underprovision can occur only if information is imperfect and transactions are costly. Such an outcome was referred to in 1776 by Adam Smith when he argued that the sovereign has the duty:

> of erecting and maintaining those public institutions and those public works, which, though they may be in the highest degree advantageous to a great society, are, however, of such a nature, that the profit could never repay the expense to any individual or small number of individuals and which it therefore cannot be expected that any

individual or small number of individuals should erect or maintain (1961, vol. II, p. 244).

■ 7.6 Externalities

An *externality* arises when social costs and benefits do not coincide with private costs and benefits – for example, where the market fails to reflect all the economic costs and/or benefits resulting from an undertaking, or where an economic agent fails to take account of the effects of his own activities upon others. Consider a chemical factory polluting a river which is used by a brewery downstream. The neoclassical argument is that the actions of the chemical firm generate an external diseconomy causing a divergence between marginal private cost (*MPC*) and marginal social cost (*MSC*). Chemical production is at $0Q_1$ (**Figure 7.2**) instead of the socially optimal level of $0Q_2$ and this causes a loss of welfare.

Where individuals have clearly assigned property rights, Coase's work again shows the above outcome to be unstable. *Property rights* (conferred either by law or by custom) allow an economic agent exclusive rights to a particular property. A good or an asset is deemed to be *private property* if three distinct sets of rights are associated with its ownership: the exclusive right of use (including the right to exclude other individuals from its use), the exclusive right to receive any income generated, and the full right to transfer ownership. The property does not have to be tangible – it could, for instance, be an idea that has been patented. The owner of a property right can seek legal protection against infringement, and is at liberty to transfer the property right as he chooses. Any infringement of property rights can be legally defended, and the ownership of property rights may be transferred. Such rights with respect to private property form part of the institutional environment (**Section 1.5**).

Where property rights are clearly assigned, a welfare loss may not occur because of the gains (equal to the size of the welfare loss) which can be realised through negotiation. Assume that the brewery has been granted a property right to unpolluted water. The chemical firm now faces the prospect of successful litigation if it pollutes. It will choose the cheapest of the following options. It could fully compensate the brewery for the infringement of its property right and continue polluting at the original level. It could eradicate the pollution, or it could partly control the pollution, paying reduced levels of compensation. Alternatively, the property right could be owned by the chemical works, allowing it legally to pollute the river. In this case, the brewery will be willing to pay the costs of reducing the level of pollution generated by the chemical works

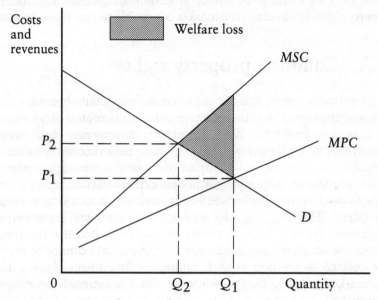

Figure 7.2 *The externality argument for market failure*

if this proves to be cheaper than installing a water purification plant. Whichever approach to the pollution problem results (and regardless of which firm owns the property right), output corresponds to the socially optimal level because the chemical firm is now operating on the marginal social cost curve.

However, without the assumptions of perfect information and zero transaction costs, this socially optimal outcome is an unlikely event. Consider a factory whose pollution affects a large number of people who have a legal right to clean air. This right will not be effectively enforced if the transaction costs in taking legal action outweigh the potential gains. Nor will it be enforced if many of those affected choose to free-ride, hoping to benefit from a successful legal action, without sharing in the costs. In such circumstances, externalities must reduce society's welfare.

The situation is further complicated if property rights are not clearly assigned. The chemical factory may be unclear as to its right to pollute and the brewery as to its right to draw clean water. Ambiguity over ownership of property rights may encourage litigation in the hope of establishing legal rights. More often such ambiguity will reduce the willingness of individuals to use the judicial system, since it both increases the costs of litigation and reduces the chance that the action will be successful. In a sense, this is not an example of 'market failure', but of a failure of the institutional environment (**Section 1.5**). Because property rights are unclear, the market is less able to function effectively.

■ 7.7 Common property rights

Where property rights are not assigned to individuals but are held in common, there will be little incentive either to conserve or to improve the *common property*. With imperfect information and positive transaction costs, a loss of welfare may result because one co-owner has no reason to pay regard to the impact of his own actions upon other co-owners of the property right. For instance, there may be heavy costs in trying to reach agreement between all individuals, or in trying to exclude 'free-riders'. This explains why seas are overfished and common land overgrazed. There is little to rectify the situation because the returns consequent on restocking fisheries or improving land cannot be entirely appropriated by the person undertaking the investment. Again, this is not 'market failure', but a failure of the institutional environment (**Section 1.5**).

7.8 Differences between private and social time preference rates

Economic actions are usually effective over time rather than at a point in time. A firm's investment decision, for example, requires a current commitment of resources in exchange for anticipated future benefits. The problem arises of comparing benefits received at different points in time.

For the individual with perfect information, this is fairly easily resolved. An individual saves (or borrows) in order to improve his pattern of consumption over time. Current consumption is generally more highly valued than future consumption, if only because the individual is not certain about his life-expectancy. Consider a consumer who is just willing to forgo £1's worth of current consumption in exchange for £1.10's worth of consumption in one year's time. He is said to have a *marginal time preference rate* (MTPR) of 10 per cent per year. With a real market rate of interest of 12 per cent, this consumer would increase his welfare by saving (abstaining from current consumption). £1 saved would result in repayment, of principal plus interest, of £1.12 in a year's time. In these circumstances, saving leads to an enhancement of the individual's welfare, but there are forces to limit the total amount of saving individuals undertake. According to the law of diminishing marginal utility, the lower the level of current consumption (as a result of saving) the more highly each unit of consumption will be valued. Conversely, the extra consumption in the future made possible by this saving would become progressively less valuable. The consumer's MTPR would increase with his level of saving. His welfare would be maximised when his MTPR equals the market rate of interest.

Whilst individuals differ in their preferences between current and future consumption, if they face a common rate of interest their marginal time preference rates will be equal in equilibrium. Differences in the income tax positions of individuals, taxes on companies' profits and different interest rates for borrowing and lending complicate but do not fundamentally alter the analysis. (Evaluation of business investment projects, using the 'net present value rule' follows a similar procedure, and can likewise be shown to maximise welfare.)

Social time preference is analogous to individual time preference. It refers to the rate at which society evaluates returns arising in different time periods. Markets fail if the rate of interest does not reflect the social time preference rate. This occurs when there is a divergence between the time preference rate for all individuals and that for society as a whole. One reason for such a divergence is that the composition of individuals within society is constantly changing. Individuals may be faced with the choice of forgoing consumption now to invest in a project whose main benefits will be to future generations. Here the MTPR of individuals is likely to be higher than a social MTPR which includes welfare effects on future generations. Conversely, it could be argued that the social MTPR is greater than individuals' MTPR. This could be the case where there is rapid technological advance, and it is likely that future generations will enjoy much higher standards of living. In both these situations, the level of investment undertaken will be sub-optimal, and there may be a case for government intervention.

7.9 Government intervention to correct market failure

An analysis of the exact circumstances in which markets fail is a prerequisite to the examination of corrective policy measures. It is crucial to recognise that the case for industry policy depends on uncertainty, imperfect information and – as a result – the presence of transaction costs. This means that neoclassical economic theory is an inappropriate basis for policy prescriptions. Furthermore, when it is recognised that the governments too may fail, it becomes even more difficult to provide an economic rationale for industry policy.

A large literature on public choice theory (see, for example, Downs, 1957; Buchanan, 1968; Tullock, 1965, 1976) suggests that many political acts can be understood by assuming that the objective of politicians is to maximise chances of re-election (**Section 1.4**). Such acts may be inconsistent with welfare maximisation. A vote-enhancing strategy causes politicians to intervene in cases where market failure arguments do not apply. The consequence is that governments may be willing to implement industry support programmes even where the result is to reduce the overall level of welfare. Import controls to protect workers from foreign competition are a good example (**Section 8.14**). While such policies benefit clearly identified groups of voters (usually involved with production) their costs are widely distributed (and hence less acutely felt).

The ability of politicians to pursue non-welfare-maximising objectives stems from the presence of imperfect information. (This also explains how, where competitive forces are weak, managers in private sector firms are able to pursue objectives of which the shareholders would disapprove.) If the electorate were fully aware of the costs of intervention as well as its benefits, then any policy that failed to enhance overall welfare would lead to a net loss of votes.

Even where motives are altruistic, government intervention to correct market failure may not be merited. Government intervention is unlikely to be warranted where few parties are involved, property rights are clearly assigned and transaction costs are low. In such circumstances market failure is unlikely. For instance, with just one party involved, the brewery (**Section 7.6**) is easily able to identify the source of polluted water and arrive at an optimal solution by negotiation. However, with air pollution, market failure is more likely, even where inhabitants have been assigned a right to clean air. The costs to an individual of enforcing his rights will be high in relation to the benefits to be gained from clean air. Here legislation and effective enforcement procedures to limit pollution, commonly found in advanced economies, may increase economic welfare.

The government may find it difficult to identify cases of market failure. In the absence of perfect knowledge, costs are incurred in acquiring the necessary information to intervene successfully. All this is very different from the view portrayed by many economic texts. As Kay argues:

> More usually in the neoclassical literature it has been traditional to presume that if some decision maker is at an informational disadvantage, optimality can be rescued through the intervention of

some omniscient policy maker with privileged access to informational secrets (1984, p. 4).

Even when a case of market failure has been correctly identified, the government faces a further problem in that it cannot know with certainty the most appropriate form of intervention. A decision widely perceived as 'correct' in the current time period may lead to an undesirable outcome in the future. For example, controls on a monopoly to improve the current allocation of resources may lead to reduced innovation. Only where the optimal prices, products and technologies of the future are currently known could intervention be guaranteed to bring an improvement in welfare.

Another reason why the presence of market failure is not a sufficient condition to support intervention is that government action uses scarce resources. Resources are used in the administration of the policy; furthermore, intervention may take the form of transferring resources towards favoured areas. There is also a dynamic impact. Government actions may induce changes elsewhere in the economy. Taxation to finance grants to small firms, for instance, may deter other firms from undertaking the investment required to maintain their own future competitiveness.

Let B represent the benefits available from the correction of a 'market failure'. A market solution depends on how these benefits compare against the resource costs of identifying and correcting the failure (M), and will come about if:

$$B > M \tag{7.1}$$

If this condition does not hold, government action may be justified, depending on the costs to the government of identifying and correcting the failure (G), which are likely to differ in magnitude from M. Government intervention is worthwhile if:

$$B > G \tag{7.2}$$

However, there will be many instances where action cannot be justified, or where:

$$B < M \text{ and } B < G \tag{7.3}$$

Logically, government should confine its attention to cases where:

$$M > B > G \tag{7.4}$$

It is impossible ever to know whether industry policy has been successful. Intervention itself alters the future state of the world, but is not the only force leading to economic change. In order to evaluate the impact of policy, those changes which are the result of intervention need to be identified. However, this requires knowledge of the state of the world which would have prevailed in the absence of intervention. Consequently, the success of a policy can only be judged qualitatively.

These problems leave governments with a dilemma. The type of policies that are more acceptable politically are those directed at improving the dynamic performance of the economy. Such policies cannot be addressed under neoclassical theory. The theories of the new institutional economics can give support to intervention that is designed to improve the workings of the market economy and to remove impediments to the competitive process. This intervention would include measures aimed at improving information flows, at strengthening legal rights and improving the framework for their enforcement. (An example of one such policy was the transformation of common property into private property in England under the enclosure movement of the eighteenth century.) But politicians concerned with re-election are often reluctant to restrict themselves to such policies, since their benefits would be widely distributed, and hence largely invisible to voters. In consequence, much of the intervention undertaken by governments cannot be supported by any theoretical analysis.

■ 7.10 Different approaches to intervention

Given the limited theoretical basis for industry policy, government involvement is very much a matter of judgement and it is not surprising that there are many differences of opinion about the best approach to adopt. Moreover, these approaches cannot be precisely evaluated. Nevertheless, certain desirable features of an industry policy can be specified. First, any policy should be capable of performing well in an environment where transaction costs are the norm, and where economic agents lack knowledge and are continually having to adapt to change. Secondly, the opportunity cost burden of the policy must not exceed any perceived, potential benefits, having regard to its static and dynamic effects on the industries involved and also on the rest of the economy.

Four distinct approaches to industry policy can be identified:

1. *laissez-faire*;
2. supportive;
3. active;
4. planning.

The *laissez-faire approach* is founded on the presumption that information flows are perfect, and holds that the market is a better judge of desirable actions than government agencies. Most types of intervention commonly pursued under the name of industry policy are rejected. Appropriate policies are those aimed at strengthening and promoting a competitive environment (for instance, through the control of monopoly or measures to remove ambiguities in the assignment of property rights).

The *supportive approach* also believes in the underlying superiority of market forces, but acknowledges the presence of imperfect information and transaction costs. Proponents of the supportive approach would agree with the *laissez-faire* approach in advocating policies to help markets function more effectively, but would often disagree over the form of desirable measures. In particular, the supportive approach would argue for intervention to improve the allocation and enforcement of property rights, to encourage education and entrepreneurship in order to foster the process of economic change. This approach also recognises that external constraints may force the adoption of less desirable, or 'second-best', policies. For example, if Japan were to adopt protectionist measures then Europe would be justified in adopting similar policies, with the ultimate intention of enforcing trade liberalisation.

The *active approach* argues for wider and more direct government involvement in the industrial sector. This approach differs crucially from the previous ones in that market judgements are often supplanted by those of government agencies. Selected industries would typically be given financial support to promote restructuring and be protected from external competition by tariff and non-tariff barriers. Although protected from external competition, measures would again be taken to promote competition domestically.

The *planning approach* is a more extreme version of the active approach. Its rationale is that welfare can be improved through centralised planning. It argues that central planners are in a better position – because of their superior, economy-wide information – to make welfare-enhancing decisions than individual firms. This advantage is greater where information flows are imperfect and where the economy is changing rapidly. Intervention is much wider-ranging and more comprehensive than under the active approach.

These policy prescriptions vary because of different perceptions about the efficiency of markets and the ability of government agencies to identify and to correct market failures. The basic dichotomy in these views is between advocacy of non-interference (the *laissez-faire* and supportive approaches) and advocacy of a large element of government involvement which includes targeting policies to particular firms, sectors or activities (the active and planning approaches). Cowling provides a distinction. In the *laissez-faire* and supportive approaches, the state is acting 'as an adjunct to the market, working at the edges of the market system' whilst in the other approaches 'the state acts to shape the industrial landscape, taking a leading role in the industrial economy – a *proactive* rather than a *reactive* role' (1990, p. 176). The greater the belief in the efficacy of the market and in the impotence of government agencies, the greater the tendency to reject intervention and to favour an essentially 'hands off' industry policy. Similarly, the greater the doubt that the principal objective of politicians is the enhancement of society's welfare, the greater the tendency to advocate an industry policy that involves minimal government intervention.

The choice between the *laissez-faire*–supportive approaches and the active–planning approaches therefore turns on views as to which uses information more efficiently, state agencies or the market. Whilst it is undoubtedly true that state agencies have the ability to be better informed about government intentions and have wider sources of information than an individual agent, this does not necessarily imply that they have an informational advantage. Hayek (1945) argues that one of the main strengths of the market mechanism is its ability to collate and to make full use of widely dispersed information. Although each agent commands but a tiny fraction of total information, by responding to price signals from the market each agent reacts as if he were much better informed (see **Section 2.16**).

Even so, most governments have chosen to intervene heavily in the operation of industry. In some cases, intervention has taken the form of accelerative policies designed to improve the speed at which the market operates. In others, a decelerative policy stance has been used to retard the operation of the market. More commonly, both stances have been adopted simultaneously for different areas of the economy. Few governments have chosen to make use solely of neutral policies (aimed simply at reinforcing the efficiency of the market). These would be more consistent with a *laissez-faire* or supportive approach, although they have sometimes been included as part of an active or planning approach. **Table 7.1** summarises the types of policy consistent with these different approaches.

■ *7.11* Accelerative industry policy

The objective of *accelerative industry policy* is to speed up the innovation process by providing financial support to the most promising firms,

Table 7.1 *Taxonomy of industry policies*

Policy approach	Policy form
Laissez faire	Very limited intervention through neutral policies
Supportive	Neutral policies
Active	Accelerative and/or decelerative policies
Planning	Accelerative and/or decelerative policies

markets or technologies (Burton, 1983). The premise behind such a policy is that an economy benefits from adopting innovations ahead of its trading rivals. This owes little to traditional arguments about intervention to correct market failure. Moreover, the essentially dynamic nature of the intervention proposed means that neoclassical theory has little to contribute.

Many countries have adopted accelerative policies. In the UK, the Industrial Reorganisation Corporation (IRC) was set up in the late 1960s to speed up the market process by promoting structural change. The mergers between the General Electric Company, Associated Electrical Industries and English Electric and between the British Motor Corporation and Leyland Motors were amongst those encouraged. In the mid-1980s selective intervention was directed at new technologies with, for instance, assistance available under the microprocessor application project, the fibre optics and opto-electronics scheme and the robot support scheme.

In Japan, the Ministry of International Trade and Industry (MITI) has a number of programmes designed to support particular sectors of the economy and emerging technologies. MITI identifies sectors of the economy which have the best prospects for growth. It then encourages and aids their emergence through the support of R&D programmes, capital programmes and government procurement policy. Boonekamp notes:

> the government plays an essential role in formulating industrial strategies, but it does so more by acting to coordinate and establish a consensus on these strategies than by directing the force or pace of resource allocation (1989, p. 15).

For instance, government and industry worked in partnership in developing electronics (Majumdar, 1988). The aims of the 1957 Electronics Industry Development Emergency Law were to train workers, raise production and quality, and promote exports. A detailed programme, with specific targets, was established that covered R&D, and then moved on to the development, and later the rationalisation, of production. Low interest loans were made available, and competition policy rules were waived to encourage cooperation in R&D, which was also supported by the government's research laboratories.

MITI's work is often heralded as the classic example of an active approach, showing that:

> the role of the state should be limited to the strategic oversight of development, rather than getting involved with the operational detail, and that strategic oversight is only essential in the case of a limited array of key industries, many sectors being left to market processes without strategic guidance (Cowling, 1990, p. 178).

Cowling goes further to suggest that the success of the Japanese economy could not have taken place without its industrial policy.

France has similarly supported promising sectors through assistance for R&D, aid for industrial restructuring, government investment and protectionist policies, but this is more comprehensive and closer to the planning approach. State enterprises have been used to promote the desired policy through their purchasing and pricing policies. In the early 1980s, four sectors – chemicals, health, electronics, and materials – and those industries which are economically related to them, were selected for special support.

It is doubtful whether such government intervention to accelerate the introduction of desirable new products and processes is worthwhile. Three main problems can be identified. First, uncertainty and information costs make the correct anticipation of market trends, technological developments and new market opportunities very difficult. The proportion of new products which are commercial failures and the relatively high rate of closure (even among firms producing established products) testify to such difficulties. In an uncertain environment, the greatest chance of success comes from those who are best able to gather relevant information. These are the entrepreneurs most closely involved with a particular area. Government agencies are less likely to have the necessary specialist information about particular market developments.

Secondly, having identified areas to support, how should the policy be implemented? General support to all new firms in a favoured area would lead to a considerable waste of resources given the high failure rate of new firms. (Ganguly (1983) notes that half the firms first registered for VAT (sales tax) in the UK in 1977 had left the register by 1982.) Directing funds to potential 'winners' is ruled out by the absence of a mechanism to identify such firms. Advocates of selective intervention may argue that uncertainty can be reduced by supporting firms with a proven record, but past success is not an infallible guide to future performance. Clive Sinclair was successful with the home computer only after failing with previous watch and calculator ventures. Subsequently his introduction of a small electrically powered vehicle proved a commercial failure.

Thirdly, the opportunity cost of accelerative policy must be taken into account. While favoured firms are nurtured, the development of other sectors is hampered. Extra taxes or higher interest rates are imposed on firms and their customers to finance industry policy, resulting in an overall reduction in the demand for goods and services. These other sectors, although not apparently promising, may turn out to be the real winners. The EC appears to accept these arguments:

> stimulating research and development, improving the training of European workers and developing European infrastructures would be far more effective in improving the competitiveness of Community industry (CEC, 1992a, p. 43).

■ 7.12 Decelerative industry policy

Decelerative policies can be of two types. If an essentially viable concern is facing temporary financial difficulties, bankruptcy or liquidation may be avoided by providing assistance to help it rationalise production methods or to improve its product range. Typical examples from the UK are the support given to Rolls-Royce in 1971 following problems in developing the RB211 engine and to British Leyland, which was rescued from commercial difficulties in 1974–5. If rescue is not viable then help can be given to phase the closure, giving time for retraining and for new firms to set up in the area. In the 1970s and early 1980s West Germany gave financial aid to restructure the shipbuilding industry, while most European countries have subsidised and/or protected their textile industries.

In the case of a firm facing terminal problems, the intention of decelerative industry policy is to moderate the externality effects of its closure and to attain a better utilisation of resources. Proponents argue that, while economic forces may quickly lead to a firm's collapse, markets operate too slowly in re-absorbing displaced resources. Instead of suggesting intervention designed to enhance market forces they seek to maintain the employment of resources in their current use. They propose intervention because of the length of time markets will take to re-establish equilibrium. Neoclassical theory can give little support to this because it implicitly assumes that adjustment is instantaneous.

Decelerative policies have been justified on social grounds, the argument being that preventing (or slowing down) firm closure leads to the attainment of a more equitable and less divided society. However, the most frequent justification for support to 'failing' firms is that their collapse will lead to adverse effects on economic welfare. Externalities may arise from the closure of a major employer in a particular locality, causing a large proportion of the population to become unemployed with consequent ill effects on the rest of the community. There may also be *domino effects* on other companies. For instance, the failure of a motor manufacturer will harm firms supplying components to the motor vehicle industry. It would also lead to difficulties among firms involved in the distribution of motor vehicles. These domino effects would also follow from the failure of a small firm although, in most cases, decelerative policies have been biased in favour of large firms. The explanation for this is probably political, stemming from the widespread publicity given to the failure of large firms. Moreover, smaller firms are generally less experienced in lobbying for government assistance.

Despite the externalities generated by the premature collapse of a potentially viable firm, the economic case for government intervention to help it through its temporary difficulties is dubious. If financial markets are efficient, a basically sound company should be able to obtain financial support from the private sector. Conversely, if a firm cannot convince lenders of its basic soundness, then government resources should not be advanced to try to improve its operation. Even if financial markets do sometimes fail to recognise an inherently successful company (for example, because of transaction costs) this does not invalidate the basic argument. The government is likely to be at an informational disadvantage compared with firms already operating in similar lines of business. Such firms are more likely to possess the information on future demand relevant to identifying a failing company, taking it over and turning round its performance. Furthermore, financial support from the government may fail to promote efficiency, for it enables management, which has demonstrated its incompetence, to retain control of the company. This is compounded by the reduced pressure on management and unions to adapt and change. Lindbeck argues:

> bargaining with the government may become a more attractive way of raising profits than are attempts to remove inefficiencies within the firms (1981, p. 397).

Evidence on the performance of many industries assisted by the state supports these points. For instance, the National Enterprise Board (NEB) in the UK made a loss of £40.3 million in 1978 on its assets of £1.4 billion. Similar experiences were recorded by the IRC in the UK and the Instituto per la Riconstruzione Industriale (IRI) in Italy.

As with firms in temporary difficulties, support cannot be given to every firm in terminal decline, otherwise the economy would ossify and become progressively uncompetitive. Since funds are likely to be limited, selection is required and here the government encounters another information problem. Choice of unsuitable subjects will lead to a waste of resources.

In most cases, it is expected that financial support will be required for a short period, but the process of readjustment is often protracted. For instance, British Leyland took well over a decade before it began to regain its competitive position. Devoting resources (particularly over long periods) to the pursuit of decelerative policies incurs significant opportunity costs. Again, the success of companies elsewhere in the economy will be hampered by higher taxes or higher interest rates causing a reduction in demand for their goods and services. In other words, the financing of decelerative policy generates its own domino effects leading to the contraction, reduced growth or even accelerated failure of companies in the unsupported sector. In principle, it is impossible to say how the domino effects of government policy on the employment of labour and capital compare with the domino effects consequent on the natural decline of firms. However, the overall effect is to reduce welfare because resources are switched from areas where revenues exceed costs of production to areas of failure, implying revenues below cost. There is also the cost incurred in the administration and implementation of the policy.

There is a real opportunity cost – in the form of a burden placed on the rest of the economy – incurred by the pursuit of decelerative industry policies and their 'success' or 'failure' can be established only after taking these costs into account. For instance, Jong (1984) argues that support to large, dominant firms throughout Europe in the 1970s prolonged the period of crisis and undermined profitable firms. This point is poignantly illustrated by the case of the European steel industry. A downturn in world demand for steel products together with increased competition from Japan and the newly industrialising countries meant that, left to the market, there would have been a rapid and substantial decline in the European steel industry. Decelerative policies applied during the 1970s and early 1980s cushioned the fall in employment. Although employment declined from 350 000 to 150 000, the industry remained internationally uncompetitive. Geldens (1984) estimated the cost of support at $70 billion for the ten years to 1980. This represents a substantial opportunity cost for the EC and – for the same resource effect – Geldens calculated that a new, fully competitive, European steel industry could have been established. The European Commission adopts a similar view: 'aid helps to maintain unstable jobs artificially, at the expense of viable ones' (CEC, 1992a, p. 21), as does the OECD: 'the growth of subsidies and other protective measures has distorted competition and blurred market signals, thereby delaying the necessary adjustments and creating unexpected distortions' (1989, p. 141).

What is the alternative to decelerative policies? In the absence of government support the assets of the failing firm would be sold to the highest bidder. It can be argued that this would be a better way of ensuring an efficient use of resources because the entrepreneur willing to pay the most for the firm will be the one (often already operating in a similar area) which sees the most profitable uses for the resources of the failed company. Company failure is an important aspect of the competitive process, serving to transfer resources from the hands of a management which has incorrectly predicted market developments. (This is the view of many economists, most notably Mises (1949) and Hayek (1944).)

■ 7.13 Neutral industry policy

Neutral policy seeks to improve the market framework within which economic agents operate. This type of policy is consistent with economic theories that explicitly recognise the presence of transaction costs. It is often advocated by those who recognise the difficulties involved in trying to pursue accelerative and decelerative policies. As Lindbeck argues, the task of government should be: 'to try to create an economic, social and political environment that is conducive to efficiency and new initiatives' (1981, p. 395). Likewise Stout considers that:

> the government is not responsible for picking 'winner' industries, but for increasing labour mobility, improving long-run employment prospects, and hence reducing the resistance to change (1981, p. 127).

Specific examples of neutral policy include attempts to ensure that property rights are clearly assigned. The more certain it is that the legal system will enforce such rights (and the cheaper it is to seek legal redress against infringement), the greater the incentive for citizens to acquire private property. Similarly, the easier and cheaper it is to transfer rights over property, the more desirable it is to own property. Following Coase's work, clearly assigned property rights would help to eliminate many cases of market failure. The pursuit of increased competition – for instance, by the elimination of institutional barriers which prevent the entry of new firms – could also be regarded as a neutral policy. Stimulating competition within the legal profession might be particularly beneficial. This would improve the efficiency of the system for enforcing property rights.

Industry policy in many advanced economies has been moving away from the accelerative/decelerative approach. In Italy (where it was common for the government to intervene widely in the operation of industry, providing heavy subsidies to declining sectors) more recent programmes have sought to promote R&D and training and to establish competition policy. The OECD considers that:

> A certain convergence has now been reached around a set of principles that broadly favour policy measures which do not interfere with the market process directly and instead attempt to improve its mechanisms. Such policies tend to be of a horizontal nature; they are market-correcting or market-enhancing, aimed directly at specific and known market flaws, or at promoting industry generally, and in particular the (labour and infrastructural) inputs available to industry (1992, p. 11).

Typical measures include the prevention of monopoly, enforcement of property rights, improving access to information and training, and improving the infrastructure. However, in implementation, the principles of neutral policy have been interpreted in a variety of ways and have not always been applied.

A reason why governments have difficulty adopting a 'hands off' approach is that it may be politically unacceptable not to be visibly tackling issues of 'industry policy'. This factor seems to be relevant to the USA. Here there has been little in the way of accelerative policy, but government assistance to particular industries such as steel, textiles, footwear and colour televisions could be classed as decelerative. As Behrman argues:

> In principle only, the government stands ready to see the United States develop industrially in whatever ways the international markets and transnational companies decide. The principle is violated whenever it begins to hurt seriously, and political hurt is more likely to catalyze interference than is economic hurt (1984, p. 48).

In the light of increasing concern about the performance of the US economy (Chapter 10), it is possible that the administration of President Clinton will bring a more active stance to industry policy.

Governments are missing an opportunity where they fail to adopt neutral industrial policies. These seem more likely to generate a net welfare gain than either accelerative or decelerative policies: first, the informational requirements they place on governments are less demanding; secondly, the opportunity costs are lower since their implementation requires relatively few resources.

■ 7.14 Conclusion

In developing their industry policies governments have often paid little attention to economic arguments. One reason is because of a difference in objectives. Economists are concerned with the enhancement of economic welfare, but this may not ensure re-election for the politician. Secondly, neoclassical economics has little contribution to make to many of the issues which governments usually consider vital. This is because traditional analysis is unsuited to problems where change is endemic because of its generally static thrust and tendency to ignore problems of uncertainty and lack of information. Thirdly, the approach of the new institutional economics, which can explicitly deal with such an environment, is generally hostile to the type of *ad hoc* intervention favoured by politicians.

Many governments have adopted an active or planning approach to industry. Evidence from particular countries appears to suggest that accelerative industry policies have been more successful than decelerative ones. For instance, Behrman (1984) argues that the apparent success of industry policies in Japan and West Germany arises from their concentration on selected industries. In contrast, the poor performance of France is seen as the result of attempts to counter market forces in declining sectors such as steel and textiles. Waelbroeck sums up the situation:

> Some of the strength of Japan's successful industries stems from that country's willingness to phase out less successful ones: and some of Europe's inability to break into the markets of the future is the result of excessive efforts to prop up ailing firms and industries (1984, p. 103).

However, it is impossible to say categorically whether these successes and failures are directly attributable to government policies.

It is also impossible to judge how successfully an economy might have developed without the opportunity cost burden imposed by the operation of industry policies. The opportunity costs associated with accelerative and decelerative policies are likely to be high. Given that markets fail and that there is a need for some government intervention in industry, neutral policies as part of a supportive policy aimed at improving the operation of market forces would appear to be the most promising.

■ *Chapter 8* ■

Industry Policy in Practice

> the great majority of things are worse done by the intervention of government, than the individuals most interested in the matter would do them, or cause them to be done (J. S. Mill, 1909, p. 947).

■ *8.1* Introduction

Chapter 7 discussed four types of industry policy. The *laissez-faire* and supportive approaches view the role of the government as reinforcing the operation of market forces. The active and planning approaches argue for government intervention in the operation of industry. Whichever approach is adopted, industry policy will relate to four main areas: competition policy, regional policy, innovation policy, and trade policy. These policies can have wide-ranging effects on the operation of individual firms or particular industries and, consequently, on economic welfare. Although economic theory cannot always provide either a rationale or a justification for many of the measures implemented, it is still important to gauge their impact, even where such evaluation can be only qualitative.

■ *8.2* Policy implementation

Even well-designed policies may fail if they are badly implemented. To be effective in promoting economic welfare, an industry policy should possess certain features. The variety of different measures should be coordinated, so that benefits from their implementation in one area are not outweighed by adverse effects elsewhere. This problem is more likely to occur where policy is implemented by several agencies operating separately. Measures may even conflict; for example, financial assistance to firms located in selected areas, or controls on imports into a particular market, may not only distort competition but may also run counter to other government actions taken as part of competition policy. Similarly, a policy of trade liberalisation may adversely affect sectors of the economy which the government supports through decelerative policies. It may also prove difficult to coordinate industry policy with macroeconomic management.

To minimise opportunity costs, programmes should be designed for ease of administration and for effectiveness in implementation. A rules-based programme may score over one based upon discretion. Rules clearly define the way the programme operates, and so monitoring is facilitated. Costs of obtaining information about government programmes are reduced if awards are mandatory – for instance, in the form of specific tax concessions – rather than discretionary. The use of computers might be more readily encouraged by reducing the VAT (sales tax) rate than by asking firms to submit a grant application. Discretionary action (such as awarding subsidies on a case-by-case basis or penalising monopoly only after a thorough investigation of specific circumstances) not only incurs greater decision-making costs for the firms and the government, but is also more likely to lead to disputes. In its favour, a discretionary programme offers the prospect of targeting and tailoring the policy to increase its effectiveness.

Actions by government agencies may discriminate unintentionally against certain types of firms. A separate policy approach may be necessary for small firms, which are less likely to take advantage of assistance for three reasons. First, with fewer specialists, the small firm may be unaware of the government programme. Secondly, the fixed costs associated with a grant application bear disproportionately heavily on the small firm. Thirdly, if they have been under-represented in discussions between business and the government agency responsible for formulating policy, the programme itself may be of limited relevance to small firms. Such neglect can have serious effects. If larger firms are more likely to be operating in mature, slow-growing sectors of the economy, government policy may have an unintended bias against the promotion of newly developing sectors.

Policies to enhance economic welfare rarely go hand in hand with vote maximisation, since government actions invariably create changes that benefit some but adversely affect others (**Section 7.9**). This may lead to lobbying by the losers. Perceiving that the support of these voters is necessary to ensure re-election, the government may bow to pressure and take steps to ease the cost of adjustment. These palliative measures may then work against the original objective. For instance, the government may act to slow an industry's decline by subsidising employment in current jobs. This must freeze the economy's industrial structure and adversely affect its international competitiveness. Once the precedence has been set that the government intervenes to shelter those adversely affected by the changes consequent on the operations of the market, demands for support become more vociferous and may come from an alliance of employers and employees (Lesourne, 1984).

There is more prospect of achieving an enhancement of economic welfare if these potential problems are recognised at the policy-formulation stage. By acknowledging that the promotion of economic welfare has inequitable effects, it is possible to anticipate (and so reduce) them. It can be argued that shareholders must accept the possibility of poor returns and so their losses should elicit little sympathy. More concern may be justified over the plight of employees (who are also likely to form a larger part of the electorate). It may be possible to facilitate change, without losing political support, by devising at the outset a programme of direct assistance to employees (such as redundancy payments or retraining grants). This would be an example of a 'second-best' policy. Because of the opportunity cost incurred, the improvement in society's welfare will be less than if the two objectives of welfare and vote maximisation coincided. However, it can be argued that the overall welfare improvement from adopting this second-best policy will be greater than if the government were forced into a programme of industry support.

■ 8.3 Competition policy

Competition policy encompasses measures designed either to promote a more competitive environment or to prevent a reduction in competition. Economists have different opinions as to the market conditions which best promote competition (Chapter 2) and so differ in their views of the desirable form of competition policy. In fact, some might go as far as to suggest that competition policy is largely unnecessary because efficiency prevails regardless of market structure (Chicago School, Section 5.4; contestability, Section 2.6).

According to the structure–conduct–performance (SCP) approach, competition policy should be directed towards modifying market structures and imposing constraints on firms' behaviour. This is an essentially static view. The principal problem to be tackled concerns the welfare losses arising whenever a private firm holds a dominant market position that is protected by entry barriers. Competition policy should seek to break up or to regulate existing monopolies. It should also control firms' attempts to acquire such positions by merger. More generally, competition policy should try to prevent firms undertaking practices which adversely affect competition. Examples of practices deemed anti-competitive include the operation of resale price maintenance (RPM) and of restrictive price agreements by groups of firms, and 'full line forcing' by a single firm (where customers are faced with a choice between taking the entire product range or nothing at all). These measures would typically be incorporated as part of an active or planning industry policy.

Such issues are of little concern from the Austrian perspective. Austrian economists argue that policy should be focused on those factors which make it difficult for an entrant to compete with established firms. It should concentrate on removing obstacles to competition so as to allow the development of new products and processes and ease entry by rival firms. As noted earlier (**Section 5.15**), Austrian economists believe that it is those barriers imposed by government that are the most effective block to the operation of the competitive process. Typical measures would be the elimination of import controls and the removal of licensing or statutory restrictions on entry into markets. These measures would be consistent with a supportive attitude to industry policy.

■ 8.4 Competition policy in practice

Governments in most advanced economies have been persuaded of the merits of a rigorous and comprehensive competition policy. Italy, once the notable exception, introduced legislation establishing competition policy in 1990. Governments have tended to adopt elements of both an SCP and an Austrian approach, although the emphasis has varied. In the EC, the Commission of the European Communities (CEC) favours the latter approach, and states its objective as promoting market competitiveness and structural readjustment through the elimination of factors reducing competition, which it regards as:

> the mechanism whereby the economy adapts to changing situations and preferences as reflected in the individual decisions of producers and consumers in markets (1985, p. 11).

Table 8.1   *Competition powers of the European Community as given in the Treaty of Rome*

Article affecting private firms	Article affecting states or state enterprises
85: Agreements between firms	7: National discrimination
86: Monopolies	37: State Monopolies
91: Dumping	90: Public Enterprises
	92–94: State aids to firms

Nevertheless, although the EC has widespread powers (**Table 8.1**), the most developed aspect of its policy is the SCP-based control of agreements between firms (Article 85).

The Commission has jurisdiction to intervene only in matters which affect competition between member states, and has no powers regarding intra-state competition. It considers that:

> a vigorous competition policy ... is a key element in maintaining both the efficient functioning of markets and competitive pressures. Experience ... has shown that competition is an effective tool for ensuring that producers remain dynamic, concentrate on innovation, listen to the market, reduce costs and provide high-quality goods and services at the lowest possible prices. Continued enforcement of the competition rules therefore is of paramount importance in bringing out the best in Community industry (CEC, 1992a, p. 16).

Moreover, competition policy is seen as having a major role in establishing the single European market by eliminating practices which distort competition across the frontiers of member states.

The USA has a long-established and comprehensive competition (antitrust) policy which is enforced by the Federal Trade Commission and the Department of Justice. The main legislation giving substance to this policy is contained in the Sherman Act 1890, the Clayton Act 1914, the Federal Trade Commission Act 1914 and the Robinson–Patman Act 1936. Competition policy as operated in the USA until the early 1980s was largely consistent with the SCP approach. In recent years, there has been a greater tendency to accept the ideas of the Chicago School and so recognise that monopoly may have redeeming features. Neumann notes:

> In quite a few cases mergers and contractual arrangements in restraint of trade which only a decade ago would have been banned have been

permitted on the ground that their consummation is conducive to increasing international competitiveness (1990, p. 562).

In the UK, competition policy dates from the Monopolies and Restrictive Practices (Inquiry and Control) Act 1948, but has been substantially revised and extended, notably by the Competition Act 1980. Consideration of the *public interest* requires the authorities to pay attention to several criteria (including effects on innovation, regional balance and export competitiveness) of which the effect on competition has been the most important in practice. The approach to competition policy in the UK has always been pragmatic, not leaning in the direction of any particular theoretical approach.

■ 8.5 Policy towards monopoly

By a simplistic interpretation of the SCP approach, monopoly would be condemned universally as representing a departure from maximum attainable levels of economic welfare. This is an extreme view. In practice, the presence of an uncontrolled monopoly is usually regarded as grounds for further investigation because of the possibility that the actions of the monopolist might reduce economic welfare. Article 86 of the Treaty of Rome, for instance, prohibits:

> Any abuse by one or more undertakings of a dominant position within the common market ... in so far as it may affect trade between Member States.

Abuses detailed include the imposition of unfair prices or trading conditions, the limiting of production or technical development and the tying of sales. In the USA, it is the *process* of monopolisation that is the subject of concern. Section 2 of the Sherman Act (1890) states that:

> Every person who shall monopolize, or attempt to monopolize, or combine or conspire with any other person or persons, to monopolize any part of the trade or commerce ... shall be deemed guilty of a felony.

Interpretations as to what constitutes a 'monopoly' vary. In the UK, it is where market share exceeds 25 per cent. In the USA, a much larger market share is generally required (although this is not the only characteristic taken into account): for instance, Eastman Kodak with shares of 95 per cent and 60 to 67 per cent in relevant markets in the

1970s was considered to have a clear monopoly position. The EC defines a 'dominant position' as conferring the ability to operate largely independently of competitors. Since market share is just one – albeit important – consideration in determining dominance, the EC does not specify a critical market share. However, Michelin was considered to have a dominant position as a result of its market share of around 60 per cent of the Dutch market for replacement tyres compared with less than 10 per cent for each of its main competitors.

In all investigations the reasons for the monopoly position are considered. This means that monopolies earning high profits are not automatically condemned. Even firms with very large market shares can avoid censure where such positions are seen to be the result of superior efficiency or innovation. For instance, the US Supreme Court ruled that Kodak's introduction of the Instamatic camera and cartridge film in 1972 was not an abuse of its monopoly position. In the UK, Pedigree Petfoods (Monopolies and Mergers Commission (MMC), 1977) held 50 per cent of the market for canned cat and dog foods in the UK. Its high profits were found to be the result of exceptional efficiency. Pedigree continually reformulated recipes to use lower-cost ingredients and operated a single canning factory intensively, with four shifts per day, seven days per week. Likewise, Nestlé's rate of return on capital employed of over 100 per cent was attributed to operating efficiencies and the development of products and brands perceived by customers as good value for money (MMC, 1991).

In contrast, Tetra Pak, investigated by the EC in 1991, provides a classic example of monopoly abuse. Tetra Pak had a 95 per cent share of the EC carton market for the aseptic packaging of long-life liquids (and for its associated machinery). The European Commission concluded that Tetra Pak had excluded competition by eliminating rivals, by designing contracts which stipulated that customers must use only Tetra Pak cartons on Tetra Pak machines, and by predatory pricing. Tetra Pak was fined Ecu 75 million and ordered to alter its behaviour (CEC, 1992a).

■ 8.6 Policy towards mergers

Mergers have been brought within the scope of competition policy (for instance, in the UK under the Monopolies and Mergers Act 1965) because they can lead to the development of a monopoly position. In the UK, the MMC has the powers to investigate mergers which would create a firm with a 25 per cent share of the market and/or in which assets valued at over £30m are taken over. In the EC mergers were not explicitly covered by the Treaty of Rome, but since the early 1970s the Commission has argued that mergers leading to a monopoly position can be considered a monopoly abuse under Article 86. In September 1990, an explicit merger policy came into effect, giving the EC power to investigate all mergers involving firms with a combined worldwide turnover of Ecu 5bn (provided that at least Ecu 250m of the sales of at least two of the undertakings are conducted in the EC and that less than two-thirds of the business is derived from any one EC state).

Following the 1950 Celler–Kefauver amendment to Section 7 of the Clayton Act 1914, the USA adopted a comprehensive and strict approach to horizontal mergers: all were prohibited unless they were within guidelines set down by the Department of Justice. Efficiency enhancement and other potential advantages from the merger were ignored. The 1984 Horizontal Merger Guidelines indicated a softening in attitude: efficiency advantages could now be balanced against competitive risks. Coate summarises the changes in the US attitude as:

> moving from a situation in the mid-1960s where almost any significant horizontal merger could be illegal to a situation where only a few horizontal mergers are illegal (1992, p. 997).

The 1984 Guidelines used a variant of the Herfindahl–Hirschman measure of concentration (**Section 3.3**) to specify the circumstances in which a merger was unlikely to be challenged (so-called 'safe harbors') (**Table 8.2**). Otherwise 'clear and convincing evidence' was needed to show that the merger 'may be reasonably necessary to achieve significant net efficiencies'.

Whilst the 1984 Guidelines moved the US approach closer to that of the UK, merger proposals were still less likely to be regarded favourably. Griffiths and Wall (1993) provide an illustration. They cite the merger between Morgan Crucible plc and Manville Corporation investigated by the MMC in 1991. This related to a 36 per cent share of the market for refactory ceramic fibre, and was allowed by the MMC on the grounds that other competitors were expanding their market shares. Under the US approach:

> the adverse initial movement of the [Herfindahl–Hirschman] index would certainly have created a context in which subsequent investigation in the US was less likely to decide in favour of the merger than in the UK (1993, p. 108).

This conclusion is drawn because the merger would increase an HHI value already substantially greater than 1800 by well over 100 points

Table 8.2 *Likelihood of challenge under the Department of Justice Horizontal Merger Guidelines for the USA*

Change in HHI	Post-merger Herfindahl–Hirschman index[1]		
	0–999	1000–1799	1800 and over
0–49	Zero	Low	Low
50–99	Zero	Low	High
100 and over	Zero	High	Certain

[1.] See Section 3.3 for an explanation of the Herfindahl–Hirschman index of market concentration as used by the Department of Justice.

(**Table 8.2**). However, Coate (1992) would be more wary. He notes that the US courts have not adhered strictly to the 1984 Guidelines, and have been unlikely to find against a merger unless barriers to entry were considerable.

In 1992, the Department of Justice published revised Horizontal Merger Guidelines. These maintain the attitude that mergers should not be challenged unless they are likely to enhance market power and the 'safe harbors' remain unchanged. Greater emphasis is placed on analysis of the potential effects on competition with a five-step procedure for merger evaluation specified. Entry considerations play a larger role, both in the definition of the relevant market and in the consideration of the likely impact on competition. It remains the case that a merger leading to a detrimental impact on competition will not be allowed unless the potential for considerable gains in efficiency is demonstrated.

In the UK, mergers have tended to be regarded as welfare-enhancing so that, in most years, only a few of those mergers satisfying the criteria for investigation have been referred (8 per cent in 1992). Moreover, market share has not been an overriding concern in deciding the public interest. The merger between Gillette and Parker Pen (MMC, 1993a), leading to a 62 per cent share of the market for refillable pens, was permitted. An increase in market power was considered unlikely because of the large number of other suppliers, ease of entry and the power of the retailers. In contrast, the merger between Kingfisher and Dixons (MMC, 1990) was refused despite a combined market share of only 26 per cent in the retailing of electrical appliances. A significant weakening of competition leading to higher prices and worsening terms of sale was envisaged because the merged firm would have dominance in certain products (such as washing machines) and in the expanding out-of-town market.

The EC policy implemented in 1990 recognises that mergers may promote efficiency, but is concerned to prevent mergers which would create or strengthen a dominant position. Between September 1990 and March 1993, 137 mergers were referred, but only one merger was blocked: the proposed takeover of de Havilland by Aérospatiale of France and Alenia of Italy. The new company would have had 50 per cent of the world market and 67 per cent of the Community market for 20–70-seater commuter aircraft, and no offsetting benefits – in the form of cost savings from scale economies or lower research and development expenditures – were envisaged.

▌ 8.7 Policy towards restrictive and anti-competitive practices

Restrictive practices are agreements between firms that have the effect of reducing competition. *Anti-competitive practices* are activities undertaken by an individual firm, which restrict, distort or prevent competition, generally through the erection of entry barriers. From an Austrian perspective firms lack the power effectively to retard the competitive process, unless there are entry barriers established by the government. In concerning themselves with anti-competitive practices in the private sector, governments are implicitly adopting an SCP stance.

In the USA, a particularly strong line is taken on restrictive and anti-competitive practices. Unlawful practices include price- and market-sharing agreements between firms and the refusal to supply customers. For instance, Section 1 of the Sherman Act (1890) prohibits: 'every contract, combination ... or conspiracy in restraint of trade or commerce'. This makes illegal all agreements between firms intended to enhance their position at the expense of other firms and/or the consumer. Similarly the Clayton Act (1914) has outlawed practices whose effect is 'substantially to lessen competition'. Price-fixing, bid-rigging, territorial and customer allocation schemes are amongst the practices regarded as crimes:

> The [Antitrust] Division [of the Department of Justice] believes that these crimes impose welfare losses on the economy as a whole and transfer income from consumers to producers engaged in the crime. Furthermore, the Division believes that any social benefit from these crimes is so frequently outweighed by the costs that further close weighing of the costs and benefits is wasteful (McAnneny, 1991, p. 525).

In the period 1981–7, over 500 prosecutions were brought on cases of restrictive practices, leading to fines of $140m and jail sentences for many individuals.

This *per se* approach (which automatically condemns certain practices) contrasts with the *rule of reason* used by the EC and the UK. In the EC, Article 85 of the Treaty of Rome prohibits:

> agreements between undertakings, decisions by associations of undertakings and concerted practices which may affect trade between Member States and which have as their object the prevention, restriction or distortion of competition within the Common Market.

The EC takes the view that:

> large cartels in which competitors fix prices or allocate markets amongst themselves, are a most serious violation of the competition rules. They are particularly pernicious because they shield an entire Community industry from exposure to effective competition and because they make the European consumer pay the price for cosy industry arrangements (CEC, 1992a, p. 15).

Exemptions are made if an agreement is considered to lead to an improvement in either static or dynamic resource allocation (by improving production and distribution or enhancing innovation), and if it does not eliminate competition. Exclusive dealing agreements (where one firm supplies goods to another for resale within a specific geographical region within the Community) are one class of agreement which have been granted *block exemptions* on the grounds that they may benefit consumers.

In the UK, restrictive practices (agreements between firms with respect to prices and terms of supply) must be registered, the form of the agreement being the prime criterion for registration, rather than its likely effects (a contrast with the EC approach). Registered agreements are presumed to be against the public interest unless the firms can show certain net economic benefits as prescribed in the legislation. Only eight *gateways* are allowed under the Restrictive Trade Practices Act 1976. In addition, the firm must satisfy the *tailpiece* that benefits stemming from the operation of an agreement are not outweighed by detriments to persons not party to the agreement. The Association of British Travel Agents (ABTA) has been one of the few to defend its agreement successfully. It was accepted that the arrangement whereby ABTA members (tour operators and travel agents) would only deal amongst themselves protected the consumer. The ability of a firm to enforce a given retail price for its product is similarly presumed to be against the public interest under the Resale Prices Act 1976. A White Paper *Opening Markets: New Policy on Restrictive Trade Practices* (HM Government, 1989) proposed to bring UK policy into closer conformity with that of the EC, but has yet to result in legislation.

Individual firms may try to create barriers against the entry of potential competitors by such means as tying the sale of one product to the sale of another, forcing customers to stock the entire product range, refusing to supply an outlet that stocks competitors' products and adopting uncompetitive discount practices. These fell outside the UK's restrictive practices legislation, but are now within the scope of the Competition Act 1980. Here there is no presumption that the practice is against the public interest. There is a preliminary investigation by the Office of Fair Trading (under Section 3 of the Competition Act 1980) and a reference to the MMC under Section 5 if an anti-competitive practice is identified and the parties refuse to abandon it.

The rule of reason approach taken by the UK and the EC appears, superficially, to be more attractive than the *per se* approach of the USA since it recognises that there may be cases where agreements between firms are welfare-enhancing. However, the *per se* approach has the advantages of reducing the uncertainty facing firms and of reducing the costs of implementation (because inquiries only need to establish the existence of a proscribed practice).

■ 8.8 Policy towards state entry barriers

A less developed area of competition policy is that directed at removing government-imposed obstacles (either deliberate or unintentional) to the operation of the competitive process. It is only since the Competition Act 1980 that the MMC has had more than token powers to investigate UK public bodies. Section 11 of the Competition Act 1980 permits consideration of 'efficiency and costs' or 'abuse of a monopoly situation'. In the first sixteen public sector investigations (which included the Post Office and the electricity boards) 634 recommendations for improved efficiency were made (National Audit Office, 1986). However, important state activities such as education and the health service remain outside the scope of the legislation.

The EC has wide powers to control policies which adversely affect competition, including (under Article 90) the activities of member governments. Furthermore, Articles 92–4 aim to control support given by member states to individual firms, specifically:

any aid granted by a Member State or through State resources in any form ... is incompatible with the common market.

The form of aid covered under Article 92 remains as stated in the Fourteenth Report on Competition Policy:

not only constituted by grants or advances, but also by loans on more favourable terms than are available on the market, guarantees, tax concessions, relief of social security contributions, and by the State putting up new capital for enterprises in circumstances in or on terms which a private investor would not do so (CEC, 1985, p. 129).

For instance, in 1991 the EC argued that Toyota had been indirectly granted state aid in purchasing government-owned land at a price below market value (CEC, 1992a). Exceptions are allowed (for example, regional aid and assistance to the research and development of generic technologies) but these have to be cleared by the Commission in advance of their implementation. Articles 92–4 also prevent national governments treating public sector companies in a different way from private firms, and so effectively preclude nationalisation as a means of protecting particular industries. But although these articles appear to constrain industry policy, the rules have been hard to enforce, partly because of the failure of national governments to disclose aid payments.

■ 8.9 Evaluation of competition policy

Whether or not competition policy is judged a success depends on the theoretical stance adopted. For instance, the MMC has been accused of inconsistency in failing to condemn automatically monopolies earning high profits (Sutherland, 1969). This accusation is justified only if a narrow, SCP-based approach is adopted. Developments to traditional theory, such as Demsetz's efficiency hypothesis (1973) and Baumol's contestable markets (1982), make it less obvious whether monopolies and mergers are undesirable. In fact, Demsetz recommends:

Consider blocking horizontal mergers only if this keeps an industry from becoming very concentrated, but allow an efficiency defense of such mergers (1982, pp. 53–4).

Demsetz (1992) is also opposed to the *per se* prohibition of price agreements on the grounds that this fails to consider potential efficiencies.

From an Austrian viewpoint, competition policy is flawed if it devotes resources to transitory problems (such as private sector monopoly) while failing to tackle the government abuses which more effectively constrain the operation of the competitive process. Mergers are an integral part of the competitive process, playing a valuable role in eliminating inefficient firms. Some Austrian economists may therefore argue that it is unnecessary to investigate them; action should be taken if and when the merger leads to an undesirable monopoly. Littlechild (1989) and Neumann (1990) adopt a less extreme position in advocating the prevention of those mergers which would strengthen entry barriers.

Developments to neoclassical theory, and the Austrian view, suggest that cases should be investigated individually. Consequently, in the USA, dogmatic, but administratively simple, rules on mergers are being replaced. Unfortunately a case-by-case approach adds to administrative costs as demonstrated by the fact that the MMC in the UK published an average of less than three dominant firm reports per year during the 1980s. Moreover, the selectivity such an approach imposes makes the policy less clear and predictable, and can introduce inconsistencies. For instance, Fairburn notes that, in the UK, market share is not a clear guide to the likelihood of a merger being referred:

> in a substantial number of cases, mergers creating a strong presumption of danger of monopoly abuse were not even put before the Commission (1989, p. 211).

The EC approach on monopoly tries to reduce inconsistencies in treatment by specifying particular forms of conduct which constitute an abuse and so are unlawful.

An effective competition policy is one where issues of competition are the overriding concern. This has not always been the case in the UK (Colenutt and O'Donnell, 1978). The MMC is required to acknowledge a public interest criterion which encompasses considerations other than competition, although, as Weir (1993) notes, during the period 1974–90 a merger had a significantly greater chance of approval if competition was expected to increase or remain unchanged. The gateways of the restrictive practices legislation are similarly wide-ranging. Proposed changes in restrictive practices legislation should remedy this: agreements restricting, distorting or preventing competition would become unlawful.

Competition policy should also concentrate on areas where the potential benefits are greatest. In the UK, the MMC (1975, 1982) twice investigated the London Rubber Company which had a dominant position in the market for contraceptive sheaths and was earning an 80 per cent rate of return on capital employed. Even this classic monopoly was calculated to have generated an annual welfare loss of no more than £1.5 million (Ferguson, 1985). In contrast, the investigation of the postal service in Inner London (MMC, 1980) resulted in annual savings of £23 million. Since the welfare gain is likely to be directly related to the size of the market, competition policy investigations would do better to concentrate on potential abuses in the largest markets. Moreover, priority should be given to the investigation of those markets characterised by high entry barriers, which confer the greatest opportunity to exploit market power.

Transaction cost economics and public choice theory raise doubts about the whole rationale of competition policy as a means of improving economic welfare. As Ginsburg argues:

> Ironically, whenever government asserts that a particular transaction or business practice should be prohibited under antitrust law, it imposes its own monopoly decision on the market and thus displaces the multiple decisions that would otherwise be made by consumers, with their diverse tastes and preferences … A supposedly benevolent (public) monopolist, that is, exerts its power to prevent the emergence, which it claims to foresee, of a malevolent (private) actor, a firm with market power or a monopoly (1991, p. 96).

Lack of information and bounded rationality limit the government's ability to identify accurately potential threats to competition and to propose remedies likely to enhance economic welfare. Moreover, the motives of the politicians and bureaucrats may not be altruistic:

> As rational maximisers of their own welfare, politicians must find something valuable about antitrust, because they spend considerable resources to obtain more of it (McChesney, 1991, p. 790).

From these perspectives, there can be no presumption that competition policy will enhance society's welfare.

■ 8.10 Regional policy

The case for policies to direct the spatial location of industry to ameliorate regional problems turns on the failure of the market to achieve adjustments in the economy either quickly or equitably. Firms must adjust to changes in tastes and incomes. With firms unevenly spread in terms of number, size distribution and activity among regions, change has differential effects. Some regions may become prosperous, whilst others face decline. In a region suffering industrial decline, high unemployment is expected to lead to reductions in local wages. This raises the attractiveness of the region to migrant firms. At the same time, relatively higher wages in more successful regions stimulate immigration by the unemployed. The more imperfect the market mechanism, the longer it will take to reduce regional disparities.

It has been argued that the process of readjustment can lead to externalities and that these also provide a case for regional policy. For example, migrants tend to be younger, more educated and more highly skilled than the population left behind. This may worsen the prospects of the remaining unemployed, since firms generally require a mix of skills. The lack of certain types of labour may reduce firms' willingness to locate in a problem region. In addition, migration out of a region is also likely to lead to adverse domino effects (**Section 7.12**). These further exacerbate the impact on the depressed region's income and unemployment. At the same time, the economic infrastructure in the problem region (roads, sewers, schools, hospitals) is under-used. In contrast, infrastructure in the receiving regions requires expansion, while the additional population may cause or compound congestion problems.

Proponents of an active regional policy argue that the best way to improve economic welfare at the national level is by government intervention. To deal with the externality effects of regional disparities, intervention usually involves policies designed to attract firms to problem regions. This may take the form of grants to firms which locate or expand in particular areas, or of a refusal to permit development in more prosperous regions.

The precise form of intervention depends on which regional disparities are to be redressed. For example, high unemployment may be the result of a relatively sluggish regional growth, perhaps because of a disproportionate number of declining industries. In this case, regional unemployment might be reduced by policies to raise demand for the region's output. Clearly such a policy would fail if the unemployment were a consequence of a mismatch between labour skills in the region and the needs of local employers. An active approach here would be either to initiate retraining or to attract those firms that could make use of existing labour skills.

In sharp contrast, adherents of the *laissez-faire* approach to industry policy believe there is no role for such measures. They argue that using resources to alter firms' location decisions simply switches employment around the national economy. This is a waste from the point of view of the economy in that resources are tied up in policy implementation and firms are being transferred to higher-cost locations. Furthermore, the competitiveness of firms in those sectors not supported is reduced because they have to contribute to the finance of regional policy. A *laissez-faire* approach would not deal specifically with regional problems. Rather, policies to reduce imperfections in product and factor markets would be viewed as bringing benefits to the regions, as well as to the economy as a whole.

One measure would be to tackle labour market imperfections – such as centrally determined (or minimum) wage agreements, which prevent wages from reflecting local market conditions. Government welfare payments to the unemployed may similarly be viewed as discouraging labour mobility. Another measure might be to remove restrictions from the housing market so that labour can move more freely between regions. This is appropriate to the UK where rent controls have led to the demise of private rented housing and where there are barriers to mobility within the public rented sector.

Empirical findings apparently refute the hypothesis that firms choose the lowest-cost location (Townroe, 1971; Sant, 1975). Rather, they show that firms choose to expand close to their current operations. The existence of market power and/or principal–agent problems (**Section 1.5**) allows management to indulge personal preferences. (It may be a plausible assertion that managers prefer a location near a major city because of the extensive social and recreational facilities it offers.) Removing barriers to competition in capital and product markets would discipline managements to locate in the lowest-cost locations. If the problem regions are lowest-cost, then this would automatically ease the regional problem. Alternatively, if problem regions are not the lowest-cost regions, these measures would exacerbate regional disparities (but would still be justified because national economic welfare would be enhanced).

The fact that favoured sites are not those with the lowest production costs is (by itself) insufficient evidence that a firm is not attempting to maximise profits. Transaction and management costs (**Section 2.17**) should be taken into account: expenses incurred in trying to evaluate all potential sites are a relevant part of the location decision. A site which fails to offer the lowest production costs may be profit-maximising when such costs are taken into account. This might allow an alternative prescription consistent with a supportive regional policy. By setting up an agency to provide information on relative prices throughout the country, the government may be able to reduce a firm's transaction costs and enable it to extend the search for a lower-cost site. Similar arguments would justify an agency to reduce the costs of labour mobility by providing information about job opportunities, housing, schooling and social facilities in other regions.

Differences between the four theoretical approaches to industry policy are very clearly seen in the arguments about the extent to which retraining costs (consequent on inappropriate workforce skills) should be borne by state agencies. All would agree that intervention could be justified on externality grounds: enhancing the skills of one individual may raise the productivity of his workfellows. If this occurs, the social rate of return exceeds the private rate of return. Income taxes also mean that the social rate of return exceeds the private rate of return because the individual captures only part of any increase in earnings.

Externalities are the only arguments for intervention that might be accepted by the *laissez-faire* approach, which takes the view that government support is unwarranted. Since retraining generally enhances future earnings, the individual should be able to arrange – and justify taking – a loan. Furthermore, in areas of skill shortage firms may be willing to pay for retraining. As long as there are no alternative sources of employment for the newly trained worker, then the firm can be sure of reaping the benefits of its investment. Where many employment opportunities exist, there is less incentive for a firm to train its employees, but the gain to the individual from undertaking retraining would be greater because of the large number of employers demanding the skill.

Adherents to the supportive approach would argue that this fails to recognise transaction costs. Uncertainty about future labour market developments may cause individuals to under-invest in skill acquisition. Also lenders may be unwilling to make loans available because of the risk that an individual might not obtain employment. Recommendations would be that government should subsidise retraining (or, indeed, education generally) to offset the distorting effect of income taxes, and also perhaps loan funds at market rates (without risk premia).

The active and planning approaches would go further. Individuals require information on relative earnings and the likely demand for different skills before embarking on a retraining programme. Current labour market information is only a crude indicator of the pattern of future labour demand. The active–planning approaches would attempt to overcome this difficulty by specifying likely future skill demands according to the view taken of how the economy will develop under the guidance of industry policy. Retraining programmes would then be provided either by government agencies or through support to private sector initiatives.

■ *8.11* Regional policy in practice

There is no explicit regional policy in the USA, although particular programmes may have a regional impact. In contrast, the UK has had an explicit regional policy since the Special Areas Acts of 1934. For many years, the UK adopted an active stance in which financial support was prominent. A main arm of policy was the Regional Development Grant, which provided grants of up to 15 per cent to eligible firms investing in new plant and equipment. Between 1947 and 1981, firms proposing a new development were required to apply for an Industrial Development Certificate which was withheld if the location was considered inappropriate. Since 1979 there has been a switch to a more supportive approach, culminating in 1988 with the abolition of the Regional Development Grant. Financial support continues to be available, but on nothing like the scale of the mid-1960s to mid-1970s and there has been a switch from automatic to discretionary assistance. Regional Selective Assistance provides discretionary grants to both service and manufacturing firms in cases where projects can be demonstrated to safeguard or create jobs and will benefit the economy. Regional Enterprise Grants aim to encourage small and medium-sized firms.

The EC faces a wide regional diversity with income per head in the ten least developed regions less than one-third of the average for the ten most advanced regions (CEC, 1991b). Since the adoption of the Single Act in 1987, the EC has attached greater importance to achieving social and economic cohesion. Reform of the structural Funds (including the European Regional Development Fund (ERDF)) in 1988 has both increased and focused the financial assistance available. For instance, two-thirds of the funding in the period 1989–93 was to be directed towards 'Objective 1', increasing the development of lagging regions (such as the whole of Ireland and Portugal, and the regions of Sicily and Calabria in Italy). Resources are targeted to priorities. As an example, 29 per cent of the funds allocated to Objective 1 were to be directed to improvements in basic infrastructure and 21 per cent were to be spent on enhancing human resources. The philosophy behind the reform is:

> Instead of encouraging action in a particular sector – aid to the textile industry or to shipyards in a certain member state – as in the past, the EC wished to tackle all the structural problems facing the less favoured regions and the most deprived citizens. Since investment is the key to development, these regions must be given the best chance of attracting firms by giving them production and economic

conditions as close as possible to those in developed regions (CEC, 1992b, p. 10).

This is a supportive approach to regional policy.

A difficulty in evaluating the success of regional policy is that social equity may be a more important objective than economic efficiency. Reduction of differences in unemployment rates between regions, largely for non-economic reasons, is often a primary aim. As Armstrong and Taylor note in respect of the UK:

> The justification for regional policy has relied heavily upon the fact that significant disparities in employment opportunities are socially and politically unacceptable (1985, p. 43).

Pursuit of such objectives may conflict with the wider industry policy aim of enhancing national economic welfare.

The ninth report of the ERDF (CEC, 1984) estimated that (between 1975 and 1983) 570 000 jobs were created or maintained because of joint assistance from national bodies and the ERDF. Moore, Rhodes and Tyler (1986) calculated that the UK's active regional policy over the two decades from 1960 created or safeguarded 945 000 jobs. Such figures demand careful interpretation, for they relate only to the situation within problem regions. They say nothing about the opportunity cost (in jobs and welfare) on the rest of the economy, which will be substantial. For instance, the White Paper *Regional Industrial Development* reported the average financial cost per job created in the 'assisted areas' of the UK during the 1970s as £35 000 (1982 prices) and noted that:

> Many of the jobs said to be created would otherwise have come into existence elsewhere in this country and should thus be described as 'transferred' (Department of Trade and Industry, 1983, p. 2).

Furthermore, Regional Development Grants during the 1970s were essentially capital subsidies, and hence their net job-creating effect could have been negative. Firms operating labour-intensive production methods in the unassisted regions may have relocated in the problem regions using more capital-intensive operations.

Opportunity costs are increased where regions or countries seek to attract firms away from rival locations. In the case of foreign firms, governments seek to outbid rivals by offering assistance to make a particular location the most profitable for the firm. Whilst much political capital is made of the job opportunities created, the impact upon domestic welfare is more problematic. Incentives offered may well exceed the level required to attract such firms. For instance, several states offered incentives to the German car manufacturer BMW following its decision to open a plant in the USA. The winning bid, from South Carolina, was reported to total $130 million (Reich, 1992). As Stopford and Turner argue with respect to the UK electronic and mechanical engineering sectors:

> By failing to understand the motives of prospective investors, civil servants have probably acted unnecessarily so as to enrich foreign shareholders rather than to focus their efforts on the creation of jobs in Britain in cases where, without public assistance, they would have gone elsewhere (1985, p. 141).

In addition, more favourable treatment to such firms hands them a competitive advantage over domestic rivals. For example, Nissan (established in a development area in north-east England) was reported in September 1986 to have a cost advantage of around £300 per car over the long-established General Motors' subsidiary Vauxhall. Much of this was the direct result of grant aid and, partly as a consequence, Vauxhall was forced to cut its workforce by 1000 (*Financial Times*, 5 September 1986).

■ *8.12* Innovation policy

Although innovation generally enhances economic welfare (Chapter 6), firms may not undertake the 'desired' level of innovatory activity. They may be deterred because the returns on any project are uncertain, and the size or time scale of the project may be too daunting for an individual firm. Even where an innovation is successful, the higher profits resulting may quickly be eroded. In contrast, lack of knowledge about competitors' developments may lead to the wasteful duplication of investment and research effort. Any one of these arguments can be used to justify innovation policy.

There are also externality arguments for government involvement to expand the level of innovation. As well as enhancing the profit opportunities of the innovating firm, benefits will accrue to consumers, rival firms and the government itself. Consumers' welfare is improved where innovation leads to lower prices or improved products. By imitating, rivals are sooner or later able to profit from the innovation. The government gains from the higher tax receipts generated. These externalities create a divergence between private and social rates of return. For a sample of seventeen product and process innovations,

Mansfield *et al.* (1977) estimated that the social rate of return was around 2.5 times higher than that realised by the innovating firms.

Adherents to the *laissez-faire* approach would give no credence to such arguments for government involvement as they turn on imperfect knowledge and uncertainty (**Section 7.10**). But for those adopting a supportive approach, they provide a case for government action to improve the R&D infrastructure or to reduce the costs to firms of information-gathering (perhaps by setting up a government agency). The net welfare effects of such intervention are ambiguous. On the one hand, it should improve sales, increasing the innovator's profits, but on the other, faster rates of imitation made possible by the improved flow of information will mean a more rapid erosion of these profits.

An active or planning approach would advocate additional forms of intervention, including the adoption of a patent system, financial support to innovative activity and government sponsorship of academic research programmes. A danger here is that the deployment of a plethora of instruments may decrease the uptake by small and medium-sized firms, which are both at an informational disadvantage and subject to higher administration costs.

A patent gives a legally enforceable right to prevent others from making, selling or using an invention for a specified number of years. The rationale is that this provides the incentive to innovate since it slows down the speed of imitation and the rate at which innovatory profits are eroded. Higher prospective rates of return provide an incentive to devote more resources to innovation. Robinson refers to this as the *paradox of patents*:

> A patent is a device to prevent the diffusion of new methods before the original investor has received profit adequate to induce the requisite investment. The justification of the patent system is that by slowing down the diffusion of technical progress it ensures that there will be more progress to diffuse (1956, p. 87).

A patent system may encourage innovation in a second way which is often overlooked. When seeking a patent, the firm has to disclose information which is then made generally available to others a few months later. Rivals can utilise this to avoid duplication of effort or to refocus their R&D programmes on more promising lines of research. While this aspect of a patent system would appeal to those advocating a supportive innovation policy, there remains a doubt. Patents may actually foster the duplication of research efforts because of the rewards in being the first to file a patent application. Alternatively, the patent system may encourage premature R&D expenditures, which would increase the costs of invention.

The bureaucratic costs involved in a patent system must not be ignored: the opportunity costs of the resources used may be considerable. These comprise the resource cost of the patent agency and that of using the system (management time and the costs of patent agents). There are also substantial costs consequent on preventing patent infringements. McGee (1966) cited legal fees of $3 million in the fifteen-year court action on petroleum-cracking patents, whilst Scherer (1980, p. 454) estimated that annual administration costs in the USA totalled $330 million at 1978 prices. Additional costs are borne by society through the use made of the system by firms who would have undertaken innovation even in the absence of patent protection. For these cases patents simply slow down the market process and cause a reduction in economic welfare.

An active innovation policy could also incorporate direct assistance to all (or to a selected sub-set) of firms – for instance, through sales tax exemption for firms using advanced technology products, through tax allowances or through grants to firms undertaking R&D. Such programmes have several drawbacks. A patent system essentially provides a reward to firms who make successful innovations (generating abnormal or entrepreneurial profits). On the other hand, financial support is usually made available at an earlier stage in the innovatory process and so tends to benefit firms regardless of whether they eventually deliver marketable ideas. Intervention agencies again face the problem that their expenditure may not actually increase the level of R&D activity. Although a firm may argue that support is necessary to finance a specific project, that research may have been undertaken anyway, so that state finance is used for other purposes. Finally, selective assistance schemes require an agency to decide which sectors merit support and which do not. Centralised 'strategic' choices are unlikely to be better than those of the firms closest to the technologies and markets concerned. They may be worse, upsetting the market mechanism and wasting resources by assigning aid to inappropriate projects and the wrong firms. This argument can also be used to counter proposals to enhance innovation by sponsoring research activity in universities and other institutions.

Patents and financial assistance to R&D are examples of policies directed principally to stimulate invention and innovation. This is not necessarily the most effective approach; consideration should be given to the potential merits of policies that encourage diffusion. This recognises that commercially successful innovations require the development of a supply of specialised inputs and the establishment of markets for the products. For instance, Geroski (1992) notes that biotechnological innovation was encouraged by mergers which gave specialist firms access to the manufacturing expertise and distributive networks of established chemical and pharmaceutical firms. He suggests that an appropriate industry policy would be to use public procurement to create the markets that will stimulate innovation.

The stance of competition policy has implications for innovation. It has been shown that a perfectly competitive market structure is unsuitable for innovation (**Section 6.4**). Rather, markets with a higher level of market concentration (particularly oligopoly) appear to be more favourable. Indeed such structures appear to evolve in industries where technological change is rapid. Consequently any competition policy which adopts perfect competition as its ideal will tend to hamper innovation. Similarly, measures intended to prevent the distortion of competition by restrictive agreements between firms must avoid penalising joint R&D ventures. Competition policy should also recognise that mergers can benefit innovation, for instance by eliminating duplication and allowing economies of scale (George and Jacquemin, 1992). On the other hand, government support to innovation may itself distort competition by selectively advantaging certain firms.

■ *8.13* Innovation policy in practice

Most advanced economies operate an active innovation policy aimed at accelerating the rate at which new products and processes are introduced. This usually incorporates both a patent system and financial assistance, although the latter may unintentionally discriminate against small firms who often lack the information to take advantage of such support. Some governments also adopt a supportive approach by providing the infrastructure that will facilitate innovation, such as technical and contract R&D services.

The objective of policies to provide financial support to innovation often seems to be the promotion of national prestige and national security, rather than welfare enhancement. In the USA, UK and France the support to military, nuclear and space programmes has been a major component of innovation policy. These are often loss-making projects. In the UK, loans to aircraft manufacturers to finance civil airframe and engine development ('launch aid') have exceeded $2 billion (excluding Concorde) since the Second World War. Subsequent lack of commercial success has meant the repayment of only 10 per cent (*Financial Times*, 26 February 1986). In contrast, Vogel (1979) argues that a key reason for Japan's industrial success is that virtually no resources are tied up in government-sponsored, non-commercial defence and space projects.

Without patent protection many innovations may not have taken place, although empirical evidence suggests that patent protection is crucial in only a few industries. Mansfield (1986) studied 100 US firms in 12 industries between 1981 and 1983 and found that 65 per cent of pharmaceutical and 30 per cent of chemical inventions would not have occurred without patent protection. In contrast, there were no inventions for which patent protection was essential in the office equipment, motor vehicles, rubber and textiles industries.

Patent systems have a number of operational limitations. Firms operating internationally face the costs of meeting patent requirements in different countries, although these costs have been reduced by extensive developments in recent years. The European Patent Office (which has operated since 1978) has reduced the transaction costs of patent protection in Europe. Similarly, the Patent Cooperation Treaty (1970) requires only one patent application for cover in the countries party to the agreement.

There is a view that the life of a patent (twenty years under the EC system, seventeen in the USA) may be too long. Nordhaus (1969) argues that a patent life of between fifteen and twenty years is optimal for projects which yield a cost saving of only 1 per cent and whose end products are price-inelastic. Any project likely to yield more substantial cost savings merits a shorter patent life because the costs of the innovation can be recouped more readily. However, calls for a variable patent life ignore the associated heavy administrative burden.

One disadvantage of the US patent system is that it does not prevent the practice of 'ringing' a new field. This is where a firm increases its monopoly power by taking out patents on a series of different innovations all in the same area, and refusing to make licences available to others. The firm then uses the least-cost innovation while other firms are denied use of the others. This is largely avoided in the UK, where the possibility exists that compulsory licences may be granted to others when the patent is not being commercially worked.

The White Paper *Realising Our Potential* (HM Government, 1993) proposes (for the UK) a Technology Foresight Programme whose intention is to 'pick winners' in the form of technologies and areas of research that should provide the best opportunities for enhancing economic and social welfare. These are to be identified by three criteria: real scientific promise, the availability of strong research groups, and the existence of firms that are willing and able to exploit the results. This is an example of an active approach to innovation policy.

Efforts to prevent conflict between innovation and competition policies have been mixed. The introduction of the National Collaborative Research Act in the USA in 1984 has helped reduce the chance that joint ventures to promote innovation are considered anti-competitive. EC competition policy offers block exemptions, but runs the risk that firms may act opportunistically, cloaking agreements in the guise of R&D in order to gain approval. In contrast, UK competition policy has accorded no special treatment to collaboration between firms in R&D.

■ *8.14* Trade policy

The use of trade policy to achieve industrial objectives has a long history. Protection is frequently used as part of an active or planning approach to industry policy. By restricting foreign competition, it is possible to influence the operation of particular firms and industries; to accelerate the growth of an infant industry; or to decelerate the decline of a mature industry. It may also (as part of a supportive industry policy) be used as a 'second-best' measure to try to force other nations to adopt liberal trade policies.

Figure 8.1 illustrates how a declining industry may be helped by the imposition of a *voluntary export restraint* (VER) (the effects of quotas, tariffs and other forms of protection are similar). Under free trade, supply (S_w) is assumed to be perfectly elastic at the world price P_w. Domestic production is limited by the domestic supply curve S_d to $0Q_1$ so that imports equal to Q_1Q_2 meet the remaining demand. A VER is a market-sharing agreement: exporters agree to restrict the quantity of goods they trade in a particular economy (they may be willing to do this because their export prices rise and/or because they fear the imposition of even more restrictive controls). In **Figure 8.1**, the VER limits imports to Q_1Q_3. Adding this to S_d, the effective supply in the economy is shown by S_v. The equilibrium price rises from P_w to P_v, domestic production increases to $0Q_4$ and consumption falls to $0Q_5$.

The use of trade policy to achieve domestic industry policy ends has several attractions. It appeals to politicians concerned with re-election, because the benefits are readily perceived by the favoured industry. The government is saved any direct expense; quite the reverse if tariffs are used, for these increase government revenues. However, the costs of such policies are substantial. The protection of one sector may bolster local employment but the overall effect on welfare – and even on overall employment levels – may be negative because protection insulates and supports domestic firms by raising prices and reducing competition. Area 1 + 2 + 3 + 4 in **Figure 8.1** represents part of the consumer surplus

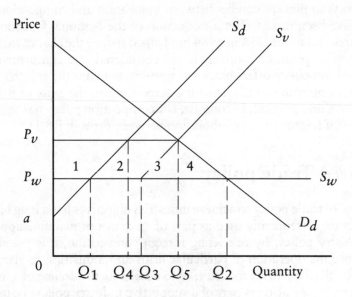

Figure 8.1   *The effect of a voluntary export restraint*

available under free trade. In increasing price and reducing sales (from $0Q_2$ to $0Q_5$) protection reduces the welfare of consumers (although this effect may be negligible to any given individual). The VER transfers areas 1 and 2 to domestic producers in the form of increased revenues. Their net gain is only area 1 since area 2 is absorbed by production costs. Area 3 represents a transfer to foreign producers. The net cost of the VER is equal to the sum of areas 2 and 4, which is a deadweight loss to society.

In many respects, protection of a declining industry suffers from the same disadvantages as financial support. The respite from foreign competition is rarely used as a 'breathing space' for adjustment, but rather tends to be seen as an opportunity for inaction. This may be profit-maximising from the firm's viewpoint. If it fails to see a long-term future for the sector (and so regards the investment necessary to regain international competitiveness as uneconomic) then it may be prepared to suffer production inefficiency and enjoy the benefits of protection. Even if the firm could have a viable future, it may be less profitable to make the changes necessary to become competitive. If these would involve large job losses, politicians might consider that supporting another industry instead would now offer the prospect of gaining more votes. Protection therefore tends to preserve jobs in their current employment. This takes place at the price of the ossification of the structure of the economy, reductions in market flexibility and adverse effects on long-term competitiveness, leading to reduced living standards for the country's citizens.

■ *8.15* Trade policy in practice

Before the Second World War, trade policy was the principal method of supporting domestic industries, with tariffs and quotas the main instruments. There has been a reduction in the use of these traditional measures, particularly in manufacturing. This is a result of the formation of the General Agreement on Tariffs and Trade (GATT) in 1947 (culminating in tariff cuts in the Kennedy and Tokyo rounds) and the emergence of free trade areas and customs unions (such as the EC). The North American Free Trade Area (NAFTA) proposed between Canada, the USA and Mexico is expected eventually to enhance welfare by some $15 billion per year (*The Economist*, 20 March 1993). Despite the benefits of free trade, advanced economies continue to rely heavily on trade policy. Unlike other industrial policy instruments, such policies are frequently used to protect firms in the agricultural and service sectors, as well as in manufacturing. Within manufacturing, they tend to be concentrated on a narrow range of products, including textiles, footwear, steel, automobiles, electronic products and components.

Tariffs have been increasingly replaced by non-tariff barriers (such as voluntary export restraints or 'health' and 'safety' standards to be met by imports) and by the use of selective assistance to industries. Between 1966 and 1986, the World Bank (1991) noted an increase of around 20 per cent in the share of imports subject to non-tariff barriers by the USA, a 40 per cent increase for Japan, and a 160 per cent increase for the EC. In the early 1990s, there were almost 300 voluntary export restraint agreements known to GATT, mostly imposed by the USA and the EC against imports from Japan and other Far Eastern countries. As an example, the EC made an agreement with Japan in 1991 that would partially insulate European car manufacturers from competition until the year 2000.

Whilst trade policy might be used to help firms with healthy growth prospects to become internationally competitive, the aim, in many cases, has been to assist an industry in difficulty. The OECD is highly sceptical of the effectiveness of protection:

> It is ... questionable whether the policies in place have actually helped advance these goals or have done so at a reasonable cost (1992, p. 15).

Australia is cited as an example (OECD, 1989). With domestic firms isolated from international trade, the opportunities for economies of scale have been limited and relative prices have been distorted. As a result, resources have been misdirected into sectors where Australia lacks a comparative advantage.

There have been many attempts to gauge the costs of protection. For instance, Collyns and Dunaway (1990) investigated the impact of voluntary export restraints limiting Japanese car imports into the USA. In raising prices, the cost of the VER to US consumers (area 1 + 2 + 3 + 4 in Figure 8.1) during the period 1981–4 was estimated at almost $17 billion. Of this, $6–12 billion was transferred to domestic producers as extra revenue (area 1 + 2). The transfer to foreign producers and the deadweight loss (area 3 + 4) was estimated at between $5 billion and $11 billion. Consumers were further penalised by the effects of the VER on product choice and quality as the limitation on potential sales encouraged the Japanese to offer their larger models and those with extra equipment.

Collyns and Dunaway also considered the effects on employment in the US car industry. The VER saved 40 000–75 000 jobs at a net cost of $110 000–145 000 each. This is but an illustration of a general feature: it is typical for such studies to show protection to be an expensive means of preserving jobs. Another example is that of Silberston and Ledic (1989) who analysed the effects on the UK of the Multi-Fibre Arrangement (MFA) which manages world trade in textiles. They argued that prices of imported textiles and clothing would fall by 8 per cent in the absence of quotas, which implied that 33 000 jobs in the UK textile industry were preserved at a cost to consumers of £980 million per year (£29 700 per worker).

There are many examples of nations protecting themselves against 'unfair' trade. The US government has used powers under Section 301 of the 1974 Trade Act to punish countries whose trade practices it considers unacceptable (typically by threatening a 100 per cent tariff on selected products). Low (1993) is critical of this approach: only one-third of the actions between 1975 and 1990 had the desired result, and many led to retaliation and fostered a climate hostile to liberal trade. Similar criticisms can be made of the EC's use of antidumping duties, in force on some 50 products (including photocopiers and CD players) in the early 1990s. Finger argues that instead of enhancing economic welfare by operating to counter distortions in trade:

> Antidumping ... is a harnessing of state power to serve a private interest: a means by which one competitor can use the power of the state to gain an edge over another competitor (1992, p. 141).

This is in keeping with Finger's definition of dumping: *'whatever you can get the government to act against under the antidumping law'* (1992, p. 122).

▌ 8.16 An integrated industry policy – the case of the EC

Industry policy must integrate the variety of policy measures in a coherent approach in order to attain the overall welfare objective. Nowhere is this problem more visible than in the EC. Not only must the Commission achieve harmony between its own policies, but it must also achieve this coordination between its policies and those of member states.

Until the 1970s, European industry policy was limited to competition policy and to the removal of barriers to trade between members. The *Memorandum on the Community's Industrial Policy* (CEC, 1970a) signalled a wider role for industry policy and identified five broad objectives which were adopted in 1973:

1. to pursue the establishment of a single market by the removal of barriers such as national preference by state bodies;
2. to move towards the harmonisation of the legal, financial and fiscal environment in which firms operate;
3. to promote mergers between the firms of different member states;
4. to facilitate adaptation by firms to changed market circumstances, particularly with regard to new industries plus a science and technology policy to facilitate the emergence of new industries;
5. to adopt a common policy with respect to economies outside the Community to ensure fair competition in foreign markets.

Industrial Policy in an Open and Competitive Environment (CEC, 1990a) specified 'three axes' on which an effective industrial approach should be based:

1. maintaining a favourable business environment;
2. implementing a positive approach to adjustment (that is, one that avoids protectionist and decelerative policies);
3. maintaining an open approach to markets (both inside and outside the EC).

This is a supportive approach to industry policy:

> The role of public authorities is above all as a catalyst and pathbreaker for innovation. The main responsibility for industrial competitiveness must lie with firms themselves, but they should be able to expect from public authorities clear and predictable conditions for their activities (CEC, 1990a, p. 1).

and:

> The provision of a horizontal framework in which industry can develop and prosper by remedying structural deficiencies and addressing areas where the market mechanism alone fails to provide the conditions necessary for success is the principal means by which the Community applies its industry policy (CEC, 1992a, p. 42).

The textile and clothing industry provides a specific example of the implementation of EC industry policy (CEC, 1991a). The EC is concerned to achieve fair and open trade, to improve information and training, to foster innovation and to introduce a special initiative encouraging diversification in those areas heavily dependent on textiles.

Competition policy plays an important role in EC industrial policy, but is potentially in conflict with regional policy. Regional support favours certain firms and industries and hence distorts competition. The EC tries to reduce this distortion by channelling regional assistance into those areas that are most disadvantaged; in the early 1990s assistance is focused on regions whose development is lagging, areas affected by industrial decline and rural areas. It is argued that aid to such regions is justified because the gain from regional development compensates for the distortion to competition. The EC employs competition policy to further its regional objectives. By restricting the aid given by member states to the more prosperous regions, programmes aimed at the least prosperous regions are more likely to reduce regional differentials.

Innovation policy is generally consistent with the aims of competition policy because it promotes dynamic competition through the development of new products and processes. Despite this, problems may arise if the innovation support is applied at an inappropriate stage, or the amount given is badly judged. Financial assistance to applied research acts in a way similar to an operating subsidy and gives supported firms significant commercial advantages. The Commission therefore provides guidelines to direct national support to basic research. Too much support may misdirect R&D activity towards projects that gain subsidy but may not be intrinsically desirable. In consequence, the EC advocates that assistance to basic research should not normally exceed 50 per cent of the gross costs of the project.

Although agreements between firms are normally regarded as anti-competitive under Article 85, block exemptions have been given to permit cooperation between firms on R&D activity. The EC itself has a number of innovation programmes (such as ESPRIT which focuses on information technology and RACE targeting developments in telecommunications) aimed at fostering the competitiveness of European industry whilst avoiding duplication in R&D. Through its 'framework programmes' (the third running from 1990 to 1994, and listing – with financial allocations – the main areas of activity) the EC is seeking to establish a more effective and coordinated approach to technological development and research in Europe.

It is less clear that EC trade policy is consistent with competition policy or even in line with the industry policy objectives of maintaining open markets. Clearly the removal of trade barriers of all types to establish a single European market is pro-competitive. Widespread use of antidumping duties and voluntary export restraints does more than shield EC firms from the competitive pressure of imports. However, conflicts may arise from the EC's approach to external trade. George and Jacquemin argue:

> a protectionist external policy would not only limit the benefits of competition; it would also reduce the effectiveness with which anticompetitive practices are controlled (1992, p. 156).

In adopting a protectionist stance the government in effect sanctions anti-competitive behaviour, and adversely affects the climate within which competition policy is operated.

Much of the conflict between Community industry policy and that of member states turns on differences in objectives and in approach; member states frequently adopt a more active stance on industry policy. In certain cases the EC has been forced to accept decelerative policies, including support to the textile, steel and shipbuilding industries. But even here the underlying philosophy of the EC is revealed by the type of support permitted. In 1982 the EC applied Articles 58 and 61 of the European Coal and Steel Community to declare a situation of 'manifest crisis' in the steel industry. This gave the Commission the power to impose minimum prices and production quotas on firms. The aim was to phase out uneconomic plants and to generate a competitive industry. Temporary subsidies were to replace national support programmes. An end date for EC assistance was always clearly specified.

The same view that decelerative policies are second best is evident from the EC's proposals to tackle the recurrence of problems in the steel industry in 1993. Financial support of around Ecu 1 billion is likely to be offered in order to achieve a reduction in crude steel-making capacity of some 30m tonnes. Any assistance will be subject to producers' commitment to a programme of closures to be fully implemented by a particular date. Governments have been warned not to try to prevent the industry's decline by awarding state aids (*Financial Times*, 19 February 1993).

This latter point shows that the EC continues to see a role for itself as a 'policeman', restraining members from policies involving excessive intervention. Where governments give different levels of support to the same industry, competitiveness may be determined more by the level of support than by intrinsic efficiency advantages. This may give perverse results such as the elimination of unsupported low-cost producers in one member state because of the high level of subsidies given to inherently higher-cost producers elsewhere. A framework has been developed to prevent each member state simultaneously pursuing a policy of strategic protection to selected industries. Textiles was the first industry to be subject to guidelines on state support (see CEC, 1972, pp. 135–6). The guidelines were that:

1. Price subsidies are unacceptable because they reduce the incentive to restructure ailing industries;
2. Aid should be tied to the requirement to reduce excess capacity;
3. Aid should be designed to enhance the industry's international competitiveness.

In general, member states are required to notify the Commission of any plans to grant or to alter aid. Despite the EC's efforts to limit state aid, the level remains very high (an annual average of Ecu 89 billion in 1988–90). Moreover, member states continue to resort to aid programmes without prior clearance. Where illegal aid has been given, the Commission can take (and has taken) steps to recover it from recipient firms.

■ 8.17 Conclusion

In implementing industry policy, most governments make use of a combination of competition, regional, innovation and trade policies. The objectives of these policies are often political and social rather than the enhancement of economic welfare. Furthermore, policies are often conceived without any theoretical justification, although occasionally lip-service may be paid to the externality case for market failure. The notable exception to this is competition policy, which often draws on views of the SCP approach, Chicago and Austrian Schools.

Careful economic analysis can reveal those policies that seem most likely to offer the chance of improving welfare without causing harmful effects on the rest of the economy. Although quantitative evaluation is often impossible, the policies likely to be most successful in meeting these aims can usually be determined. For instance, governments may fail to recognise the extent to which measures in one area impinge upon those elsewhere, in which case industry policy is an amalgam of policies which fail to complement each other. Policies advocated may presume a level of knowledge and influence for the government that is unrealistic in a world where change and uncertainty are endemic. Policies may impose heavy (if perhaps hidden) costs on the economy. This is likely to be the case where many of the policies involve a high degree of government intervention in the operation of firms and industries.

Overall, it is the supportive policies that appear most attractive. This is significant as such an approach has often been rejected in favour of more active involvement in industry. Even in the USA, where industry policy is less extensive, the measures used as part of trade policy and innovation policy rely on active intervention by the government. The industry policy of the EC is the most promising. It is closer to the requirements of a supportive policy, although even here the Commission is often forced to intervene actively in support of ailing industries. Furthermore, the EC sets an example by showing that a common policy framework can be devised to ensure consistency and coordination between policy elements.

■ *Chapter 9* ■

State or Private Control?

> If Government control had supplanted that of private enterprise a hundred years ago, there is good reason to suppose that our methods of manufacture now would be about as effective as they were fifty years ago, instead of being perhaps four or even six times as efficient as they were then (A. Marshall, 1925, p. 338).

■ 9.1 Introduction

Even where governments generally favour the operation of market forces, there is often state control of the production of certain goods and services. This involves either *state ownership* of the industry or *state regulation* of the way in which private sector firms operate. Recent developments in economic theory have increasingly questioned the benefits and usefulness of this type of intervention, and these views are reinforced by the relatively poor performance of industries under state control.

In consequence, ideas as to the appropriate boundary between the state and the private sector are being revised in many countries. Although, for much of the twentieth century, there has been a trend for greater state involvement in the provision of goods and services, this has been reversed since the 1980s. Moves to reduce state regulation and state ownership have been proceeding apace, not only in the UK and the USA, but also in France, Japan and New Zealand and even in less advanced economies such as Chile, Mexico and Malaysia. Between 1980 and 1991, almost 7000 state-owned enterprises (including some 2000 in developing countries and 4500 in the former East Germany) were transferred to the private sector (World Bank, 1992).

Privatisation is set to continue. In 1993 France has announced plans for a second wave of sales involving 21 state firms, including Renault, Air France and the steelmaker Usinor Sacilor. Developing countries are starting to transfer larger enterprises (such as banks, telecommunications companies and airlines) to the private sector. Privatisation also forms a major element of the transition to a market economy in Hungary, Poland, Russia and other former Eastern bloc states.

9.2 Theoretical arguments for state control

There are several theoretical arguments for state control which merit careful consideration. In some cases, state control stems from the operation of either an active or planning approach to industry policy. For instance, in the UK, state ownership (in the form of a majority shareholding) was extended to British Leyland and other 'lame duck' firms as a means of supporting sectors in decline. As **Section 7.12** has shown, the rationale for government intervention in such circumstances is flawed. In most other cases, state control is advocated because the product is deemed to be a merit or a public good, or the industry is regarded as a natural monopoly. In such circumstances, it might be argued that state ownership or regulation is necessary to preclude underprovision of the good or to prevent abuses which might reduce economic welfare.

The *merit good* argument has been applied most strongly for education and health. Economic analysis usually assumes that individuals are best able to judge their own welfare. If this assumption is dropped, it is possible for an individual to make decisions against his own best interests – for instance, by consuming too little education. This provides an argument for state intervention to ensure that provision is at an optimal level. This argument is reinforced if individuals suffer from bounded rationality, such that their information is partial and cannot be evaluated fully. The case for state control of merit goods ignores the possibility of government failure and largely turns on paternalistic and normative judgements beyond the scope of economic analysis (although some externality arguments will apply: for instance, failure by one person to request medical treatment for an infectious disease may lead to an epidemic).

Defence, law enforcement and the judiciary are *public goods*. For this reason, state control may be advocated. As shown in **Section 7.5**, where information is imperfect and transaction costs are positive, private provision of a good which is non-rival and non-excludable will be non-optimal. This argument provides a necessary, but not a sufficient, condition for state control. A government, too, operates under uncertainty and is disadvantaged by imperfect information, in which case it is impossible for the state to identify the optimal level of provision.

The *natural monopoly argument* (**Section 5.5**) is most commonly advanced for state control of the utility and transport sectors of the economy. A natural monopoly is said to exist where scale economies are not exhausted, even when one firm produces the entire market output. (This is illustrated by the continually declining long-run average cost curve in **Figure 9.1**.) In such a market, output is produced at least cost when there is only one firm. Monopoly is the natural outcome, but it leads to several problems.

According to traditional neoclassical theory, a profit-maximising monopolist would produce an output level of $0Q_m$ and set a price of $0P_m$ (**Figure 9.1**). This leads to abnormal profits and a welfare loss equal to the shaded area ABC as compared with the socially optimal level of $0Q_{opt}$ (see also **Section 5.3**). This welfare loss may persist, and even increase over time. The high profits of the monopolist may fail to attract the entry of new firms because of the shape of the long-run average cost function. For instance, another firm may find entry into the market unattractive if it believes that its extra output would drive the market price down to a level which fails to cover costs. Furthermore, if the monopolist feels safe from the threat of entry, and if the capital market is imperfect, it may be less concerned to operate efficiently. If, as a result, average costs rise, then society's welfare is further reduced. Even if entry were profitable, it may be unwelcome from the social welfare point of view. Although entry constrains the profits of the original firm (while moving price and output towards socially optimal levels) duplication *per se* misallocates resources. In other words, the costs of the two firms combined would necessarily exceed those incurred by one firm. This was recognised by Mill in 1848:

It is obvious, for example, how great an economy of labour would be obtained if London were supplied by a single gas or water company instead of the existing plurality ... Were there only one establishment, it could make lower charges consistently with obtaining the rate of profit now realised (1909, p. 143).

The government therefore faces a dilemma. Monopoly is the most efficient market structure, but a profit-maximising monopolist behaves in a way that is detrimental to society's welfare. The traditional solution is for the state to control the operation of such an industry.

■ 9.3 State control of natural monopoly

The options open to a government seeking to control natural monopoly are to take it into state ownership or to regulate the industry (keeping it in private ownership, but constraining the way in which the firm operates). The USA has favoured the regulatory approach, while in Europe nationalisation has been more common.

Regulation in the USA began in 1877, following a Supreme Court decision to control the market prices of companies operating grain elevators in Chicago. Railways, trucking, air transport, telecommunications, electricity and gas are among the sectors that have been regulated. The regulatory agencies were charged with devising methods of control that prevented abuse of market power while ensuring efficient operation. In the USA, only the postal system and some utilities are owned by the state. State ownership has also been quite limited in Japan (only posts, telecommunications and the railway system have been nationalised). In contrast, in Austria, Italy and France most communications, utilities and transport industries have, at some point, been operated by the state. In the UK, the coal, gas, electric, transport (road and rail), and steel industries were taken into state ownership during the period 1945–51. Shipbuilding and aircraft manufacture were nationalised later.

The rationale for state regulation is largely economic, based upon market failure arguments. However, these do not necessarily apply where an industry is taken into state ownership. For instance, much UK nationalisation was for social and political reasons, although it was also believed that direct control of important sectors would facilitate macroeconomic management. This has caused conflicts. Policies oriented to these wider goals have not always been compatible with the efficient operation of the industry (National Economic Development Office, 1976).

9.4 Pricing and profits under state ownership

Although state-owned natural monopolies sell their output in the market, they are, to a large extent, isolated from the market's disciplines. Direct finance from the state isolates them from the pressures of capital markets. Product market pressures are often reduced by their privileged status (they often have a statutory monopoly). This is also true of regulated industries where entry is restricted by the state. As a result, the state must attempt to replace market disciplines with economic groundrules for pricing, investment and other aspects of firm behaviour.

Where an industry is taken into state ownership, it may be directed to set prices which eliminate abnormal profits. The earliest groundrule for nationalised industries in the UK, and contained in nationalisation Acts, was to 'break-even' (over an unspecified number of years). However, this tended to encourage *cross-subsidisation*. Cross-subsidisation uses profits from certain activities to sustain others and leads to a misallocation of resources. In the profitable areas, consumers pay a price that exceeds marginal cost; in the loss-making areas, the price is below the marginal cost of the output. The result is a level of production in excess of $0Q_{opt}$ (**Figure 9.1**). The incentive to cross-subsidise arises from the attempt to attain simultaneously the break-even objective and the wider social obligations placed on these industries. As an illustration, the unprofitable supply of electricity to remote homes may be advocated on social grounds; to avoid making losses, the nationalised industry is forced to finance this service by raising the price it charges in lower-cost markets.

Another option is to direct that prices be set on the basis of marginal costs (*marginal cost pricing*). This instruction was given to UK nationalised industries in the 1967 White Paper (HM Treasury, 1967). However (with the exception of electricity) this directive was largely ignored: there were information problems and it was incompatible with other objectives. The calculation of marginal cost depends on knowledge of the value of the next best use of the resources employed, and such evaluation is necessarily subjective.

Beyond such practical difficulties, marginal cost pricing has other, economic limitations. The attraction of setting price equal to marginal cost (price $0P_{opt}$ in **Figure 9.1**) is that – in the neoclassical paradigm – it maximises economic welfare arising in this industry (see also **Section 5.3**). But when this price is below average cost, the industry operates at a loss. This might be financed in a number of ways. Revenue might be raised by fixed charges (such as a standing charge for connection to a

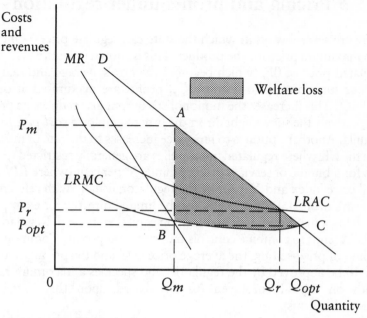

Figure 9.1 *Natural monopoly*

electricity distribution system) but this reduces welfare. Some small-scale users are likely to be deterred because the consumer surplus they would obtain from consuming units priced at marginal cost is outweighed by the standing charge. A similar problem occurs with multi-part tariffs, where the price per unit decreases as more units are consumed, until eventually price equals marginal cost. This avoids the financial loss, but again results in reduced welfare for small-scale users. Another device is for the state to finance the deficit through taxation – but unless these are lump-sum taxes they will generate a loss of welfare elsewhere in the economy.

If all other sectors of the economy were perfectly competitive, there were no externalities and no taxation, then marginal cost pricing in the case of the state-owned industry would improve economic welfare. This is a *first best solution*. But where these conditions are not met, instructing only certain industries to adopt marginal cost pricing may reduce economic welfare. This is because a movement towards marginal cost pricing in one industry is merited only when the gain in marginal benefit in the regulated industry exceeds the marginal loss induced elsewhere by the reallocation of resources. Marginal cost pricing may therefore not even be a *second best solution* (Lipsey and Lancaster, 1956).

■ 9.5 Pricing and profits under regulation

There are several ways in which the state can regulate prices. One is to set a maximum price for the product. This is shown in **Figure 9.1**. At the regulated price of $0P_r$ (which becomes the firm's average and marginal revenue functions up to output $0Q_r$) profits are maximised at output level $0Q_r$. This increases the monopolist's output and reduces its profits. Alternatively the state might direct the firm to employ a *cost-plus pricing* formula. Another option is to link price increases to the rate of inflation, as in the UK where regulated monopolies are generally restricted to price rises for a bundle of services of '*RPI* minus X' per cent (where *RPI* is the retail price index and X is set by the regulator, usually with reference to the firm's profits). Profits might also be limited directly, for example by specifying a maximum rate of return on capital employed. Regulation in the USA tends to combine controls on prices and profits. Commonly the method of price-setting, the average price level and the pricing structure have to be approved by the regulator who specifies a maximum rate of return on capital employed (usually based upon that earned by comparable firms).

These methods of regulation are not without drawbacks. As presented so far the problem has been essentially static, and it has been implicitly assumed that the regulatory body has the information necessary to exercise effective control. To set maximum prices or cost-plus pricing rules, regulators must be able to identify efficient methods of production. They also require information on market demand and the competitive level of factor prices. This information may be difficult to acquire, especially where cost and demand conditions are subject to rapid change. Often the regulator must rely on information provided by the firm, which has an incentive to misrepresent the data to ensure that the regulatory controls imposed still enable it to earn a high rate of return. For instance, cost-plus pricing gives the regulated firm an incentive to exaggerate its costs to secure higher absolute margins.

The adoption of a cost-plus pricing regime may reduce a firm's willingness to lower costs, either through the adoption of new work methods and innovations or through bargaining to gain the lowest factor prices. Forsyth and Hocking (1980) and Albon and Kirby (1983) noted evidence of such *cost-padding* (generating productive inefficiency) in the case of the regulated Australian airlines. Firms could again be discouraged from pursuing cost reductions if price increases are subject to regulation using an '*RPI* minus X'-type formula: the regulator might respond by raising X when the pricing formula is reviewed. The incentive for cost reduction depends upon the length of time between regulatory reviews. The longer the period, the greater the incentive to undertake innovation and reduce costs. Even so, when the review becomes imminent, the firm will have little incentive to reduce costs.

Restrictions on profits also tend to reduce a firm's incentive to control costs. Moreover, they have another drawback, which was first identified by Averch and Johnson (1962). Imposition of a maximum rate of return on capital employed causes the regulated firms to adopt more capital-intensive production techniques. This distorts allocative efficiency because capital in the regulated sectors of the economy becomes relatively less productive than that in the unregulated sectors.

Littlechild (1986b) and Yarrow (1989) argue for the use of *yardstick competition* as a means of reducing the information difficulties facing the regulator. Here, the performance of similar companies would be used as a benchmark. For instance, where water or electricity distribution is organised on a regional basis, the prices set for one company can use information and examples of efficient practices taken from all the regional companies. Critics of this approach, however, suggest that it is inappropriate because, for example, there will always be fundamental differences in circumstances – and, hence, costs – between firms (see Foster, 1992).

■ 9.6 Investment under state control

Where industries are regulated by the state, there are generally few controls on investment behaviour. The instruction to limit the rate of return on capital to levels achieved elsewhere means that regulated firms encounter little difficulty in attracting finance. This does not, however, guarantee that the level of investment undertaken is socially optimal. The Averch–Johnson effect (**Section 9.5**) can lead to over-investment. Under-investment is also a possibility in the case of long-lived projects which are highly asset-specific (that is, sunk costs are incurred). Uncertainty about the future regulatory framework may lead managers to 'over-discount' future returns on such investments (by using a discount factor in excess of the firm's cost of capital) (Helm and Yarrow, 1988).

Firms in state ownership often face problems obtaining finance for investment. In the UK, nationalised industries are generally barred from private sources of funds and face *external financing limits* which restrict borrowing from the government (or, for 'profitable' industries, specify a surplus to be contributed to state funds). Choice of the appropriate cost of capital by the state is crucial because it affects both the volume of investment undertaken and the capital intensity of production.

Nevertheless it has proved difficult to devise effective guidelines. The 1967 White Paper required investment projects to meet a *test discount rate* of 8 per cent (later 10 per cent). This was thought to be comparable with the real rate of return achieved by large private sector firms. Projects failing to meet this criterion might still be justified on 'social or wider economic grounds', but this argument was often used to side-step the test discount rate. In consequence, the 1978 White Paper (HM Treasury, 1978) amended the investment groundrules to require a real rate of return of at least 5 per cent (8 per cent since 1989). Less profitable projects may still be accepted on wider social grounds but, overall, this target must be met.

All these approaches to investment appraisal consider *social opportunity costs*, since it is assumed that investment by the nationalised industry displaces an equivalent amount of private sector investment elsewhere. Hence, for allocative efficiency, the rate of return on marginal projects must be the same as in the private sector. However, since private sector consumption is displaced as well, then this approach suffers the defect of ignoring the problems of social time preference discussed in Sections 7.3 and 7.8.

■ 9.7 Problems of enforcing state control

In consequence of various unintended effects of regulatory controls, there is a tendency to extend the scope of regulation over time. For example, to counter the risk that firms adhere to price controls at the expense of product quality, regulators may introduce specific quality targets. This is part of a wider problem that, under state control, it may be hard to discipline management so that it works to achieve the objectives desired by the state. The problem can be illustrated by reference to the chain of principal–agent relationships involved in state ownership in the UK. Parliament (through government ministers and civil servants) is charged with monitoring managers to ensure that they operate in the interests of the general public. Difficulties arise if the various agents pursue their own objectives, and if the means for controlling their performance is weak. As Vickers and Yarrow note:

> in the British context at least, a system of control that relies heavily upon the agents' internalization of public interest objectives is unlikely to produce good performance. In the event ... the results of policy failure have included goal displacement, lack of clarity in corporate objectives, overlapping responsibilities, and excessive ministerial intervention in operational decisions. These, in turn, have

had detrimental effects on the pricing, investment, and internal efficiency performance of the nationalised industries (1988, p. 151).

This is despite the progressive tightening of constraints on management in the nationalised industries in an attempt to reduce the room for inappropriate actions. For instance, under the 1961 White Paper (HM Treasury, 1961) nationalised industries were simply required to achieve a specified rate of return on assets, which was formulated to take account of expressed social obligations. By 1978 they had to satisfy external financing limits; they had pricing guidelines and financial targets, and they also had to publish additional non-financial performance indicators to enable international comparisons. Since 1980 nationalised industries have also faced the possibility of a review of their efficiency by the Monopolies and Mergers Commission (**Section 8.8**).

Regulation of those industries which have been transferred from state to private ownership has also proved difficult. This is illustrated by the case of British Gas, transferred to the private sector in 1986. Two years later, it was subject to a reference to the Monopolies and Mergers Commission, accused of abusing its monopoly position. Its failure to supply adequate information to potential competitors on the costs of access to the distribution network and its practice of charging different prices based on the ease with which customers could switch to other fuels were condemned as being 'against the public interest' (MMC, 1988). There has been ongoing conflict over access to information, with the regulator heavily dependent on data provided by the firm. This has led, for example, to a wide divergence in opinions on an 'acceptable' level of profits. This is judged with reference to the cost of capital, which the regulator has estimated at between 2.5 and 5 per cent. British Gas itself claims that a rate of 6.7 per cent on existing assets and 10.8 per cent on new investments is more appropriate (*Financial Times*, 14 June 1993). British Gas referred itself to the MMC in 1992 to settle this and other conflicts with its regulator.

In the USA, several models have been developed to show how regulation has favoured particular groups rather than the wider national interest. The term *regulatory capture* was coined by Stigler (1971) to describe situations where the consumer loses out from regulation because potential gains are captured by producers. Stigler's analysis provides a radically different view of the process of regulation. He argues that it is the industry itself that lobbies for state control. The regulatory body then acts in the interests of the producer rather than for society as a whole. For instance, the Civil Aeronautics Board (established in 1938) served the interests of firms in the airline industry by refusing to allow any new entry during its 40-year life. Another example comes from the transport industries, where high-cost firms have been protected from competition by the statutory maintenance of minimum charges.

A similar view, advanced by Peltzman (1976, 1989), is that regulation is the result of different interest groups 'bidding' for the right to transfer wealth from the community as a whole. Politicians select areas for regulation according to the likely impact on political support. Under the regulatory framework, there may well be resistance to new technology or to changes in demand: while benefiting some, such changes may adversely affect others, to an extent that the politicians' chances of re-election are reduced. In trying to contain change, regulators will seek to adopt policies which 'share the gain and share the pain'. This may moderate distributional effects, but with the result that cross-subsidisation becomes endemic.

There is substantial evidence in support of these contentions. With the extension of regulation from US railroads to other sectors of the transport industry in 1935, the status quo was maintained by setting trucking rates in line with rail freight charges. Furthermore, the extension of regulation in the first place (and its later extension to waterways and airlines) may be seen as a way of minimising damage to the railroads from technological developments. Studies of the US and Canadian trucking industries (Moore, 1978; Kim, 1984) suggest that regulation principally benefits labour- and capital-owners rather than consumers.

■ 9.8 What is privatisation?

In recent years, there has been increasing dissatisfaction with the performance of industries controlled by the state, and the failure of state control to achieve its objectives. For instance, Cornell and Webbink argue that regulation is equivalent to saying to a firm that:

> Because in an unfettered market you may exercise or you have in fact exercised your monopoly power, we're going to give it to you in perpetuity. In addition, we will let you control the relevant information so we cannot tell whether you are abusing your monopoly power (1985, p. 38).

At the same time, developments in economic theory have questioned the rationale for state control in cases of market failure. There has been a change of emphasis, the suggestion increasingly being made that greater benefits to society might follow from shifting provision to the private sector and allowing market forces to operate more freely.

The term *privatisation* is often used to describe the process of switching ownership from the state to the private sector, but this is a narrow definition. It is better to refer to privatisation as the general removal of state controls on economic activity. This embraces not only change of ownership (*denationalisation*), but also actions to remove regulatory constraints and general attempts to expose more economic activities to the rigours of market forces (sometimes termed *deregulation* or *liberalisation*). These three elements can be readily illustrated for the UK. Jaguar, British Telecommunications (BT) and British Gas are just three companies whose ownership has been transferred to the private sector since 1979. Deregulation has occurred in several sectors: solicitors have lost their exclusive conveyancing rights; opticians have lost their monopoly in the dispensing of spectacles; long-distance coach services and local bus operations have been given more freedom in determining routes and fares. Where activities have been kept within the state sector, efforts have been made to foster greater use of the market. This is illustrated by the instruction to the National Health Service to put out to tender their 'hotel services' (cleaning, catering and laundry), and by contracting out of municipal street cleaning and refuse disposal.

▮ 9.9 The natural monopoly argument revisited

Recent developments in economic theory question the rationale of the natural monopoly argument for state control. According to neoclassical analysis, the case for state control turns on the welfare losses that arise from the private operation of a natural monopoly. This is static analysis and it ignores two important considerations. Over time, natural monopolies may face competition from new products and processes. This is so for telecommunications where established technologies are threatened by radio-based, microwave and cellular-radio systems. Paradoxically, state control may bolster a natural monopoly by slowing down the rate at which new technologies emerge, because state agencies may actively prevent new forms of competition developing. Such results would be anticipated by Austrian theorists. From their dynamic perspective on competition as a process, a natural monopoly is not immune from the process of competition, although governments may be able to slow down the speed of new entry. This is a return to earlier thinking. Wide recognition of the natural monopoly argument dates from Adams (1887). Prior to this, the conventional wisdom was that private sector monopolies were essentially ineffective against all-pervasive, irrepressible competitive forces and that, if monopoly were a problem, then it was because it was state-owned (Hazlett, 1985a).

New institutional economics would also criticise state control of natural monopoly on the ground that it ignores many practical difficulties. Successful regulation of a natural monopoly requires accurate data on costs and demand. In a world where information is imperfect, transaction costs exist and change is endemic, it is impossible to obtain the information which neoclassical theory takes for granted. As Hazlett argues:

> Faced with a complicated world and complex long-term relationships in that world, regulators are seen as a low-cost mechanism for imposing rules on monopolists. Yet by the very same problem, that of limited information, we are led to question the ability of regulators to know what rules efficiency dictates or, divining such wisdom, their altruism in implementing such to the detriment of more profitable opportunities (1985b, p. 104).

Marginal cost pricing and other regulatory solutions cannot be practised with any certainty, and may consequently worsen rather than improve the performance of natural monopoly.

Theorists are reviewing the natural monopoly argument. Traditionally it has been argued that the natural monopoly stems from a continuously declining long-run average cost curve resulting from technical economies of scale. Recognising the presence of transaction costs, substantial economies in organisation (such that one firm is able to organise production at lower per unit cost than two or more firms) may create a natural monopoly even where there are no technical economies of scale. Conversely it is possible that, even for a single-product firm, falling average production costs do not confer a natural monopoly, because they are outweighed by organisational diseconomies.

The theory of contestability (Baumol, 1982) also suggests that the conditions necessary for a natural monopoly are more restrictive than commonly supposed. It is not sufficient for long-run average costs to decline relative to market demand. Consider the case of oceanic freight shipments. Indivisibilities in capital lead to substantial economies of scale and falling long-run costs and may mean that costs are minimised when any particular route is in the hands of one firm. But this situation does not free that firm from the threat of other firms using the same route. Capital costs are salvageable, since it is relatively easy to switch ships to other routes. In consequence, other shipping lines may enter the market if they see the incumbent firm earning high profits. This threat may force the incumbent firm to price more competitively so that the welfare loss is reduced. The essence of the contestability argument is that the unregulated natural monopolist is forced to charge $0Q_r$ (**Figure 9.1**), earning normal profits. (This is the case for single-product firms. The multi-product case is considerably more complex, see Reid, 1987.) It is only where there are non-recoverable sunk costs which act as a barrier to exit that the natural monopoly argument applies.

The argument that multi-firm provision in a market characterised by the conditions of natural monopoly leads to higher prices and wasteful duplication may be faulty. Conditions of natural monopoly imply that a single firm has the potential to offer products for sale at lower prices, but Primeaux (1989) notes that this may not be realised if, through lack of competitive pressure, the monopolist becomes inefficient, so that costs rise. Furthermore, entry by another firm need not automatically lead to duplication of facilities. Take the case of gas supply. Suppose a new entrant attracts custom away from the incumbent firm by offering to set up a service at a relatively lower price. If it also sets up a distribution system, that of the incumbent firm becomes redundant. It is in the interests of both firms for the incumbent to sell or lease all, or part, of its existing system to the rival. Duplication is unlikely to occur if (as implicitly assumed by neoclassical theory) products and processes are identical. Recognising differences in costs and variations in products introduces another qualification. Duplication is less wasteful in such circumstances since it opens up additional choices.

It should also be noted that the natural monopoly may not extend to the whole of a firm's activities. In the utilities, it is generally only the distribution system that meets the criteria for a natural monopoly. With electricity, the distribution network is a natural monopoly, but the generation of electricity and the sale and maintenance of consumer appliances are not. Moreover, competition in the supply of electricity to the consumer can be introduced by allowing any supplier equal access to the distribution network: that is, operating a *common carrier* (or *interconnection*) *system*. This suggests that in many instances it is unnecessary for state control to encompass the entire area of a firm's operations.

■ *9.10* Ownership arguments

It is feasible for goods to be provided either by the state or by the private sector in all but a few cases (a government would not readily agree to the private provision of the armed forces or police service, because of the risk of being overthrown). Proponents of privatisation argue that (*with no change in the competitive environment*) the switch to private provision will enhance welfare by improving performance because the change of ownership increases the motivation of managers. There are two reasons. First, in the private sector it is more common for financial remuneration (the 'carrot') to be linked to company performance (for instance, through share option schemes). Secondly, the 'stick' – in the form of increased pressure resulting from exposure to the capital market – is likely to be more effective in disciplining management.

Under state ownership, managers' financial remuneration is less clearly related to the performance of the firm. Without the prospect of reward, there is less incentive for efficient management. Equally there is less risk of personal loss if management is poor. The inference is that there is greater scope for managers in state-owned firms to pursue personal objectives that are not in the best interests of the firm (that is, the principal–agent problem is greater under state ownership). Managers may resist change if the introduction of new products or processes disrupts existing work procedures and requires increased effort. They may also be more willing to concede improved working conditions to placate the workforce, produce to an excessively high standard to minimise complaints from customers, and pay 'over the odds' for inputs (Alessi, 1974).

Bureaucrats employed by the state face the same weak incentive system, so may be less likely to expose poor management. (This may be a vicious circle if inefficient management results from the frustrations of bureaucratic delay and political interference.) In contrast, principal–agent problems should be less pronounced in the private sector where the capital market is likely to be more effective in monitoring managers' performance. The threat of takeover may focus minds more sharply on the task of efficient operation because of the likelihood of dismissal by the new owners. There may also be more pressure on private sector management from the need to satisfy shareholders, especially if these have large holdings and are well-informed (as, for instance, in the case of pension funds).

North's transaction cost approach (1990) (**Section 1.5**) suggests an alternative explanation for any differences in management performance as a result of a change of ownership. Managers adapt their behaviour, and firms evolve, according to the constraints and incentives imposed by the institutional environment in which they operate. In the private sector the 'institutional rules' differ from those in the state sector. Much greater priority is accorded to the pursuit of profit, and there is less concern with social and political factors. In state hands, a firm may find itself subject to interference in its operations as the government seeks to achieve macroeconomic objectives. For instance, borrowing by state-owned firms in the UK and in Italy has been restricted because of the need to control the public sector borrowing requirement. Transfer of ownership to the private sector not only removes such a constraint – which may have prevented the implementation of viable investment projects – but may also open up additional sources of finance (such as bank borrowing and issuing shares). Moreover, in the private sector, the firm is freed from government interference in its pricing or employment decisions (such as being directed to contain price increases on the grounds that this will help the government restrain inflation). Veljanovski considers:

> The great influence of politics in the nationalised industries is a matter too often forgotten by economists analysing the difference between public and private enterprise. One of the major attractions of privatisation is that it takes politics out of the day-to-day operation of these industries (1989, p. 36).

Where governments transfer ownership to the private sector, they are implicitly accepting that the institutional rules they imposed are no longer appropriate.

A number of economists have questioned the strength of these arguments in favour of private sector ownership (for instance, Vickers and Yarrow, 1988). Principal–agent problems, for example, may still arise in the private sector. Estrin and Pérotin (1991) also question the superiority of private sector ownership. They suggest that, where shareholding is widely diffused or where firms do not rely heavily on the capital market for finance, performance may be the same (or even superior) in the state sector. Moreover, they argue that if objectives are clearly defined and remain stable, government stands a better chance of monitoring managers' behaviour (particularly if the firm operates in a competitive environment that provides a clear point of reference for judging performance). In addition, state sector managers are more likely to pursue efficiency in those economies where labour moves readily between state and private sectors. Experience of employment in the private sector, or the expectation of holding a private sector job in the future, will colour their approach to the management of the state-owned firm. In effect, the differences in the institutional arrangements between sectors are moderated by the cross-over of culture, rules and routines as staff move between private and state-owned firms.

In countries making the transition from a command economy, institutional factors can explain why a change in the firm's ownership by itself could have little impact on economic welfare. With financial markets undeveloped and individuals unfamiliar with share ownership, the discipline imposed by the capital market lacks force (a problem in developing countries too). Compounding this, managers are without the

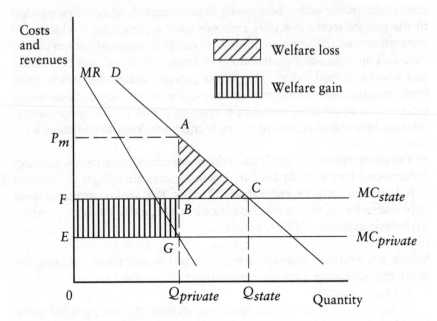

Figure 9.2   *Gains and losses from privatisation*

experience of running a firm in a market situation. McDonald describes the position of a Polish baby-food manufacturer:

> Alima had an accountancy department, but its clerks merely collected data on inputs and outputs and prepared statistical reports for the government. They did virtually no analysis of the statistics they compiled and no management accountancy worthy of the name. There was no finance function at all, so factors like the cost of capital and the effect of inflation were ignored. Surprisingly, Alima did have a marketing department, but its two employees spent 90 per cent of their time doing work for the personnel department (1993, p. 53).

The benefits of a change in ownership therefore depend on managers' rapid acquisition of the skills required for the effective management of a private sector firm (Ferguson, 1992). In this respect, it has been argued that assistance from firms operating in established market economies could be of considerable value. For instance, Polkolor of Poland has been transformed swiftly into an internationally competitive producer through a joint venture with Thomson of France (McDonald, 1993).

If changes in management performance do occur as a result of the change of ownership, these may, paradoxically, reduce economic welfare. Whilst the elimination of X-inefficiency will improve resource allocation by reducing costs, greater efficiency may also be displayed in more aggressive exploitation of market power. This can be illustrated in **Figure 9.2**.

Before privatisation of a monopoly, average and marginal costs are equal to OF and, because of a directive to set price equal to marginal cost, price is also equal to OF. After privatisation the situation is represented by price OP_m and cost level OE. These changes follow from the assumption that management is brought under greater pressure from share-owners: prices are raised to monopoly levels, and costs reduced. Privatisation results both in a productive efficiency gain equal to the cost reductions (area $EFBG$) and an allocative loss occurs (equal to area ABC). From a static viewpoint, privatisation enhances economic welfare only if area $EFBG$ exceeds area ABC. However, static loss may be offset by beneficial changes over time. Managers have more reason to foster new products and processes if any increase in profits increases their income. A higher rate of successful innovation will soon overcome the short-run allocative loss and advance the welfare of society.

9.11 Empirical evidence on ownership arguments

There are three possible approaches to a study of the impact of ownership changes:

1. comparison between private-sector firms and state-owned counterparts in the same country and industry;
2. comparison between a large sample of private-sector firms and firms in state ownership, irrespective of industry or country;
3. tracking the performance of a firm whose ownership is transferred from state to private sector (or vice versa). This may involve comparison with firms whose ownership remains unchanged.

Most studies discussed below have taken the first approach. With their analysis of the largest 500 manufacturing and mining corporations in the world (outside the USA) in 1983, Boardman and Vining (1989) exemplify the second approach. Such studies must ensure that samples are large enough to overcome any industry- or country-specific effects in the data. The third approach involves a time-series study. With a growing number of firms switched from state to private sector ownership since the start of the 1980s, there are ample subjects for investigation, although many have insufficient experience of private sector ownership to permit definitive conclusions. (Studies of this type are discussed in **Sections 9.16–9.18.**)

Any attempt at efficiency comparisons between the private and state sector is fraught with problems. Adjustments need to be made for differences in product mix, in the cost of factor inputs, and in product quality. Whilst it may be reasonable to assume profit-maximising behaviour on the part of private sector firms, this cannot automatically be applied to firms in state ownership. For instance, the statutes of nationalisation in the UK require consideration of wider social objectives. In addition, governments have often directly intervened in the activities of state industries in order to attain other national objectives. Typical examples of such intervention include price restraint, curtailment of investment programmes and directives to buy inputs domestically. A simple comparison of firms under private and state ownership overlooks the extent to which state industries attain these wider social and macroeconomic objectives. At the same time, there is the risk that management may use these to excuse poor performance. The comparison between state and private sector ownership is also complicated because the performance of firms within each group may vary considerably. Whereas a state firm facing a weak system of controls and incentives may prove substantially inferior to its private sector counterpart, this may not be true of a state firm operating within a tighter and more appropriate framework.

The difficulties of making valid comparisons are clearly illustrated in Pryke's study of relative efficiency in the private and state sectors in the UK. Pryke (1982) recognised bias in his sample. British Airways (state) had the advantage over British Caledonian (private) of being able to operate from Heathrow Airport. Sealink and British Rail Hovercraft (state) were in a better position to take ferry passengers without cars than European Ferries or Hoverlloyd, while cross-subsidisation gave gas and electricity board showrooms (state) an advantage over private sector retailers. Even so, Pryke discovered several instances where the management of state-controlled firms had missed opportunities to improve or develop their operations. Sealink failed to react to the integration by European Ferries of the carriage of commercial vehicles and passenger cars. The company also had much older ships, and was less astute in price-setting. British Airways was overmanned by 15 per cent in 1978 while the Electricity Board showed a reluctance to close down loss-making activities. Pryke concluded that:

> public enterprise has performed relatively poorly in terms of its com-
> petitive position, has used labour and capital inefficiently and has
> been less profitable (1982, p. 70).

Comparison problems may account for the failure of US studies to produce clear-cut results. Several studies have analysed differences in cost levels between private and state electricity generators in the USA. Some studies (for instance, Moore, 1970; Alessi, 1975) found the private sector to be more efficient, some found the public sector more efficient (Meyer, 1975; Neuberg, 1977; Pescatrice and Trapani, 1980), whilst others found no difference between sectors (Di Lorenzo and Robinson, 1982; Färe, Grosskopf and Logan, 1985). Studies of water utilities in the USA (Crain and Zardkoohi, 1978; Bruggink, 1982; Feigenbaum and Teeples, 1983) reveal similar mixed findings, as do studies from other economies. For instance, Caves and Christensen (1980) reported that there were no obvious differences in productivity between the railways operated by Canadian Pacific (private) and Canadian National (state) over the period 1956–75. Forsyth and Hocking (1980) noted no difference in efficiency between state and private sector airlines in Australia, but Davies (1971, 1977) found private sector firms to be up to 100 per cent more efficient.

A problem of many studies is that they consider sectors where the private operators are themselves regulated by the state. They may simply reveal that regulation itself acts as a disincentive to efficient management in the private sector. Support for this contention comes from a study by Atkinson and Halvorsen (1986) of electric utilities in the USA. On finding no difference in efficiency between private and state-owned companies, it was noted that costs were 2.4 per cent above competitive levels in both cases. This may reflect the inappropriateness of the form of regulation. If cost-plus pricing methods are being used, a more efficient private firm may increase its nominal costs in order to earn higher profits.

Parker's (1991) UK study is another which appears to give limited support to privatisation. Performance improved in five of the ten organisations investigated. However, only two – in both of which improved efficiency was noted – had been transferred from state to private sector ownership. The others (such as the Royal Mint and London Transport) had been subject to a reduction in political control, but remained in state hands. Consequently, the full force of the ownership arguments could not have been expected to apply. Duch (1991) would concur with this. From an investigation of telecommunications in Germany, France and the UK, he noted that the benefits generated by market forces declined with a movement from private to pure public ownership, and that controls and guidelines imposed by the government were a poor substitute for market forces.

Whilst the empirical evidence on differences in efficiency between private and state sector firms is ambiguous, there is some support for the contention that the discipline of the private sector is more effective. For the UK, Pryke (1982) noted that loss-making firms in the private sector tended to disappear relatively quickly from the market, their assets being transferred (via takeover or liquidation) to other firms. Even allowing for differences in objectives, elimination of loss-making activities in state-owned companies and corporations appears to be much slower. In a very different context – secondary education in Colombia, Thailand and certain other developing countries – there is evidence that the private sector outperforms the state (even after controlling for factors such as pupil background and access to resources). Jimenez *et al.* suggest this is consistent with 'inherent incentives for private schools to be efficient because of greater accountability to parents' (1991, p. 215).

Despite the variability of results, many consider the evidence to be strongly in favour of private sector ownership. In their summary, Borcherding *et al.* (1982) note that state enterprise outperformed its private sector counterparts in only nine out of more than fifty studies. Of these nine, three studies (including that of Meyer, 1975) were felt to be unreliable because of deficiencies in their methodology or data. Boardman and Vining conclude from their research that:

> the consistent direction and magnitude of the estimates across all equations provides robust evidence that state enterprises ... are less profitable and less efficient than private corporations (1989, p. 17).

The World Bank is even more dogmatic: 'ownership itself matters' (1992, p. 7). Whilst reforms can improve the efficiency of state-owned firms, the World Bank argues that this is rarely sustained for more than a few years. Moreover, within each sector, there is a considerable range of performance, but 'the median point on the private enterprise spectrum lies higher than the median point on the public enterprise spectrum' (1992, p. 6).

■ 9.12 Promotion of competition

Whilst economists may disagree over the size of the gains (if any) which stem from a change from state to private ownership, there is wide agreement that increased competition improves resource utilisation. One survey of the theoretical and empirical evidence, argues:

> the available evidence supports a presumption in favour of private enterprise. However, when market power is significant, and particularly when company behaviour is subject to detailed regulation, there

is little empirical justification for a general presumption in favour of either type of ownership (Vickers and Yarrow, 1988, p. 40).

and another that:

Numerous studies of the relative costs of public and private sector services suggest that private operators do cost less, as long as there is competition to ensure that the private operators remain efficient (Gomez-Ibanez *et al.*, 1991, p. 265).

In other words, much of the problem is not a consequence of state as opposed to private ownership, but of the absence of competitive forces, so that the greatest benefits are to be expected from a privatisation programme which combines a change in ownership with measures to increase competitiveness.

Many state-controlled firms are isolated from market disciplines and incentives. State-owned firms are often statutory monopolies: by law they can exclude potential competitors. For instance, in the UK the Post Office has, to all intents and purposes, a statutory monopoly in the provision of a letter post service, since rivals are obliged to set a high minimum charge. Where firms are regulated by the state, it is often the case that incumbents are protected from new entrants. Few states of the USA allow new firms to set up an electric utility. Austrian theorists would condemn such practices, as the resultant lack of competition adversely affects economic welfare. Without the threat of competition, there is less pressure on management to operate the firm efficiently, or to introduce new products and processes. Austrians economists would go further to argue that state monopoly is worse than private sector monopoly. A multi-product firm is always threatened by other firms capturing parts of its business; an incumbent natural monopolist would find it difficult to sustain its advantage over the entire product range, furthermore it is always under threat from technological changes. In contrast, the state monopoly is immune to many of these pressures. Its position can be eroded only by a major technological development in a substitute industry.

One of the benefits from increased competition is the elimination of cross-subsidisation (**Section 9.4**). Competition forces prices into closer alignment with costs. Goods and services formerly subsidised by revenues generated elsewhere will either be discontinued or methods devised to produce them at lower cost. Either way, society gains as resources are switched from lower- to higher-valued uses.

Increased competition may force managers to pay more attention to the absolute level of costs, since the penalty for X-inefficiency is the loss of markets to rivals. There is less scope for disparities in costs of production. Competition makes it easier for managers to assess performance. Carsberg makes a similar point:

> a regulator can rarely establish with certainty how efficiently – including at how low a cost – a particular service can be provided. Competition will seek out the answer to that question far more effectively than a regulator can. Competition gives firms and individuals the opportunity to succeed by showing that they can operate more effectively than others (1989, p. 82).

However well-motivated, managers of a state-controlled monopoly lack any frame of reference to judge the effectiveness of policies. Under competition, they can draw inferences about their own achievements by comparing their performance with that of rivals.

Baumol's concept of contestability (**Section 2.6**) introduces another slant on the relationship between competition and the promotion of economic welfare. In markets with low entry and exit barriers, potential (rather than actual) competition can provide effective stimulus for the incumbent to operate in society's interests. Contestability arguments have been made with most force in relation to the deregulation of transport markets.

Improved efficiency of state-controlled firms will not automatically be achieved by exposure to increased competition. It depends on the attitude of government. If the government is prepared to countenance increased losses, then there will be no pressure on management to reform the firm's operations. For potential gains to be realised, the government must impose (and enforce) rigorous financial targets, unless the introduction of competition is linked with private sector ownership.

9.13 Franchising as a means of promoting competition

In the case of a natural monopoly, it may be possible to retain state ownership or regulation whilst promoting competition by *franchise* (or *competitive tender*). Demsetz (1968) illustrates this by considering the sale of car licence plates in cases where drivers are required to purchase these annually as a means of paying road tax. Scale economies in this market would lead to a natural monopoly if provision were left to the private sector. On the other hand, Demsetz argues that there is no rationale for the state to issue the licences. Instead, he suggests that firms in the private sector should be asked to tender for the right to be the sole supplier of licence plates for a specified length of time. By requiring private sector firms to vie for the exclusive right to use the system, competition could be introduced into markets where it was felt that the ownership of a natural monopoly element (say, a gas or electricity distribution system or the permanent way in rail transport) should remain in state hands. Competition is reintroduced into the market at the end of each contract period.

Franchising has commonly been used to inject competition into areas of health care, education and other government services, such as cleaning and catering. Public transport provision in Sweden has been subject to competitive tender since 1988. County transport authorities are charged with planning the local bus networks, timetables and fares, but tenders are invited from potential operators of the bus services. In addition, the railway infrastructure is the responsibility of a state track authority, Banverket, and tenders are invited for the right to operate train services. Proposals for the privatisation of British Rail from 1994 advocate a similar system for the UK. Railtrack (eventually to be sold to the private sector) is to be created to manage the infrastructure, with train services operating on the basis of franchises.

A franchise is usually awarded to the private sector firm which bids the highest amount (subject to contract conditions and commercial viability). The maximum amount a bidder would offer is determined by the perceived potential profitability of the franchise. The size of the actual bid depends principally upon the number of firms expected to be involved in the tender: with a large number of bidders, firms' offers are likely to be driven closer to their profit estimates. This bidding system encourages the successful firm to operate its franchise so as to maximise profits, resulting in a price close to $0P_m$ in **Figure 9.1**. Society faces the allocative inefficiency associated with private sector monopoly (area *ABC* in **Figure 9.1**), but gains from improvements in productive and dynamic efficiency. Since the franchisee captures all the profits consequent on cost reductions, the system offers good incentives.

The gains to society should be greater where a franchise is allocated through *Demsetz–Chadwick bidding*. Here, the franchise is awarded to the firm which charges customers the lowest price for the service (subject to provisos concerning the quality of the service). In this case, the larger the number of bidders the more likely it is that the franchise will be awarded at a price of $0P_r$ (**Figure 9.1**) below the 'natural monopoly price' of $0P_m$. When the contract period expires, the original operator only retains the franchise if he again bids to sell at the lowest price.

Franchising is not without its difficulties. For the franchisee to undertake a substantial capital investment (such as the purchase of new rolling-stock to operate its railway service) the franchise period must be sufficiently long to enable the firm to recoup its outlay, since these assets are highly specific and cannot be redeployed elsewhere. This could be in conflict with the government's desire to introduce competition, which is best served by putting the franchise out to tender at frequent intervals. Furthermore, the existing franchisee is likely to be in a stronger position to offer an attractive price than other candidates when re-bidding for the franchise. The knowledge and experience gained as a current operator in the market should place the incumbent at an advantage, which would be compounded to the extent that the firm has incurred sunk costs by making investments that have no value except in their existing use.

Williamson (1976) argues that, although franchising introduces an element of competition, it may not always result in an improvement in economic welfare. This follows if the benefits to society of increased competition are outweighed by increased transaction costs. Substantial transaction and management costs may be incurred in awarding the franchise and in subsequent monitoring and policing, particularly if the contract is complex. This could apply in the case of cable television where the bidders offer a service that differs not only in price, but also in terms of number of channels offered, variety of programmes proposed, reliability and the level of disruption associated with installation. State control may be more efficient in these circumstances.

9.14 Empirical evidence on the promotion of competition

Empirical evidence supports the contention that increased competition in state-controlled industries enhances welfare. Reporting on the costs of refuse collection in the UK the Audit Commission (1984) noted wide disparities. Each refuse collector had its own local monopoly, and most were state-owned. Some provided efficiently run, low-cost operations, but others were high-cost. In a more competitive environment, these cost disparities could not persist. If inefficient firms were not reformed they would find themselves losing custom to rivals who could provide the service more cheaply. UK local authorities have since contracted out refuse collection to competitive tender. Domberger *et al.* (1986) had calculated that if all local authorities introduced competitive tendering for refuse services then substantial savings (of the order of £80 million for 1984–5) could be made. These expectations have been borne out, with cost savings (ignoring the costs incurred in managing the contracts) estimated at 40 per cent (HM Treasury, 1991) and 27 per cent (London

Business School, reported in *Financial Times*, 15 July 1993). Savas (1977) found similar results in the USA where competition between private and state refuse collectors in Minneapolis led to an improvement in the quality of the service and a reduction in costs.

Competitive tendering of bus services in Sweden is also reported to have generated cost savings, typically of between 5 and 15 per cent. Jansson and Wallin (1991) further noted that tendering reduced train fares (although the amount is not quantified). This was despite the fact that tenders were limited to local lines, and that all but one had been awarded to the state-owned incumbent, Swedish State Railways.

Primeaux's study (1985) of the costs of electricity generation in the USA revealed that competition reduced costs as long as output was less than 222 million kilowatt hours. At higher levels of output, economies of scale from a single supplier would outweigh the advantages stemming from competitive pressures. However, this can be largely discounted because only three of the 23 cities studied had power outputs near this level. In general, competition appeared to reduce costs by about 11 per cent. The average reduction in price was between 16 and 19 per cent, implying that competition had also led to a tightening of profit margins.

Privatisation appears to be eroding cross-subsidisation in the telecommunications markets. The break-up of AT&T in the USA and the entry of Mercury in the UK has led to increased competition for long-distance business. In the past, prices for these services had been set above marginal cost in order to subsidise local calls and domestic subscribers. In the USA peak coast-to-coast business rates fell by around 20 per cent over the period 1982–6. In November 1986, BT in the UK reduced its charges for long-distance calls by 12 per cent and for cheap-period local calls by 3.6 per cent, whilst increasing the price of peak-period local calls by 18.9 per cent.

Empirical studies (especially those investigating services franchised or contracted out to the private sector) may not separate out the benefits arising from a change in ownership from those arising from a change in the competitive environment. Domberger and Piggott (1986) provide evidence that it is competition that is important in promoting efficiency, not ownership. Examining cases where state firms were at least as efficient as their private sector counterparts, they noted that in all instances the firms operate in a competitive market environment. Likewise, Savas (1977) noted greater similarity in the unit costs of state and private sector firms in situations of competitive tendering.

There is also the question as to whether it is actual or potential competition that is necessary for firms to behave in ways which improve society's welfare. For transport markets, which have often been argued to display the characteristics of contestability:

Evidence so far strongly suggests that actual competition is considerably more effective in reducing market power than is potential competition (Button and Keeler, 1993, p. 1022).

The experience of the US airline industry since deregulation in 1978 provides an example (see also **Section 9.17**). Expectations that the market would prove contestable were not fulfilled as entrants faced barriers and sunk costs were present, for instance in the form of advertising needed to establish the airline's presence on a new route (Levine, 1987). However, the market appears contestable to some degree and potential competition has been found to exert some influence on fares (Keeler, 1991; Pryke, 1991).

9.15 Where are the greatest gains from privatisation?

The potential benefits of privatisation are best illustrated by the case of monopoly. **Table 9.1** shows that privatisation (options 2, 3, 5 and 6) generally offers a better chance of enhancing economic welfare than the operation of a monopoly under state control (options 1 and 4). Even where only partial privatisation is implemented, it may be possible to improve economic welfare. For example, it is possible that performance might benefit from a transfer to private ownership without any measures to increase competition (option 3). However, in this case, the need to prevent abuse of market power requires regulation of the firm's behaviour. This implies a continuance of government involvement in the firm's operations, possibly limiting the advantages from a change of ownership. Alternatively, benefits might be achieved by leaving the firm in the hands of the state whilst increasing competition (option 2). However, the greatest potential for the advancement of economic welfare is normally expected from a privatisation programme that both removes production from state ownership and improves the competitive environment (options 5 and 6).

The extent to which society's welfare will improve will depend on the characteristics of the firm being privatised. Gains from the transfer of ownership will be largest where it has been most difficult for the state effectively to control the operation of the firm. Gains from competition will be greatest where market forces have played a very minor role. On these criteria, the greatest improvement in welfare in the UK would follow from the privatisations of the health service and education.

This causes a dilemma for any government trying to sell firms in state ownership. The easiest firms to sell are those where potential purchasers can most easily appraise their prospects. These are most likely to be activities where state firms already operate in the market sector, and where the firm is already competently run and competing effectively in markets at home and abroad. In these circumstances, however, the potential welfare gains are smallest.

The way in which the firm is privatised also has an important bearing on economic welfare. There is a danger that the potential benefits of a transfer of ownership are not realised in full. For instance, if the government tries to maximise receipts from the sale of the firm, then it will sell the firm with monopoly rights intact. Another problem can be illustrated by considering BT. The provision of public telephones generates a positive externality. Prior to privatisation, public telephones earned £75 million in revenue but cost £125 million to provide. Any private firm would eliminate such a loss-making activity or reform the operation to restore profitability. The UK government avoided this problem by instructing the privatised BT to retain a network of public telephones. As an alternative, the government could have given the privatised BT (or a cheaper supplier) a contract to extend and maintain the system of public telephones. The state's role is reduced to monitoring the firm's performance to ensure that society receives the external benefits. Similarly, education could be privatised without compromising the merit good arguments. The state could continue to make education compulsory and regulate standards, whilst leaving supply to the private sector. It would also be possible to introduce competitive pressures by providing finance in the form of education vouchers which the pupil could redeem at the school of his parents' choice.

■ 9.16 Privatisation in the UK

With privatisation taking place in such a wide variety of countries (ranging from advanced economies to developing and former command economies) and with each programme differing in its characteristics, it is difficult to present a short summary of the impact of privatisation. Moreover, it is still rather early to be able to make definitive judgements, since few of the programmes pre-date the early 1980s. However, consideration of experiences in the UK, the USA and Chile provide some early indications.

In the UK, preliminary impressions suggest that the performance of some firms has improved beyond expectations. For instance, eight former nationalised industries were amongst the top 50 UK firms ranked by profit per employee (*Management Today*, May 1991). However, it is impossible to establish how well these firms would have performed in

Table 9.1   Monopoly – state control and the privatisation options

Option	Ownership pressures	Competitive pressures	Productive efficiency	Allocative efficiency	Innovation incentives	Entry possibilities	Monitoring requirements	Remarks
1 State-owned monopoly	No	No	If effectively monitored	If effectively monitored	Poor	None	Extensive to control management	
2 State-owned firm without statutory monopoly	No	Yes	Yes	If market contestable	Fair	Yes	Less than option 1	
3 State monopoly transferred to private sector	Yes	No	Depends	If market contestable	Fair	Yes, if statutory monopoly removed	If market not contestable	
4 Regulated private monopoly	Yes	No	No	Danger of Averch–Johnson effect	Poor	Yes, if allowed by regulators	Extensive	Danger of regulatory capture
5 State monopoly sold as many companies	Yes	Yes	Yes, unless natural monopoly	Yes	Good	Yes	Perhaps, to prevent collusion	Lower receipts from sale than option 3. Will be unstable if natural monopoly.
6 Franchise of state-owned monopoly (Demsetz–Chadwick bidding)	Yes	Yes	Yes; almost if a natural monopoly	Yes	Good	When franchise re-awarded	To enforce terms of franchise	Where very complicated, options 1 or 4 may be more efficient. Danger of regulatory capture.

the absence of privatisation. Bishop and Kay (1991) investigated this problem. In comparing a sample of denationalised firms against others remaining in state hands, the greatest improvements in total factor productivity between 1979 and 1983 and 1983 and 1990 were found for the state-owned British Coal and British Rail. Galal *et al.* (1992) urge caution in interpreting these results, noting that these firms have shed considerable amounts of labour and operate in stagnating markets. There is also the point that these firms too may be preparing for future anticipated privatisation.

There are a multiplicity of objectives behind the privatisation programme in the UK, economic efficiency ranking alongside aims such as widening share ownership, generating revenue to reduce the public sector borrowing requirement (PSBR), and reducing the power of trade unions. Economic motives have often taken second place to political expediency. Consequently, the form of privatisation has often been inappropriate when viewed from the economic welfare perspective. For instance, the discipline imposed on managers from the threat of takeover has often been diminished by the government retaining a *golden share* or placing limitations on the size of individual or foreign shareholdings. In part, this inappropriateness has been due to the speed of the programme (around £45 billion of state assets were sold between 1979 and 1991, comprising almost 12 per cent of the average annual GDP over the period (Stevens, 1992)). This has required concessions to win the cooperation of existing management:

> The paradox of privatisation is that the view that it contributes to economic efficiency is derived from the belief that private sector managers are subject to incentives and disciplines different from, and more demanding than, those which apply to their public sector counterparts ... But without the consent, or acquiescence, of these same managers privatisation of any sort is a difficult and protracted business (Kay and Thompson, 1986, p. 18).

Firms sold by the state have often been those where the potential gains from privatisation have been least. For instance, Jaguar, British Aerospace, National Freight and Britoil were subject to effective competition prior to privatisation, enjoying little protection in the home market. In other cases, privatisation in the UK has frequently involved the sale of state-owned firms with limited accompanying liberalisation of competition. Veljanovski comments:

> the Government's privatisation programme has sacrificed the goal of greater competition and of introducing more market forces to the

expediency of short-term considerations ... the programme relies to an excessive extent on the unproven ability of regulation to do what the market would have achieved costlessly (1989, p. viii).

British Airways is an example of a privatised firm essentially isolated from competition on many routes. This is because of the requirement to hold an operating licence from the Civil Aviation Authority, a body which has been very restrictive in granting licences.

BT is another firm transferred to the private sector with its monopoly position essentially unchanged. Mercury was the only company initially licensed to compete (this contrasts with the four firms licensed to compete with NTT in long-distance telecommunications in Japan) and, by 1993, BT still had market shares of the order of 87 per cent for business telephone calls and 97 per cent of the residential market (HM Treasury, 1993). Even so, BT's prices have declined on average by a real 27 per cent since 1984, and the provision of payphones has increased whilst the percentage in working order has risen from 77 per cent in the late 1970s to 96 per cent (UNCTAD, 1993). Galal *et al.* (1992) calculate a net welfare benefit from BT's privatisation, almost half of which accrued to consumers. Looking at prices, they consider that consumers' surplus has increased annually between 1983 and 1990, with the principal gains to those making long-distance telephone calls. Following the White Paper *Competition and Choice* (HM Treasury, 1991) the market has been further liberalised and more radical changes seem likely with the introduction of more competitors, such as Ionica (building a national radio network) and Energis (routing a fibre-optic network along the national electricity grid). Energis has announced its intention to challenge the incumbents with prices some 10–15 per cent lower (*Financial Times*, 24 June 1993).

With the privatisation of the electricity industry, the UK government began to address the competition criticism. However, many commentators considered that the initial creation of just two generating companies (plus the state-owned Nuclear Electric) presented too much opportunity for collusive behaviour. Moreover, evidence suggests that the bidding system used to establish prices paid to the generating companies has led to prices in excess of marginal costs (see, for instance, Fehr and Harbord, 1993).

Deregulation and the contracting-out of areas of state operation has been less developed than ownership transfers, but appears to have generated greater benefits. Following the deregulation of long-distance coach services there were notable improvements in the quality of services, while costs per mile and prices fell (Davis, 1984; Heseltine and Silcock, 1990). Even so, opportunities to enhance welfare further were lost as a result of the government's failure to sell off city centre coach terminals. National Bus (the established state operator) was able to prevent rivals sharing the most convenient terminals (Jaffer and Thompson, 1986). The introduction of competitive tenders for state services (such as street cleaning, catering and refuse collection) is calculated to have generated average cost savings of the order of 7 per cent, inclusive of the transaction costs of contract management (Birmingham University, reported in *Financial Times*, 15 July 1993). The UK government intends to expand contracting-out during the 1990s, applying it, for instance, to various civil service functions.

The results of the 1986 changes in local bus transport have been more mixed. Nash (1993) reports that deregulation of services outside London reduced costs per bus mile by an average of 30 per cent and that service frequency increased. However, there was little competition in price, with fares rising in real terms; passengers were also deterred from travelling by bus by lack of information and repeated changes to timetables. Evans (1990) cites the fact that route-specific fares have not been introduced as evidence that the market is not contestable. White (1990) quantifies the net effects on economic welfare. He concludes that the net benefit has been positive in the metropolitan areas, but negative in the shire counties. In contrast, both White and Nash note that there have been welfare gains in London (not yet subject to deregulation) as a result of the introduction of competitive tendering on subsidised routes. This has fostered productivity improvements, cutting costs per bus mile by 14 per cent.

Since April 1991, health care in the UK has been subject to a different form of privatisation. Although the National Health Service remains in state ownership, competitive pressures are being introduced through the creation of an *internal market*, which separates the purchasers of health care from its suppliers. Purchasers (District Health Authorities and fund-holding general practitioners (GPs)) are expected to arrange contracts with those suppliers (hospitals) which offer the best mix of prices and quality of service. Permitting some GPs to manage their own budgets and allowing some hospitals to become self-governing trusts is argued to yield further efficiency improvements by increasing the responsibility and accountability of management. Amongst early evidence of benefits is the search by GPs for the best ophthalmological and gynaecological services for their patients, and the hire of hospital consultants to provide clinics at their surgeries (Harrison, 1992). Yet, invariably, there are transitional problems: GP fund-holders' patients appear to have received priority treatment, and some hospitals face financial difficulties. It will take some time for a full picture of the impact of such major changes in the health care system to emerge, and it will depend on how rapidly managers acquire the skills appropriate to a more market-oriented environment. For instance, Ellwood (1991) questions whether NHS managers currently have the necessary expertise to set prices which convey appropriate signals. In support of this contention, she quotes prices for the treatment of an ingrowing toenail in West Midlands hospitals in 1991/2 as ranging from £91 to £656.

■ *9.17* Privatisation in the USA

Privatisation in the USA generally appears to have been more successful in promoting economic welfare than it has in the UK. A number of state-provided services have been contracted out to the private sector in the areas of health care, prison construction and management, and refuse collection. These are reported to have led to cost savings of the order of 10–40 per cent, as well as to improvements in quality of service (UNCTAD, 1993). However, the limited amount of state ownership means that privatisation has generally taken the form of deregulation – that is, directly promoting competition – and the greater success of the US programme stems largely from this fact. This is vividly illustrated by comparing the privatisation of gas in the UK and USA. In the interests of speed it was decided to sell British Gas as a single body rather than to split it into regional utilities, which could then have competed for supplies of gas (third parties have had the right to transmit gas through existing pipelines since 1982). In the period immediately following privatisation, the only checks on the market power of British Gas have been the regulatory bodies OFGAS and the MMC, and competition from alternative energies. (In essence, state control has simply altered its form from ownership to regulation.) In the USA, where there are 1500 gas utilities, the Federal Energy Regulatory Commission has (since October 1985) allowed any firm access to the gas distribution network on payment of a cost-related fee. This widening of the choice of gas suppliers available to consumers ensures that prices are kept close to competitive levels.

The results of deregulation in the USA have been generally beneficial. The experience of airlines (deregulated in 1978) provides an example (even though the market has not proved to be contestable). The initial results of deregulation were that the number of certificated carriers rose from 33 in 1976 to 98 by 1982, whilst existing carriers extended their networks (Moore, 1986). Many of the new entrants had the cost advantage of using non-union labour. Although average costs increased in real terms by 15 per cent (largely because of higher fuel costs), fares per mile fell by an average of 8.5 per cent, particularly on long hauls and flights between large cities. However, short-haul fares generally rose with the ending of the deliberate underpricing that had been practised under regulation. There were reductions in the quality of some services, but this is not necessarily against the public interest; passengers often chose the lower-quality, lower-priced alternative.

By the late 1980s, many of the new entrants had failed, and the market had become more concentrated. Hub and spoke networks (where flights are made via a central airport), frequent flyer programmes and control of computer reservation systems were among the factors permitting major airlines to create entry barriers and exercise market power. Fares from the most concentrated hub airports were substantially higher than fares in general, although passengers benefited from a wide choice of routes and frequent flights. Outside these 'fortress' hubs, deregulation has often led to a greater choice of airline, and fares overall have declined in real terms from 9 cents per mile in 1978 to 7.5 cents in 1988 (US Department of Transportation, as reported in *Aviation Week and Space Technology*, 19 February 1990). These findings are reflected in estimates that the welfare gain to consumers from airline deregulation has been positive, but could have been larger:

> Public policy towards airline mergers, airport capacity utilization, and air safety has not been responsive to the changes in the air transportation system brought by deregulation and has consequently lowered social welfare in the long run (Morrison and Winston, 1989, p. 107).

■ 9.18 Privatisation in Chile

Chile has been in the vanguard of privatisation, with programmes of deregulation and transfers to private sector ownership dating from 1974. However, the early phase is untypical in many respects in that it involved the return to their original owners of firms expropriated by the state between 1971 and 1973. The second wave of sales from 1975 involved over 200 firms and banks, but many of these experienced financial difficulties, which led to renationalisation. These firms were resold in subsequent years, along with some of the large firms and public utilities that had remained in state ownership. By 1990, the number of enterprises remaining in state hands had fallen from around 500 to less than 30.

Galal *et al.* (1992) undertook a detailed investigation of three firms, concluding that privatisation offered net benefits (a view supported by Luders, 1993). The electricity generator, CHILGENER, was transferred to the private sector in 1987. It already operated in a fairly competitive environment, and was subject to effective regulation (which, for instance, required prices to be related to marginal costs). The transfer of ownership was regarded as partially responsible for improvements in productivity. In contrast, ENERSIS (sold in 1986) held a regional monopoly in the distribution of electricity. Galal *et al.* consider that, although the firm performed well under state ownership, privatisation strengthened incentives resulting in a net welfare gain.

The privatisation of Compagñía de Teléphonos de Chile (CTC) in 1987 differs in that competitive pressures were enhanced as a consequence of the ownership change. CTC owned over 90 per cent of all telephone lines and was the dominant supplier of local telephone services. Its sale to the private sector (including foreign investors) improved access to finance, permitting more rapid expansion of networks, new technology and other services (such as the provision of public and cellular telephones). These changes have substantially improved economic welfare, with consumers realising the greatest benefits (Galal *et al.*, 1992). Private sector ownership is also acting as a spur to increase penetration of the market for long-distance services, dominated by ENTEL. (At the same time, ENTEL's switch to private sector ownership has increased its desire to enter CTC's market for local services.) Future competition between CTC and ENTEL can be expected to lead to further welfare improvements.

Privatisation in Chile has not simply focused on the transfer of firms to private sector ownership. Foreign competition has been stimulated by reduced tariffs and import quotas, while various state services, including refuse collection and the maintenance of public parks, have been contracted out. In 1979, entry into the urban bus market was opened, with fares freed between 1980 and 1984. The results of this deregulation (described by Thomson, 1992) appear similar to those in the UK. More bus services became available, but fares rose and converged for all types of service.

∎ 9.19 Conclusion

Privatisation is worth pursuing only if benefits exceed costs. Unfortunately both are difficult to quantify, so ultimately the choice depends on qualitative arguments. Supporters of privatisation are those who believe that markets rarely fail, including those economists who stress the role of competition as a process (instead of concentrating on static models of market failure and the market structure of perfect competition). They would also argue that politicians and bureaucrats are unlikely to possess (and would find it difficult to acquire) the information necessary to correct market failures and, furthermore, would lack the motivation to promote the public interest.

Those who favour privatisation in principle may object to the form it takes in any particular country. Whilst transference of a firm from state to private ownership may bring benefits by increasing the pressures on management to perform efficiently, it is the interaction of private ownership with increased competition that appears to promote the best prospects for enhanced welfare. The UK programme can be criticised because it has often involved the transfer of large state monopolies into private hands with (at best) token efforts to provide either a competitive environment or checks to prevent monopoly abuse. Deregulation in the USA appears to have been more successful.

The arguments for privatisation do not undermine every case for state control. Rather they indicate that a different perspective on state control is needed. Few sectors are likely to require regulation; even fewer warrant state ownership. Where state control is felt to be justified, the regulatory framework needs to be carefully thought out. In the past, economic welfare has been reduced because regulation has not been lifted when the rationale for it has disappeared; management has been isolated from the incentives and disciplines imposed by markets, and the controls themselves have encouraged abuses.

■ *Chapter 10* ■

Deindustrialisation

> The Prime Minister has said manufacturing matters and who could possibly disagree? But to leap from that proposition to the belief that manufacturing is more real and reliable than other forms of activity is heroic; to leap to the view that manufacturing should be specially favoured by government could prove disastrous (*Financial Times*, 8 March 1993).

■ *10.1* Introduction

Deindustrialisation refers to the contraction of the industrial (or secondary) sector which has been a notable feature of many advanced economies. It has generated widespread concern, accompanied by many calls – particularly when economies are in recession – for policies to reverse the process and to re-establish a revitalised and growing industrial base. For instance, referring to the UK, the Director-General of the Engineering Employers' Federation has stated:

> The country has expectations for living standards which the economy will be unable to deliver in the immediate future. It will be unable to deliver them at all unless industry is rebuilt (*Financial Times*, 13 January 1993).

Such concern may be misplaced. Deindustrialisation has largely been analysed from a macroeconomic viewpoint. Consideration of the changes taking place at a more disaggregated level provides important insights into the process of change. Furthermore, the decline of the industrial sector has been accompanied by a growing service (or tertiary) sector. The service sector in most advanced countries employs more people than the industrial sector – substantially more than half the workforce in many cases. But this sector has received scant attention from economists. Examination of the interaction between the service and industrial sectors is essential in order to determine whether deindustrialisation is a problem or simply part of a natural transition to a post-industrial economy.

■ *10.2* What is deindustrialisation?

There is no single definition of deindustrialisation. Many economists consider the changes that have occurred in manufacturing; some consider the industrial sector as a whole (by including mining and quarrying, public utilities and construction). For Bluestone and Harrison, deindustrialisation is: 'a widespread, systematic disinvestment in the nation's basic productive capacity' (1982, p. 6). Some focus on the changes that have taken place in industrial output but, more often, the concern is with employment.

Table 10.1 shows that the percentage of the workforce employed in the industrial sector has been in decline since the mid- and late 1960s in the UK, USA, France, Netherlands and West Germany. In Italy and Japan the share of the workforce employed in the industrial sector reached its peak later, but there too the decline has set in (although quite gradually in the case of Japan). In the European economies – particularly the UK – the trend shows a decline in the absolute level of industrial employment, although the totals for individual years reflect cyclical factors (Table 10.2). This contrasts with Japan, where industrial employment continues to increase, and with the USA where such employment remains at historically high levels.

As regards output, deindustrialisation is less obvious (Table 10.3). Although in all countries the overall trend has been upward since 1970, there have been marked differences in the rate of growth. In the UK, for instance, there have been several years where industrial output has declined, and over the twenty year period to 1990 it has grown by little more than a quarter. Japanese industrial production has increased more steadily, and has more than doubled between 1970 and 1990.

Table 10.1   *Percentage of total employment in the industrial sector*

	UK	USA	W. Germ-any	France	Italy	Neth-erlands	Japan
1960	47.7	35.3	47.0	38.4	33.9	40.5	28.5
1965	46.6	35.4	48.4	39.9	37.0	41.1	32.4
1970	44.7	34.3	48.5	39.7	39.5	38.9	35.7
1975	40.6	30.5	45.4	38.7	39.1	34.9	35.9
1980	37.8	30.5	44.2	36.0	37.8	31.4	35.3
1985	32.4	28.0	41.0	32.0	33.6	28.1	34.9
1990	29.0	26.2	39.8	29.9	32.4	26.3	34.1

Source: Derived from Organisation for Economic Cooperation and Development, *Economic Surveys* (various years).

Table 10.2   *Employment in the industrial sector (millions)*

	UK	USA	W. Germ-any	France	Italy	Neth-erlands	Japan
1960	11.3	22.2	12.2	7.1	6.9	1.7	12.7
1965	11.5	25.2	12.8	7.8	7.2	1.8	15.3
1970	10.9	27.0	12.7	8.1	7.6	1.8	18.2
1975	10.0	26.2	11.5	8.0	7.7	1.6	18.7
1980	9.4	30.3	11.4	7.6	7.8	1.6	19.6
1985	7.8	30.0	10.3	6.7	6.9	1.4	20.3
1990	7.7	30.9	11.1	6.5	6.8	1.6	21.3

Source: Organisation for Economic Cooperation and Development, *Economic Surveys* (various years).

For Singh (1977, 1979) and Thirlwall (1992) the state of a country's external manufacturing balance (the value of manufactured exports less that of manufactured imports) is the cause for concern. **Table 10.4** provides evidence on the balance of trade, whilst **Table 10.5** shows changes in countries' shares of world trade in manufacturing. The UK and the USA stand out. Both have experienced a notable decline in their share of world trade and have a deteriorating trade balance (masked in the case of the UK by sales of North Sea oil in the early 1980s). In contrast, Japan and Germany have seen an increase in their trade

Table 10.3 *Index numbers of industrial production (base 1985 = 100)*

	UK	USA	W. Germany	France	Italy	Neth-erlands	Japan
1970	83.4	63.5	83.2	75.0	74.5	71	56.5
1972	84.4	70.6	86.9	84.3	77.7	79	62.1
1974	90.0	75.2	90.8	92.2	88.6	89	68.6
1976	88.2	74.9	91.1	93.1	90.2	91	67.8
1978	95.4	86.1	92.5	96.6	92.0	92	75.1
1980	92.5	87.8	97.2	100.9	103.2	95	84.4
1982	91.0	83.4	92.3	99.2	97.8	89	85.5
1984	94.9	98.2	95.7	99.5	98.7	95	96.5
1986	102.3	101.1	102.0	100.9	104.1	100	99.8
1988	109.5	110.9	106.1	107.5	114.2	101	112.9
1990	109.2	115.7	117.2	114.1	117.9	109.0	125.4
1991	106.0	113.4	120.6	114.3	115.4	113.2	128.2

Source: Organisation for Economic Cooperation and Development (1990, 1993).

surpluses and growth in their shares of the world market in manufactures.

Whilst the statistics on employment, output and trade show that the industrial sectors of advanced economies have undergone marked (and often rapid) changes in recent years, care needs to be taken in their interpretation. First, any of the measures taken in isolation (as is often done) presents but a partial view. For instance, the output measure does not take into account changes in population. Moreover, productivity increases brought about by capital investment may cause industrial employment to fall, but have no adverse effects on output levels.)

Secondly, measurement (particularly of services) is sensitive to the way in which the activities are defined, and whether measurement is by volume or by value. For instance, Smith (1972) argues that the 2.8 per cent per annum growth of manufacturing, and 1.9 per cent per annum growth of services in the UK between 1951 and 1966 can be reversed by changing the basis for calculation. Another difficulty arises from the government's classification of firms according to their primary activity. An advertising specialist working for a chemical firm will be recorded as being employed in manufacturing, whilst the executives of an advertising agency will be classified as being in service sector employment. If,

Table 10.4   *Trade balances (billion SDRs)*

	UK	USA	W. Germ- any	France	Italy	Neth- erlands	Japan
1970	0.1	2.6	5.7	0.3	−0.2	−0.9	4.0
1972	−1.4	−5.9	7.7	1.2	0.8	0.4	8.3
1974	−9.8	−4.5	18.4	−3.2	−7.1	0.5	1.2
1976	−6.1	−8.2	14.0	−4.3	−3.7	1.2	8.5
1978	−2.4	−27.3	19.7	0.1	2.3	−1.2	20.5
1980	2.9	−19.6	6.9	−10.3	−12.6	−1.1	1.7
1982	3.4	−33.2	22.5	−14.3	−8.1	4.2	16.5
1984	−6.0	−109.9	21.8	−4.5	−5.7	5.5	43.3
1986	−10.9	−123.0	47.3	−2.1	3.7	6.2	78.6
1988	−27.2	−94.7	58.5	−6.0	−0.5	6.1	70.8

Source: International Monetary Fund, *Balance of Payments Statistics Yearbook* (various years).

Table 10.5   *Share of world exports of manufactures (percentage)*

	UK	USA	W. Germ- any	France	Italy	Neth- erlands	Japan
1970	9.2	17.8	16.6	8.2	6.5	5.1	9.7
1980	8.8	15.7	16.8	9.4	7.0	5.6	11.7
1990	7.5	14.8	17.5	8.8	7.3	5.3	12.8

Source: Organisation for Economic Cooperation and Development (1992).

say, a textile manufacturer decides it no longer wants to employ accountants or designers but to use outside consultancy firms instead, a reduction in industrial employment and a corresponding growth in service employment will be recorded. Conversely, the statistics would show industrialisation if a firm decided to employ its own specialists rather than contract out a particular job. There is evidence that as an industrial firm grows the proportion of its employment devoted to production falls quite substantially, to as little as 10 per cent in some cases. Eliasson (1984) considered that the 25 largest Swedish manufacturing firms would be better classified as international marketing institutions. A similar point can be made about the US car manufacturer General Motors, which is a major provider of financial services to its dealers and customers (OECD, 1992).

Because the statistics reflect any such changes in the organisation of firms over time, the extent of any deindustrialisation cannot be precisely measured. However, it is clear from the data that the advanced economies are not deindustrialising in equal measure. The evidence suggests that the UK is experiencing a particularly marked decline in its industrial sector. In contrast, it is only in terms of its share of employment in industry that Japan can be considered to be suffering deindustrialisation; and even this evidence is weak. In the USA, deindustrialisation is most apparent from the data on the country's trading performance.

■ *10.3* Is deindustrialisation a problem?

Many economists consider that deindustrialisation raises serious issues. If the industrial sector is contracting in absolute terms, then unemployment is a problem if the transition to alternative occupations is slow. If the sector is in relative decline, its growth may not be fast enough to absorb any increase in the working population. Another reason for concern turns on the idea that manufacturing is the *engine of growth*, because of its ability to extend markets, the scope for productivity gains and its record of technological innovation. Dertouzos *et al.* argue:

> The roots of much of the technological progress responsible for long-term economic growth can ultimately be traced to the nation's manufacturing base. Because of this connection, high-technology and high-value-added services as well as products depend on the presence of a healthy, technologically dynamic manufacturing sector (1989, p. 40–1).

Living standards and employment may be sacrificed if reductions in manufacturing exports create international payments problems. Manufacturing is the principal contributor to the current account of the balance of payments. A continuing deficit on the current account caused by a weak manufacturing sector may act as a constraint on the economy's growth. Godley argues:

> A basic premise is that Britain needs a strong manufacturing base to generate the income to pay for imports (*Financial Times*, 14 December 1992).

Issues of national security and regional balance have also been raised. The case that deindustrialisation poses a serious problem has been made with such force that Singh states: 'The implication that the UK's industrial base needs strengthening is obvious and uncontroversial' (1979, p. 202). Is this view correct?

To a large degree, calls for policy action to stem deindustrialisation have arisen from consideration of the industrial sector in aggregate and in isolation from the rest of the economy. Such a focus is misguided. The industrial sector includes many different industries, subject to a wide variety of influences and with very different performance records. Nor can the industrial sector be considered to be independent of the other sectors of the economy. As the OECD recognises:

> the clean lines separating the economy into sectors will probably have less meaning in the future. Instead of emphasizing one sector over another (e.g. 'manufacturing matters') the focus of economic development policy should be on the systemwide gains that maximise the efficiency of the integration of different industries (1992, pp. 188–9).

All areas of the economy interact and an apparently unfavourable development in one sector may be caused by (or cause) favourable developments elsewhere.

The principal consideration should be whether deindustrialisation reduces the welfare of the nation as a whole. This is not necessarily the same as concern about jobs, about the balance of manufacturing trade, or about the preservation of a particular sector of the economy, but most authors fail to spell out the link between their chosen measure of deindustrialisation and economic welfare. If welfare were enhanced it would not matter if production was entirely carried out by robots leaving people to enjoy leisure, or if the majority were employed in the service sector.

▌ 10.4 Theoretical framework for the analysis of deindustrialisation

A variety of reasons for deindustrialisation have been proposed: the stage of economic development reached, loss of competitiveness, the activities of the multinational firms, the growth of the state sector and the disruptive impact of the development of a major new natural resource (the so-called *Dutch Disease*). These explanations can be linked to a common theoretical framework by considering the Austrian view of competition as a process by which economies adapt in an uncertain and changing environment. Where market forces are allowed to function freely, changes in relative prices and profit opportunities act as signals to entrepreneurs to reallocate resources. When successful, their actions lead to an increase in economic welfare. Within this framework, changes in the size and composition of the industrial sector are considered to be the consequence of economic activity in response to changes in tastes, incomes and relative prices. It is also affected if the government or firms (via the establishment of entry barriers) seek to influence the process of change. North's institutional perspective (**Section 1.5**) adds a further dimension to this analysis. Each country's institutional environment is unique in the extent to which it is conducive to the process of change. In those economies characterised by a myriad of administrative restrictions, safeguards to employment and cultural attitudes that favour the status quo, other sectors may not be able to respond to and compensate for any adverse developments in the industrial base.

■ *10.5* The stages of growth argument

It has long been recognised that as economies mature the relative size of the industrial sector declines. **Figure 10.1** illustrates the *stages of growth* view, showing the relative importance of the primary, secondary and tertiary sectors at different points in the maturing of an economy. As development progresses, the secondary or industrial sector becomes less important while the tertiary or service sector grows. This is a long-term phenomenon, and the path of change varies between countries, but essentially there is a correlation between the level of GDP per capita and the sectoral distribution of employment.

The decline in the industrial sector occurs as market forces reallocate resources to reflect the different demand and supply conditions of a mature economy. As Kuznets recognised:

> The shift of emphasis from one area within the productive system to another in addition to knowledge, new technology, and innovation means changes in the identity of the new and rapidly growing industries. By the same token there is a tendency towards retardation in the rate of growth of old industries, as the economic effects of technical progress and innovation within them slacken and as they feel increasingly the competition of the newer industries for limited resources (1959, p. 33).

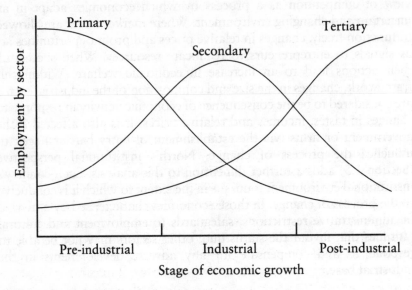

Figure 10.1 *The stages of economic growth*

Labour productivity has generally grown faster in manufacturing than in services. With an unchanged pattern of demand, this would permit a declining proportion of the workforce to be employed in the industrial sector. Moreover, greater concern with environmental factors in advanced economies has increased the costs of traditional 'smoke-stack' industries, and the industrial sector has become less attractive as a source of employment to an increasingly educated and aspiring workforce.

Two factors would suggest that changes in demand also work against industry as an economy advances. Reductions in birth rates and increases in life expectancy have led to an increased demand for social services. Secondly, as real incomes have increased there have been changes in the pattern of demand both within and between sectors: the demand for services has generally been more income-elastic than the demand for industrial goods.

The stages of growth argument also provides an insight into the reduced share of world manufacturing trade and increased import penetration experienced by some advanced nations. Developing countries often have a cost advantage in the production of relatively labour-intensive, manufactured products. Following the principle of comparative advantage, this would be expected to lead to changes in both specialisation and trade patterns. Growing competition from industrialising Third World nations is likely to have the greatest impact on those mature economies (such as the UK) whose manufactured exports are highly dependent upon low-technology products, vulnerable to price competition.

■ *10.6* Loss of competitiveness

The stages of growth argument is too simplistic to be a complete explanation of deindustrialisation. For instance, it cannot explain why the UK is deindustrialising faster than either Japan or Germany, both of which have a higher level of GDP per capita. Rather, the process of gradual adaptation of the economy, suggested by the stages of growth hypothesis, is accelerated or retarded by other factors which cause changes in supply and demand conditions. Via the operation of the price mechanism, this produces a reallocation of resources within and between sectors.

For example, the level of, and changes in, the exchange rate affect the process of economic change. An appreciation of the exchange rate will cause domestic goods traded internationally to become less price-competitive and lead to difficulty maintaining output and employment levels in the industries affected. The appreciation of sterling at the end of the 1970s produced a marked reduction in the price competitiveness of British goods. Likewise, the strong dollar between 1982 and 1985 affected the competitiveness of American industry. It allowed the Japanese to import small cars into the US at prices $2,500 below the cost of production in the USA. With the decline of the dollar against the yen in late 1985 and 1986, Japanese manufacturers believed that it might be cheaper to manufacture in the USA. As long as an exchange rate appreciation is temporary or caused by factors outside the industrial sector, it should not be interpreted as a signal for a permanent or fundamental shift of resources away from the affected industries.

Alternatively, loss of competitiveness could be the result of problems within the industrial sector, such as high labour costs, poor product quality, limited range of products or poor after-sales service. In this case, the loss of competitiveness should act as a signal for change. Production of the goods and services affected should either be cut back and resources switched to more profitable opportunities elsewhere, or the production process should be reconfigured to make more efficient use of resources so as to better satisfy the requirements of consumers. If the loss of competitiveness persists, this is a sign that the economy is changing too slowly. Adopting this viewpoint, it can be argued that deindustrialisation is a consequence of firms' failure or inability (because of an institutional environment that does not facilitate change) to respond to changing market circumstances. As Thurow noted for the US steel industry:

> Instead of junking our old, obsolete open-hearth furnaces and shifting to the large oxygen furnaces and continuous casting of the Japanese, we retreat into protection … As a result, our economy ends up with a weak steel industry that cannot compete and has no incentive to compete (1980, p. 5).

Similar comments could be applied to the UK textile industry. According to the International Labour Office (ILO), the widespread introduction of computer-based technology would instantly have led this industry to recapture its lost competitiveness (Ray, 1986b).

Many of these arguments are particularly pertinent to the UK. Its income elasticity of exports tends to be substantially lower than that for imports. To illustrate, Bariam (1993) quotes the UK's income elasticity of demand for exports over the period 1970–85 as 1.31 compared with 2.14 for imports. The figures for Germany were much closer at 1.77 and 1.92 respectively, whilst those for Japan (covering the period 1961–85) were 3.97 and 1.59. It is widely argued that this is a consequence of such factors as poor-quality products and poor marketing, a lower rate of investment relative to major competitors and a misdirection in the allocation of R&D efforts in the UK.

10.7 Multinationals and deindustrialisation

American firms also appear to have lost competitiveness, but, according to Bluestone and Harrison (1982), their response to problems of outdated plant and equipment, increased competition and high wage demands has often been to transfer manufacturing overseas. They cite the rationalisation of the American tyre industry in the latter part of the 1970s, which involved substantial plant closure and redundancy. Although some new plants were opened in the USA – relocated in the 'Sunbelt' states – much of the expansion was channelled abroad, most notably to Spain, Turkey and Brazil.

Such behaviour can be regarded as a logical response by firms to changes in the environment within which they operate and can be explained by economic theory on multinational activity. It is argued that multinational firms possess *firm-specific advantages* (such as superior management, more advanced technology or patents) which enable them to compete effectively in overseas markets. The firm must decide upon the most profitable method of exploiting these advantages from the options of exporting, making licensing arrangements with foreign producers (using the market), or operating overseas (internalising). Transaction costs play an important role in the decision. A firm may be prompted to internalise when, for instance, a foreign government imposes controls on imports or when the firm seeks to retain control of products and processes it has developed. The multinational will be attracted to locations which have low labour costs, favourable market characteristics and government policy, or other advantages for the firm

Multinational enterprises have traditionally been manufacturing rather than service firms, so their activities could affect deindustrialisation in several ways. First, there is a direct loss of jobs as a result of domestic industrial firms relocating abroad. Frank and Freeman (1978) estimated that $1 billion of direct foreign investment by US firms was equivalent to a loss of 26 500 domestic jobs and that in 1970 multinational activity led to a loss of 116 000 manufacturing jobs. For the UK, Stopford and Turner (1985) reported that between 1972 and 1983 nearly a third of all manufacturing jobs lost in the UK were cut by 58 British multinationals which (during the same period) added 200 000 jobs overseas. It was explained that these firms were attempting to reduce their exposure to the chronic problems of Britain's industrial sector.

Other studies (Hawkins, 1972; United States Tariff Commission, 1973) suggest that consideration of jobs displaced gives a biased view of the impact of multinationals, since domestic employment may be unaffected or, indeed, actually increase. One reason for this is that the direct loss of industrial jobs may be partly offset by an increase in exports of components from the home country. For instance, in 1985 it was estimated that less than half the content of US-built Japanese cars was American, with most of the engines and transmission systems being exported from Japan. In addition, foreign direct investment is likely to generate more administrative jobs at the domestic head office. These points suggest that the impact of foreign investment on employment in the home economy will vary from case to case, a view confirmed by Buckley and Artisien (1988). They surveyed nineteen British, West German and French firms in the automobile, engineering and chemical industries which had established plants in Greece, Spain and Portugal. In some instances, exports had been replaced by production in the foreign country; in others exports of components had increased. In addition, some firms reported that the foreign investment had generated jobs in the home country by opening up a new market.

Secondly, multinational activity could contribute to deindustrialisation through the decision of foreign-owned firms to uproot their operations because of a change in locational advantage. It is often argued that multinationals are 'footloose' and, being generally large firms, such mobility can result in many job losses:

> any one nation can be deindustrialised by the actions of transnational corporations – and the implication is that only when wage costs are cut, or profit taxes reduced, will capital return (Cowling, 1990, p. 170).

Nevertheless, Killick (1982) rejects this as a major explanation of the decline in industrial employment in the UK. Between 1978 and 1981 he found no significant difference between the employment performance of foreign-owned and UK-owned firms, while in the previous period, 1975–8, employment in foreign-owned plants held up rather better. Other evidence, however, indicates that during the first half of the 1980s foreign-owned companies in the UK reduced their labour force to a greater extent than indigenous firms (*Financial Times*, 29 October 1986).

Thirdly, the behaviour of multinationals is also relevant to the declining share of some advanced countries in world manufacturing exports. UNIDO (1983), for instance, attributed part of the reduced share of world trade held by US industry to the relocation of capacity overseas. Adjusting for this, the USA's share of world trade has remained virtually constant. Moreover, some manufactured imports into the USA will originate from branches of US firms overseas.

As a result of the advantages which enable them to compete successfully abroad, multinational firms are likely to be more responsive to changes in supply and demand conditions between national markets, more willing and/or able to relocate, to restructure or to identify new opportunities. In consequence it is understandable that their activities have been accused of contributing to deindustrialisation, although the evidence of this linkage is by no means clear-cut.

■ *10.8* The state sector's contribution

A different explanation of deindustrialisation is proposed by Bacon and Eltis (1976). Their thesis is that expansion of the *non-market sector* of the economy (goods and services which are financed by taxation rather than paid for directly by consumers, such as defence, police, state education systems) has deterred industrial activity by *crowding out*: the pre-emption of physical or financial resources. Although their interest is with the UK economy, the argument can be applied to other Western European countries (including Italy, West Germany and the Netherlands) and also to Japan. All of these economies have experienced substantial growth in the state sector.

For the UK, a number of points tell against the Bacon and Eltis thesis. First, unemployment levels and spare capacity since the early 1970s argue against physical crowding out although in certain areas, where particular skills are in short supply, the state sector may have attracted workers away from other jobs. Secondly, most manufacturing jobs lost were held by males whilst state sector expansion has largely increased female employment. Thirdly, evidence suggests that neither taxation nor other financial constraints have discouraged private investment. The Cambridge Economic Policy Group (1976) and King (1975) indicate that effective corporate tax rates fell at least into the mid-1970s, while the Treasury, reporting to the Wilson Committee (HM Treasury, 1977), found no signs of any shortage of funds for industry.

Following an alternative position, it may be that deindustrialisation is caused by the expansion of the state sector *per se* and the changed pattern of demand which this creates. Freeman (1979), for instance, argues that by sponsoring defence and aerospace projects in the private sector the UK government has been directing skilled scientific manpower away from research and development activity that is more 'commercial' (the European Fighter Aircraft versus improvements to the washing machine). This may have adversely affected the competitiveness of the UK industrial sector. Similar problems have occurred in Sweden with increased government expenditure in the form of industrial subsidies. Eliasson believes that:

Sweden's extremely costly industrial subsidy programme – up from one of the lowest rates in the industrial world in the early 1970s to a record breaking 16 per cent of value added in manufacturing in 1982, and in practice all structure conserving – is the major explanation of the complete collapse of manufacturing output growth in Sweden since 1973 (1984, p. 315).

■ *10.9* The Dutch disease

Deindustrialisation has been associated with the development of a major natural resource. This is often termed the *Dutch Disease* because it was first noted in connection with the Dutch exploitation of natural gas in the 1960s; with the development of North Sea oil, the concept has been applied to the UK. North Sea oil contributed to the appreciation of the pound in the late 1970s, causing a loss of price competitiveness for British goods. However, Forsyth and Kay (1980, 1981) took the argument further by focusing on the relative impact of oil production on the *traded* and *non-traded goods* sectors of the economy. Additional output is in a form that can be traded internationally, but the extra demand resulting from higher incomes is divided between tradeable and non-tradeable products (mainly services, including those provided by the state sector). The increased demand for non-tradeables can be met only by raising domestic production, and this is likely to involve the movement of resources from tradeable goods production, leaving the gap to be filled by imports. The new equilibrium for the economy is characterised by a proportionately larger non-traded goods sector whilst the traded goods sector (excluding oil) is reduced.

Forsyth and Kay's analysis can be criticised from a number of perspectives. For instance, Byatt *et al.* (1982) noted their failure to take account of the effects of rising oil prices during the 1970s. Furthermore, North Sea oil can (at best) be only a contributory factor in the deindustrialisation of the UK because the process began many years before oil came on-stream. However, Forsyth and Kay's analysis is informative because it describes the process whereby an economy adapts to changes in supply and in relative prices and incomes. Given that the UK economy has been able to respond to these developments, it seems inconsistent to suggest (as does, for instance, Aldington, 1986) that the UK will have any difficulty adjusting to the eventual, relatively slow decline of North Sea oil.

■ *10.10* Services as a substitute for industry

Widespread preoccupation with the industrial sector contrasts markedly with the lack of attention paid to services. This neglect often extends to the definition of services: activities that cannot be classified either as industrial, agricultural or extractive are regarded as services. It is also reflected in the facts that statistics on services are less detailed and less reliable, and that the major share of government assistance is directed at industrial firms. Such attitudes are surprising given that in most advanced economies the service sector has been growing steadily and employs well over half the workforce (**Tables 10.6** and **10.7**).

It has frequently been argued that deindustrialisation is a matter for concern because the service sector is incapable of fulfilling the role played by the industrial sector in creating employment, stimulating economic growth and maintaining a healthy balance of payments. This

Table 10.6 *Employment in services (millions)*

	UK	USA	W. Germ-any	France	Italy	Neth-erlands	Japan
1960	11.3	37.0	10.1	7.2	6.8	2.1	18.3
1965	12.3	41.5	10.8	8.2	7.1	2.3	20.8
1970	12.7	48.1	11.2	9.4	7.7	2.6	23.9
1975	14.0	56.1	12.0	10.6	8.7	2.8	26.9
1980	14.9	65.5	13.0	11.7	9.9	3.2	30.0
1985	15.7	73.8	13.4	12.6	11.3	3.4	32.7
1990	18.3	83.6	15.9	13.9	12.4	4.3	36.7

Source: Organisation for Economic Cooperation and Development, *Economic Surveys* (various years).

Table 10.7 *Percentage of total employment in services*

	UK	USA	W. Germ-any	France	Italy	Neth-erlands	Japan
1960	47.6	56.2	39.1	38.5	33.5	49.7	41.3
1965	49.6	58.3	40.7	41.8	36.8	51.3	44.1
1970	52.0	61.1	42.9	46.4	40.3	54.9	46.9
1975	56.7	65.4	47.6	51.1	44.2	59.4	51.5
1980	59.6	65.9	50.3	55.3	47.9	63.6	54.2
1985	65.0	68.9	53.5	60.4	55.2	67.0	56.3
1990	68.9	70.9	56.8	64.0	58.6	69.1	58.7

Source: Derived from Organisation for Economic Cooperation and Development, *Economic Surveys* (various years).

has led to widespread calls for policies to revitalise the industrial base in the UK and the USA in particular. For instance, in the UK the National Institute for Economic and Social Research (NIESR) took the view that:

> any future which holds out the hope of rising prosperity for the economy as a whole and a move back to full employment must include a reversal of the decline in manufacturing industry (1985, p. 5).

A buoyant industrial sector has long been regarded as a prerequisite for sustained economic growth, because of the opportunities it presents for productivity improvements (both because of the types of production processes involved and the large scale of many operations). In the service sector, the traditional view has been that there is, by definition, less scope for mechanisation, while the multiplicity of small organisations militates against the adoption of new techniques. This view of the service sector is becoming less valid. Distributive services, for example, have the potential to achieve economies of scale. Marked productivity advances are also possible with the introduction of computers and associated technology into banking and finance, retailing and communications. Moreover, traditional productivity measures have failed to capture gains in the form of a better quality service. Take the case of an insurance company providing personal computers to its sales force enabling them to provide more rapid and more appropriate advice to clients. Measuring productivity in terms of output per worker can only partly capture these benefits.

Balance of payments evidence suggests that it may not be possible for the service sector to offset any marked reduction in net exports of manufactures. The Association of British Chambers of Commerce (*The Economist*, 28 September 1985) calculated that a 1 per cent fall in the UK's manufactured exports required a 3 per cent rise in service exports to generate the same foreign earnings. However, Thirlwall (1992) considers that only around 20 per cent of the UK's output of services is potentially tradeable, compared with all manufactured output. Furthermore, much service trade (including banking, insurance and shipping) is dependent on industrial exports and, where service exports are growing in their own right, they are often affected by the same factors as industrial trade, such as exchange rate movements, protectionism, and competition from developing countries.

There is also a question mark over the extent to which traded services create jobs, because, whereas tourism and overseas construction are quite labour-intensive, other services are not. This is one aspect of the argument that the service sector cannot replace jobs lost in the industrial sector, but it receives little support from the empirical evidence in **Tables 10.2** and **10.6**. Jobs shed in the industrial sector since 1965 in the countries considered have been fewer than the jobs created in services. In the 1980s, around 18 million service jobs were created in the USA. However, it may well be the case that many of the service jobs are part-time, employ female workers or are located away from the traditional industrial areas.

Any failure to date of the service sector to compensate adequately for the decline of the industrial sector may be partly a reflection of variations in the time it takes for different economies to adjust. The process of transition should not be thought of in terms of the resources displaced in one sector being reabsorbed directly into another. Instead, it may be gradual and diverse, with much of the redistribution of resources occurring within the sectors, from declining industrial firms to growing industrial firms, and the same within services. Anything that hampers this mobility or deters entrepreneurship will adversely slow the rate of transition.

■ *10.11* Links between industry and services

The macroeconomic viewpoint adopted by many economists analysing deindustrialisation and developments in services can give but a partial view of the issues. Its broad perspective fails to reveal important changes consequent on linkages between the industrial and service sectors of the economy – linkages which the OECD perceives to be of increasing significance:

> economies have become more interconnected as manufacturing firms now request more inputs from service industries and visa-versa (1992, p. 188).

As an economy adapts to changes in incomes, tastes, and relative prices, both services and industry are likely to be affected. Where changes in purchasing patterns affect the industrial sector, complementary service industries will be affected; where services and industrial goods are substitutes, this may lead to changes in the form in which consumers' requirements are satisfied. Furthermore, supply side developments may influence both sectors. Increased productivity in industry may be the result of increased productivity in services (for instance, in training skilled workers or in providing superior consultancy). As Gershuny points out:

> Far from being faced with a choice between growth in services and manufacturing, it appears that those countries with the fastest growth in services also have the fastest rate of growth in manufacturing (1978, p. 111).

Services can be subdivided into four groups. *Consumer services* are those that directly satisfy final consumer demand (such as restaurants and hotels, private transport and personal services). *Distributive services* include freight transport, retailing, wholesaling: meeting either producer or consumer demand. *Social services* include health, education and administration, whilst activities such as banking and finance, accountancy and management consultancy are grouped within *producer services*. This functional classification is crude (for instance, banking serves consumers as well as producers), but it provides a useful basis for analysis because employment (and output) trends vary between areas of service provision.

Table 10.8 provides evidence of trends in employment within these service groups by considering particular constituent industries for the USA over the period 1970–2005. Whilst eating and drinking establishments have shown increases in employment well above the average, there appears to be no clear trend in consumer services as a whole. Trends in employment in distributive services are broadly similar to those in overall employment in the USA. In contrast, many social and producer services are expanding rapidly. These findings are in broad agreement with other studies of services (for instance, Bank of England, 1985; Marshall, 1988; Daniels and Moulaert, 1991).

Such variations within the service sector arise because of differences in the factors influencing each area of service provision. The demand for social services (many of which are provided by the government and are largely paid for by taxation) is affected less by income and price changes, and more by demography and government policy. In contrast, the fortunes of consumer services reflect changes in relative prices, tastes, and incomes. Where services and industrial output are substitutes, consumers may choose to switch away from provision by manufactured goods. But those services where productivity has grown slowly may have become relatively more expensive, making the manufactured alternative more attractive. For instance, television and videos have replaced many cinema visits, and the private car has increasingly replaced public transport. In other cases, consumer services and industrial output are complementary and their fortunes interlinked. Increased tourism generates a greater demand for souvenirs, hotel furnishings and catering products; home computers and stereo equipment require a retailing and maintenance network.

Employment figures may understate the contribution of producer services in the economy because producer services have made more extensive use of new labour-saving technology. The prospects of producer services (and, to a lesser extent, distributive services) depend partly – since they also supply other services – on trends within the industrial sector. For instance, General Motors counts a health insurance company amongst its principal suppliers (OECD, 1992). In part, the growth of producer services reflects their greater use, although it may also reflect an increase in the contracting-out of services

Table 10.8 *Employment in services in the USA, selected industries (percentage change over period)*

Industry	1970–80	1980–90	1990–2005
Total employment	+24.9	+20.1	+20.1
Consumer:			
Personal services	–8.9	+23.5	+25.6
Hotels and other lodging places	n.a.	+53.3	+31.8
Eating and drinking places	+79.7	+41.9	+32.7
Distributive:			
Transportation	+9.9	+20.0	+24.6
Wholesale trade	+32.1	+17.6	+16.2
Retail trade	+22.8	+26.0	+22.6
Social:			
Health services	+72.9	+48.6	+46.9
Educational services	+21.1	+45.2	+40.7
Producer:			
Computer & data processing services	n.a	+157.9	+90.6
Other business services	+66.3	+59.9	+37.5

Note: Figures for 1990–2005 are forecasts.

Source: Derived from United States Department of Commerce, *Statistical Abstract of the United States* (1990, 1992).

previously undertaken within the industrial sector. Leasing and professional services are typical areas affected (OECD, 1989). The oil company, BP, provides a notable example. It has made substantial reductions in the size of its head office staff by arranging contracts with outside bodies for the provision of computing, accountancy and corporate taxation services.

Transaction cost economics provides an explanation for such behaviour. Using the market incurs the costs of gathering information, arranging, monitoring and policing contracts. For a firm to undertake a particular activity internally, its hierarchical form of organisation must present a lower-cost alternative to coordination of the activity through the market. Kay (1984) argues that as a firm expands, the decay, delay and distortion of information flows within the firm grows. These increased costs signal an eventual limit to the growth of the firm as it becomes relatively lower-cost to incur the transaction costs of using the

Table 10.9 *Employment in manufacturing in the USA, selected industries (percentage change over period)*

Industry	1970–80	1980–90	1990–2005
Total manufacturing employment	+4.7	−5.8	−3.1
Declining industries:			
Blast furnaces & basic steel products	−18.3	−46.3	−19.3
Tobacco manufactures	−16.9	−29.0	−30.6
Textile mill products	−13.0	−18.4	−13.7
Leather and leather products	−27.2	−46.8	−45.5
Expanding industries:			
Printing and publishing	+13.4	+25.7	+20.7
Rubber and misc. plastic products	+25.3	+22.2	+17.3
Furniture and fixtures	+5.7	+9.7	+21.8

Note: Figures for 1990–2005 are forecasts.

Source: Derived from United States Department of Commerce, *Statistical Abstract of the United States* (1990, 1992).

market. Consequently, contracting-out is likely to increase as firms' service requirements become more specialised with changes in technology and growing demands for information.

■ 10.12 A disaggregated view of changes in industry

Crucial differences in performance and prospects between industries are overlooked in concentrating on aggregates and averages which:

> conceals ... all the drama of the events – the rise and fall of products, technologies, and industries, and the accompanying transformation of the spatial and occupational distribution of the population (Nordhaus and Tobin, 1972, p. 2).

As with services, it is mistaken to regard the industrial sector as a whole. It is a heterogeneous group, whose members are subject to varying influences and have very different performance records. A clear picture of the adjustments occurring in an economy emerges only if these differences are highlighted.

Trends in output and employment (but also profit records, investment trends, extent of spare capacity, rates of births and deaths of firms) are all indications of differences in the performance of particular industries. For instance, **Table 10.9** shows that declining employment in the US steel, tobacco, textiles and leather goods industries has occurred alongside the opening of new firms and the expansion of employment in other areas of manufacturing. There are also examples of US companies repatriating work from plants overseas. For instance, Tandy has switched production of desktop computers from South Korea to Texas (*Fortune*, 30 December 1991). Explanations for such actions include changes in production techniques that have made low labour costs less significant, and the improved service that can be offered if the customer is in close proximity.

Table 10.10 provides further evidence of the dynamic nature of economies. The same industry may experience similar fortunes in different countries. For instance, the manufacture of computers and office equipment achieved the highest output growth in all four countries selected, whilst ferrous metals, shipbuilding and other transportation equipment were amongst the lowest output growth industries in three out of the four countries. However, it is also true that some industries flourish in a particular economy, whilst performing badly elsewhere. Mining – a low growth sector in the USA, West Germany and Japan – was booming in the UK with the exploitation of North Sea oil. Motor vehicles were a major growth industry in Japan, but a poor performer in the UK. **Table 10.10** also indicates the variety of influences to which different industries are subject. It was largely expanding domestic demand that caused the expansion in computers and office equipment in the USA and Japan; export growth was the main influence on the industry in the UK and West Germany. Exports were important in the success of the Japanese motor vehicle industry, but contributed to the problems of this industry in the UK.

Industries in decline are often long-established (such as shipbuilding and textiles), while those in ascendancy embody newer technology. Even this generalisation can be misleading. There are signs of rejuvenation in some traditional industries. This may be due to the introduction of new production techniques, such as the increased use of electronics and robots in car production and air jet looms in textiles. Elsewhere, rejuvenation has followed exploitation of new, specialised areas of the market. The revival of the Swiss watch industry can be attributed both to new technology and to the targeting of new markets. Employment in watchmaking had more than halved between 1970 and 1984. The *Swatch* is a low-priced, plastic, electronic watch incorporating quartz movements and produced using robots. It is promoted as combining a

Table 10.10   *Industries ranked by growth in output, showing principal explanation*

	UK 1968–84	USA 1972–85	W. Germany 1978–86	Japan 1970–85
Highest output growth:				
1.	Computers and office equipment[2]	Computers and office equipment[1]	Computers and office equipment[2]	Computers and office equipment[1]
2.	Real estate and business services[4]	Electronics[1]	Aerospace[2]	Pharmaceuticals[4]
3.	Electronics[2]	Communications[1]	Communications[1]	Electronics[1,2]
4.	Finance and insurance[1]	Instruments[1]	Real estate and business services[4]	Motor vehicles[2]
5.	Mining[2]	Social services[1]	Finance and insurance[1]	Communications[1]
6.	Government[1]	Finance and insurance[1]	Plastic and rubber products[2]	Instruments[1]
Lowest output growth:				
1.	Other transportation equipment[4]	Ferrous metals[4]	Wood, cork and furniture[1,4]	Mining[4]
2.	Fabricated metal products[4]	Other transportation equipment[1]	Ferrous metals[4]	Shipbuilding[1]
3.	Shipbuilding[1]	Other manufactures[3]	Textiles[3]	Wood, cork and furniture[4]
4.	Non-ferrous metals[3]	Non-ferrous metals[4]	Mining[4]	Textiles[4]
5.	Motor vehicles[3]	Mining[4]	Shipbuilding[2]	Agriculture[4]
6.	Ferrous metals[3]	Stone, clay and glass[4]	Petrol refining[3]	Other transportation equipment[4]

Source: Organisation for Economic Cooperation and Development (1992).

Note: Superscript indicates principal explanation of output growth:

[1] changes in domestic final demand
[2] export performance
[3] import performance
[4] change in technology

'trendy' image with Swiss quality. Its introduction led to an increase in jobs by 1000 in 1985 (*The Economist*, 17 May 1986). By 1991 sales were over 17 million per year and projected to achieve 50 million by the mid-1990s (*The Economist*, 18 April 1992).

This microeconomic perspective is taken further by Baden-Fuller and Stopford who argue that 'It is the firm which matters, not the industry' (1992, p.13). They classify firms into two types. The *mature business* is ossified, unable to respond effectively to market changes, let alone influence the market. The *dynamic* or *rejuvenated business* has an organisation, strategy and approach that allow it to drive developments in the market. Even in the most depressed and declining industry, such firms can succeed in growing and earning profits. Rumelt (1991) is amongst those providing support for such a conclusion. His study of US industries found that choice of industry explained under 10 per cent the variance in business-unit profitability, whilst almost 50 per cent was explained by choice of strategy. (Similar arguments that the firm is a more appropriate focus for investigation than the market or industry were presented in **Sections 2.17, 5.13** and **5.15.**)

Baden-Fuller and Stopford cite a number of examples of rejuvenated businesses, including the UK manufacturer of steel cutlery, Richardson Sheffield. In the 1970s, Richardson was close to bankruptcy; in the 1990s it is a market leader, despite strong competitive challenges from the Far East and other European producers. Part of this transformation was due to the innovation of a knife which does not need sharpening (the *Laser*), but it was also the result of many other changes including combining high quality with low cost, meeting orders more rapidly and exploiting new markets by promoting the knife as a gift.

This approach suggests that deindustrialisation is a consequence of too many manufacturing firms with poor management and inappropriate business strategies. However, whilst addressing these issues can revitalise declining industries, it does not automatically imply that job levels will be maintained. Modernisation of the West German textile industry in the 1970s involved closure of 30 per cent of firms, the introduction of more capital-intensive production methods and improved technology, and a switch away from the production of low-quality goods. As a result, production and exports increased, but over 200 000 jobs were lost.

 # 10.13 Multinationals and the revitalisation of industry

Rejuvenation of firms and industries may be prompted by the activities of multinational firms. Their presence can stimulate competitors and suppliers alike, accelerating the structural adjustment of the economy and aiding the process of economic change. For instance, Buckley and Artisien (1988) noted skill improvements among employees as multinationals introduced newer technology and provide training. This view is supported by Thurow:

When foreign multinationals enter the United States they speed up the transmission of industrial knowledge from high-productivity areas abroad to low-productivity areas in the United States (1980, p. 92).

Multinationals are often prepared to establish themselves in locations (such as the Mid-west of the USA) where indigenous manufacturing firms are in decline. This is further evidence for the thesis that deindustrialisation reflects failures in business management.

Many Japanese firms have been highly successful in manufacturing. They perceive this success to be a consequence of their superior product reliability, flexible manufacturing systems, and a high degree of commitment from the workforce (Dunning, 1990). Studying the impact of Japanese firms on manufacturing in the UK provides a notable example of how multinationals can contribute to industrial revival:

> Having forgotten how to make cars and consumer electronics, Britain is now being re-educated by others (*Financial Times*, 16 November 1992).

The impact of Japanese multinationals has several aspects. First, there is the direct boost to employment and output from new manufacturing plants. This has been relatively small overall – Dunning (1990) puts it at around 25 000 in the late 1980s – but is made more significant by being concentrated in certain sectors (such as colour televisions and motor vehicles). In the latter industry, it is estimated that the share of UK car production taken by the UK plants of Nissan, Toyota and Honda will increase from under 10 per cent in 1989 to around 25 per cent by 1995. Over this period, car output in the UK is anticipated to rise by some 50 per cent (*Accountancy*, November 1990). Furthermore, the UK's trade deficit in motor vehicles could be converted to surplus by the mid-1990s (*The Economist*, 28 November 1992).

The Japanese presence is influencing the operations of other manufacturers in the UK:

> the activities of these firms heighten the visibility of Japanese practice to British companies, many of which regard them as a direct threat to their own competitiveness and a model to be followed (Oliver and Wilkinson, 1992, p. 213).

In the car industry, Ford (which has been adopting some Japanese ideas since the late 1970s) has taken steps to reduce stockholdings and to introduce more flexible working practices. Model introduction and quality control are two areas which have been subject to change as a result of Honda taking a 20 per cent equity stake in Rover. General Motors appears to have altered its views on the locational advantages of the UK. Whereas it had been cutting back its UK operations, in 1992 it opened a new facility to supply engines for the European market. In the longer term, to meet effectively the competitive challenge, vehicle manufacturers in the UK are likely to go further in trying to emulate those practices – such as just-in-time supply and total quality management – that have made the Japanese successful.

Suppliers to the Japanese multinationals are not only seeing their domestic market expand, but their own operations and working practices are being influenced. For instance, in order to meet Honda's requirements, Unipart has modernised equipment, introduced team-working and accorded a greater priority to quality (*Financial Times*, 9 March 1992). Firms supplying Komatsu (which manufactures earth-moving and construction equipment) have had to rethink their operations – often with advice from Komatsu – in order to achieve cost and quality targets. Should UK firms fail to meet the stringent requirements of Japanese clients they could find themselves facing more competitors as Japanese suppliers move into the UK ('local content' requirements limit the extent to which components can be imported from Japan).

The Japanese multinationals have attracted a considerable amount of publicity. As a result, in the longer term, emulation of their management practices may spread more widely amongst firms in sectors not directly affected by the Japanese firms. However, it is worth noting that Oliver and Wilkinson (1992) found that the overall impact of the Japanese on British industry to be less than they had expected, for instance, because of employee resistance to changes in working practices. This is not to deny that multinationals can have a positive effect on the UK's industrial revival: 'the imperative to change is still fixed in the minds of British managers and engineers' (1992, p. 321).

■ *10.14* Policy on deindustrialisation

Economists have suggested many policy prescriptions to counter dein-dustrialisation, reflecting their particular analysis of the dimensions and causes of the problem. As an example, Stout (1979) envisaged UK indus-try policy aimed at promoting improvements in product quality and other aspects of non-price competitiveness. General investment incen-tives or policies such as protection aimed directly at improving the balance of trade, would, he argued, be less effective, and may even oper-ate perversely. In contrast, the Cambridge Economic Policy Group

(1978), concerned with the external balance, proposed import controls, whilst those who emphasise structural causes have advocated a reduction in the size of the state sector or the more deliberately targeted use of the proceeds of North Sea oil. Rhodes suggests a broader approach involving:

> much tougher government action on behalf of manufacturing industry in several policy areas including the exchange rate, tariffs, interest rates, taxation and subsidies for modernisation, expansion, and product and process innovation (1986, p. 167).

All these prescriptions envisage some sort of intervention to correct the situation by re-establishing the industrial base (or, at least, preventing its continued decline). In the terminology of Chapter 7, they recommend active, decelerative industry policy. Such policies are misguided or even harmful, because they interfere with the process by which economies adapt to changes. The OECD takes this view where such policies have been adopted by governments:

> Broadly speaking, the growth of subsidies and other protective measures has distorted competition and blurred market signals, thereby delaying the necessary adjustments and creating unexpected distortions (1989, p. 141).

Studies of OECD countries suggest that, with good organisation and by making the best use of available technology, the demand for manufactured goods could eventually be satisfied with less than a fifth of the workforce currently employed in manufacturing (noted in Geldens, 1984). If these forecasts are correct, in absolute terms, employment in manufacturing will be comparable with the levels currently employed in agriculture. Placing this loss of jobs in a historical context, it is by no means unprecedented, and on previous occasions the long-term result has been the creation of a higher level of employment. Geldens calculates:

> this is at least the fifth time in the past century when it has been predicted that a technological or social revolution is about to bring a huge rise in unemployment (1984, p. 17).

The instances he identifies are the mechanisation of agriculture, the mechanisation of industry, the rapid rise of female activity rates, the 1970s oil price increases and (more recently) the information revolution. Robinson (1958) would also agree that other activities will eventually absorb the unemployed, citing as an example that in 1957 nearly four million in the UK were employed in industries that did not exist or were in their infancy at the turn of the century. Therefore, to the extent that the decline of industry is a manifestation of a pervasive, natural process of change and adaptation, attempts to preserve the sector will tend to ossify the economy, leading to misallocation and lower levels of economic welfare.

This suggests that, rather than try to maintain the status quo, policy should aim to speed the process of adjustment by fostering a favourable environment within which well-managed, dynamic firms can thrive. Beneficial actions would be to improve information flows (making people more aware of opportunities), to foster competition, and to reduce any factors impeding the mobility of either capital or labour (neutral, supportive policies, **Section 7.10**). Amongst advocates of such an approach is the Engineering Employers' Federation in the UK (*Financial Times*, 13 January 1993). It sees government's role as that of 'catalyst and stimulant', involving the provision of infrastructure, education and training and support for technological development. The OECD adopts a similar position:

> strengthening competition through product-market deregulation and the removal of support to industry can be expected to result not only in a more rational allocation of resources but also in an improved capacity to respond to changes in the economic climate (1989, p. 148).

■ *10.15* Conclusion

It is mistaken to regard the deindustrialisation experienced by many advanced economies as a problem in its own right or as the manifestation of underlying structural problems. Taking a general view of trends in the industrial sector as a whole gives a very partial picture of the adjustments taking place. Disaggregated data need to be considered if the changes occurring are to be better understood. These reveal marked differences in performance within the industrial sector, with some areas showing signs of rejuvenation, sometimes as a result of the activities of multinationals. It also shows that the industrial sector should not be considered in isolation. Trends in services cannot be ignored, particularly since in many cases the prospects of industry and services are interdependent.

Adopting this wider perspective, for industries to vary in importance as tastes, incomes and conditions of supply alter over time is simply part of the normal operation of the process of change. Deindustrialisation in itself is only a concern if it is an indicator of wider problems in the economy, such as ineffective management, lack of innovation, a poorly educated workforce, or an inability to create and exploit market opportunities. There is no inherent reason for certain industries to be regarded as 'desirable' for the promotion of economic welfare. What is at issue is the way in which the individual firm is operated. Some are able to develop strategies that allow them to succeed where others fail.

The fundamental concern about deindustrialisation should not be with jobs, nor with trade volumes nor with the contribution of a particular area of the economy to GDP, but with economic welfare. The best way to ensure the satisfaction of wants in an uncertain and changing environment does not come from preserving particular sectors, but from allowing change to take place. An economy that is capable of rapid adjustment is an economy that has the potential for rapid growth. Policies typically advocated to counter deindustrialisation are harmful, because they seek to interfere with (and slow down) the process of change.

■ *Chapter 11* ■

Concluding Note

> But it is often more important to raise the right questions, even if they are highly tentative and there are no clear answers, than to come up with analytical answers to more precise but less important or even the wrong questions (B. Carlsson, 1985, p. 12).

After many years with few developments of note, since the mid-1970s industrial economics has evolved – and continues to evolve – in several directions. Neoclassical microeconomics remains well entrenched as the dominant body of theory underpinning industrial economics, but is being continually refined and modified. It is often argued that, in following the neoclassical tradition, industrial economics (along with microeconomics in general) took the 'wrong road'. For example, Nelson and Winter consider:

> What today's orthodoxy represents is, above all, a particular (and not inevitable) refinement and elaboration of the core ideas from that broader tradition relating to market functioning and self interested behaviour. The price paid for the refinement has been a considerable narrowing of focus and a tendency to segregate from the main corpus of theory the questions and phenomena for which the refined theory is ill-suited (1982, p. 43).

In seeking to replace the traditional approach, the new institutional economics has developed. Some economists have emphasised the role of transaction costs, incorporating an important feature of the real world into theory. This has enabled significant advances to be made in many areas of industrial economics, especially market failure and the organisation of the firm. The transaction cost approach is also of substantial interest because it places the firm (as opposed to the market or the industry) in the centre of the stage.

Other new institutional economists have begun to apply the ideas of the Austrian School. However, this view is still largely neglected. For instance, Clarke, in a textbook on industrial economics, contends:

> The alternative process analysis they [Austrians] offer is, however, somewhat thin on substantive concepts and theories, and often offers

259

little more than political support for a free market economy (1985, p. 6).

This conclusion is understandable, since a paradigm which eschews mathematical expression, and whose proponents lack interest in empirical work, must appear very alien to a modern neoclassical economist. This conclusion is also unfounded since Austrian theory is methodologically sound and theoretically elegant, and can be used to make important contributions to the study of industrial economics. Reid, for instance, believes that Austrian economics can provide the basis for 'whole new vistas of research possibilities' and suggests:

> The starting points are as with the older Austrianism – individualism, subjectivism, uncertainty and market processes – but modern analytical methods now offer the possibility of genuine theoretical advance, as distinct from barren restatement of established propositions (1987, p. 114).

Austrian economics is particularly appropriate to the formulation of policies to address issues of change in the economy, such as deindustrialisation or innovation.

The new institutional economics also introduces a different perspective on economic welfare, again with important implications for policy. It is no longer the case that issues of welfare revolve around the possibilities for improving resource allocation in a given environment. Any attempts to achieve a more equitable distribution of income, or to shelter particular groups from the impact of change, will adversely affect the growth of the economy by diverting resources and reducing incentives. Greater equity in the current time period comes at the price of reduced standards of living in the future.

The new institutional economics has its own limitations. For example, Austrian theorists assume that markets move towards equilibrium, implicitly believing that this process will be relatively rapid. In practice, the requisite preconditions for efficient markets may be missing. The supply of entrepreneurs, for instance, may not be highly elastic and, even if ample entrepreneurs were available, deficiencies in capital markets might prevent many operating effectively. Also, Austrians believe implicitly that market solutions are always superior. Hence, they fail to address issues of market failure. Despite such limitations, Austrian theory and the other elements of the new institutional economics offer a powerful alternative to neoclassical orthodoxy.

Turning to empirical work, no clear picture in support of the views of any one theoretical approach emerges. In part, this reflects deficiencies in the empirical studies: inappropriate data, poor quality data, missing variables, problems in capturing the complexity of the real world. However, the explanation probably goes much deeper. The rationale for cross-section studies rests on the assumption that all markets are in long-run equilibrium. A weaker assumption – that deviations from long-run equilibrium are randomly distributed and that these deviations are uncorrelated with the independent variables – might instead be made. Since relationships between variables often seem to be unstable over time, neither assumption appears valid.

It is plausible to suggest that, within an economy, forces which are equilibrating and those which are disequilibrating operate at the same time. The more dominant the forces driving markets towards equilibrium, the more likely it is that empirical tests will provide support for hypotheses drawn from the neoclassical paradigm. Even so, such studies will be unable to provide a complete explanation of the data. If the forces pushing the market away from equilibrium are strong, or markets are in flux such that the equilibrium to be attained changes frequently, then the contentions of neoclassical theory must fail to receive support from empirical work. This conclusion is reinforced if individual firms behave in ways different from the market as a whole, for instance as a result of efficiency advantages not possessed by their rivals. From these viewpoints, it could be argued that the general failure of economists to explain convincingly the workings of markets is indirect evidence of the presence of disequilibrating forces and of an inappropriate analytical focus.

Where does this leave the study of industrial economics? Salinger contends:

> One might argue that the primary lesson from three decades of cross-sectional studies is that general principles based on simple indicators are not to be had (1990, p. 287).

The same comment can be extended to theory: no one approach is yet sufficiently comprehensive to provide a unique theoretical basis. However, economists are generally quick to adapt successful developments and the mainstream view will continue to evolve, accreting to itself concepts from the new institutional economics as well as from public choice theory and principal–agent analysis, amongst others. The choice between theories should turn on their relative abilities to explain the phenomena that are the subject matter of industrial economics. In the twenty-first century, the standard approach to industrial economics is likely to be substantially different, although the form it will take cannot, yet, be anticipated.

■ *Appendix 1* ■

An Example of the Approach of the New Industrial Organisation

The form of analysis employed by the new industrial organisation (**Sections 1.4** and **2.6**) can be shown by considering the *Cournot model of duopoly*. In the basic Cournot case both firms are identical. Each maximises its own profits under the naive behavioural assumption that, should it alter its own output, its rival will not react. (The *conjectural variation* is therefore zero.) Assuming a linear market demand function then:

$$P = a - bQ \qquad\qquad (A1.1)$$

where: $Q = q_1 + q_2$

The profit of Firm 1 will therefore equal:

$$\pi_1 = Pq_1 - cq_1 \qquad\qquad (A1.2)$$

where: c equals average and marginal cost

To establish the profit-maximising output for Firm 1 requires equation (A1.2) to be differentiated with respect to q_1 and then set to zero. (Given the belief that Firm 2's output will be unchanged $dq_1 = dQ$.) This gives:

$$\frac{d\pi_1}{dq_1} = P + \frac{dP}{dQ}q_1 - c = 0 \qquad\qquad (A1.3)$$

which, with substitution from (A1.1), and noting that $dP/dQ = -b$, gives:

$$a - 2bq_1 - bq_2 - c = 0 \qquad\qquad (A1.4)$$

By rearrangement of this equation, the profit-maximising output for Firm 1 becomes:

$$q_1 = \frac{a-c}{2b} - \frac{1}{2}q_2 \qquad\qquad (A1.5)$$

This gives Firm 1's reaction function (that is, its most profitable output given the output level chosen by Firm 2). Since Firm 2 is identical, its reaction function is therefore:

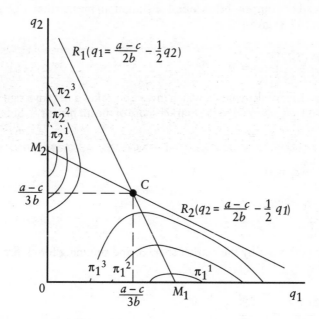

Figure A1.1 *Cournot duopoly*

$$q_2 = \frac{a-c}{2b} - \frac{1}{2}q_1 \tag{A1.6}$$

Market equilibrium is found by substituting (A1.6) into (A1.5) and solving for q_1. This gives $q_1 = (a-c)/3b$ and a market output of $2(a-c)/3b$. This solution is represented graphically in **Figure A1.1**

The reaction functions for both firms (R_1 and R_2) cut the maximum point of any particular isoprofit curve(π_i). (Note that the isoprofit curves with the *superscript* 1 represent a higher level of profits than those with the *superscript* 2.) If Firm 1 produced zero output then Firm 2 would maximise profits by selecting output M_2 (the monopoly level of output). The Cournot solution is depicted by point C where the reaction functions intersect.

The Cournot duopoly model can be extended to any number of firms in the market and to allow for variations in their costs. The assumption of linear market demand can also be relaxed. The profit for Firm i will therefore equal:

$$\pi_i = Pq_i - c_iq_i \tag{A1.7}$$

Differentiating gives:

$$\frac{d\pi_i}{dq_i} = P + q_i\frac{dP}{dQ}\frac{dQ}{dq_i} - c_i = 0 \tag{A1.8}$$

Maintaining the Cournot behavioural assumption means that $dQ/dq_i = 1$. Rearranging (A1.8) gives:

$$P\left(1 + \frac{dP}{dQ}\frac{Q}{P}\frac{q_i}{Q}\right) - c_i = 0 \tag{A1.9}$$

But price elasticity of demand (ε, which invariably takes a negative sign) is (dQ/dP). (P/Q) and q_i/Q is equal to the market share of the ith firm or S_i. Substituting gives:

$$P\left(1 + \frac{S_i}{\varepsilon}\right) - c_i = 0 \tag{A1.10}$$

$$\frac{P - c_i}{P} = -\frac{S_i}{\varepsilon} \tag{A1.11}$$

Multiplying both sides by the market share S_i and summing for all firms in the market gives:

$$\frac{(P\Sigma S_i - \Sigma c_i S_i)}{P} = -\frac{\Sigma S_i^2}{\varepsilon} \tag{A1.12}$$

$\Sigma S_i^2 = HHI$ (the Herfindahl–Hirschman Index). If c_m represents the weighted marginal cost of the market, then (A1.12) becomes:

$$\frac{(P - c_m)}{P} = -\frac{HHI}{\varepsilon} \tag{A1.13}$$

(With the value of ε negative, the price–cost margin in this equation is positive.)

This shows that a profit-maximising firm's price–cost margin is determined by structural variables, namely the number and size distribution of the firms in the market (as measured by the Herfindahl–Hirschman index) and the price elasticity of demand of the product. In contrast to the traditional SCP approach, performance is not determined by market structure; rather structure and performance are determined simultaneously.

The result derived in equation (A1.13) is contingent on the firms following the Cournot behavioural assumption. This conduct assumption can be changed by adopting different conjectures regarding the reactions of other firms to one firm's change in its own output, i.e. dQ/dq_i will not equal 1. In this more general case structure, *conduct* and performance are simultaneously determined.

■ *Appendix 2* ■

The Dorfman and Steiner Condition for Optimal Advertising Levels

Dorfman and Steiner (1954) show that, for a profit-maximising monopolist, the optimal level of advertising expenditure is dependent upon price and advertising elasticities:

$$\frac{A}{PQ} = -\frac{\varepsilon_a}{\varepsilon} \tag{A2.1}$$

where: A = advertising expenditure
P = price
Q = sales
ε_a = advertising elasticity
ε = price elasticity of demand (which invariably takes a negative sign)

This condition is derived as follows. Sales (Q) depend on the levels of both price (P) and advertising expenditure (A). Total costs comprise the costs of production (CQ) and advertising (A). Profit (π) is therefore:

$$\pi = PQ - CQ - A \tag{A2.2}$$

where: $Q = f(P, A)$

Partially differentiating to find the price and advertising levels which maximise profit gives the first-order conditions:

$$\frac{\partial \pi}{\partial P} = Q + P\frac{\partial Q}{\partial P} - \frac{\partial C}{\partial Q}\frac{\partial Q}{\partial P} = 0 \tag{A2.3}$$

$$\frac{\partial \pi}{\partial A} = P\frac{\partial Q}{\partial A} - \frac{\partial C}{\partial Q}\frac{\partial Q}{\partial A} - 1 = 0 \tag{A2.4}$$

From equation (A2.3), dividing by $P\,(\partial Q/\partial P)$ gives:

$$\frac{Q}{P}\frac{\partial P}{\partial Q} + 1 - \frac{\partial C}{P\partial Q} = 0 \tag{A2.5}$$

This can be rearranged to give:

$$\frac{P\partial Q - \partial C}{P\partial Q} = -\frac{Q}{P}\frac{\partial P}{\partial Q} \tag{A2.6}$$

and then:

$$\frac{(P - \frac{\partial C}{\partial Q})}{P} = -\frac{Q}{\partial Q}\frac{\partial P}{P} \tag{A2.7}$$

but:

$$\varepsilon = \frac{\partial Q}{Q}\frac{P}{\partial P} \tag{A2.8}$$

Substituting (A2.8) into (A2.7) gives:

$$\frac{(P - \frac{\partial C}{\partial Q})}{P} = -\frac{1}{\varepsilon} \tag{A2.9}$$

This is the familiar result that profits are maximised when the price–cost margin (Lerner index) equals the reciprocal of the price elasticity of demand (ε).

Equation (A2.4) can be rearranged to give:

$$(P - \frac{\partial C}{\partial A})\frac{\partial Q}{\partial A} - 1 = 0 \tag{A2.10}$$

This can be further rearranged to give:

$$\frac{\partial Q}{\partial A} = \frac{1}{P - \frac{\partial C}{\partial Q}} \tag{A2.11}$$

Multiplying by P gives:

$$P\frac{\partial Q}{\partial A} = \frac{P}{(P - \frac{\partial C}{\partial Q})} \tag{A2.12}$$

but from (A2.9):

$$\frac{(P - \frac{\partial C}{\partial Q})}{P} = -\frac{1}{\varepsilon} \tag{A2.13}$$

therefore:

$$\frac{P\partial Q}{\partial A} = -\varepsilon \tag{A2.14}$$

The Dorfman–Steiner condition can then be derived multiplying by A/Q:

$$\frac{P\partial Q}{\partial A}\frac{A}{Q} = -\frac{\varepsilon A}{Q} \tag{A2.15}$$

and rearranging. Since the expression for the advertising elasticity of demand is:

$$\varepsilon_a = \frac{\partial Q}{Q}\frac{A}{\partial A} \tag{A2.16}$$

Equation (A2.15) becomes:

$$\frac{A}{PQ} = -\frac{\varepsilon_a}{\varepsilon} \tag{A2.17}$$

Dorfman and Steiner assume that the effects of advertising are fully realised in the current time period. Nerlove and Arrow (1962) modify the analysis to recognise advertising's effects in both current and future time periods:

$$\frac{A}{PQ} = -\frac{\varepsilon_a}{\varepsilon\,(r+d)} \tag{A2.18}$$

where: r = rate of discount
d = depreciation rate of the advertising capital

Adopting this approach, the longer-lived the effects of advertising, and the lower the rate at which future earnings are discounted, the higher will be the optimal advertising intensity.

■ *Appendix 3* ■

Harberger's Method of Estimating the Welfare Effects of Monopoly

From the geometry of **Figure 5.1**, the triangular area 3 (the deadweight welfare loss, W) is equal to:

$$W = \frac{1}{2}\Delta P \Delta Q \qquad (A3.1)$$

where ΔP and ΔQ are respectively the discrete absolute differences in price (P) and in output (Q) between perfect competition and monopoly.

Since arc price elasticity of demand (ε) is defined as:

$$\varepsilon = \frac{\Delta Q}{Q}\frac{P}{\Delta P} \qquad (A3.2)$$

substituting for ΔQ in (A3.2) from equation (A3.1) gives:

$$W = \frac{1}{2}\Delta P \frac{\Delta P}{P} Q\varepsilon \qquad (A3.3)$$

This can be rearranged to give the formula used by Harberger (1954) to calculate welfare loss:

$$W = \frac{1}{2}\left(\frac{\Delta P}{P}\right)^2 PQ\varepsilon \qquad (A3.4)$$

■ *Appendix 4* ■

Cowling and Mueller's Method of Estimating the Welfare Effects of Monopoly

Since total revenue (TR) is equal to selling price (P) multiplied by the quantity sold (Q) or:

$$TR = PQ \tag{A4.1}$$

marginal revenue is:

$$MR = \frac{dTR}{dQ} = P + Q\frac{dP}{dQ} \tag{A4.2}$$

Rearranging gives:

$$MR = P\left(1 + \frac{Q}{P}\frac{dP}{dQ}\right) \tag{A4.3}$$

Noting that price elasticity of demand (ε), which is invariably negative, is defined as:

$$\varepsilon = \frac{dQ}{Q}\frac{P}{dP} \tag{A4.4}$$

Substituting (A4.4) into (A4.3) gives:

$$MR = P\left(1 + \frac{1}{\varepsilon}\right) \tag{A4.5}$$

For profit maximisation $MC = MR$, therefore equation (A4.5) can be rewritten:

$$MC = P\left(1 + \frac{1}{\varepsilon}\right) \tag{A4.6}$$

which can be rearranged to give the Lerner condition (see also equation (A2.9)):

$$\frac{P-MC}{P} = -\frac{1}{\varepsilon} \tag{A4.7}$$

Hence:

$$\varepsilon = -\frac{P}{P - MC} \qquad (A4.8)$$

Since $P - MC = \Delta P$ (in absolute terms), equation (A4.8) becomes:

$$\varepsilon = \frac{P}{\Delta P} \qquad (A4.9)$$

Substituting for ε in equation (A3.2) gives:

$$\frac{\Delta Q}{Q}\frac{P}{\Delta P} = \frac{P}{\Delta P} \qquad (A4.10)$$

Dividing both sides by $P/\Delta P$ gives:

$$\frac{\Delta Q}{Q} = 1 \qquad (A4.11)$$

This can be incorporated into equation (A3.1) in Appendix 3, which now simplifies to:

$$W = \frac{1}{2}\Delta PQ \qquad (A4.12)$$

Profits in a monopoly (π) are:

$$\pi = (P - C)Q \qquad (A4.13)$$

Where costs are constant, such that average cost $(C) = MC$, then:

$$\pi = \Delta PQ \qquad (A4.14)$$

Cowling and Mueller's (1978) first measure of welfare loss becomes:

$$W = \frac{\pi}{2} \qquad (A4.15)$$

References

Abbott, A. F. and G. L. Brady, 'Welfare Gains from Innovation-induced Rent Seeking', *Cato Journal*, vol. 11 (1991) pp. 89–97.

Adams, H. C., *Relation of the State to Industrial Action* (1887), reprinted edn (New York: Columbia University Press, 1887).

Advertising Association, *Advertising Statistics Yearbook 1992* (Henley-on-Thames: NTC Publications, 1992).

Advertising Association, *Advertising Statistics Yearbook 1993* (Henley-on-Thames: NTC Publications, 1993).

Albion, M. S. and P. W. Farris, *The Advertising Controversy* (Boston, Mass.: Auburn House, 1981).

Albon, R. P. and M. G. Kirby, 'Cost Padding in Profit-Regulated Firms', *Economic Record*, vol. 59 (1983) pp. 16–27.

Alchian, A. A. and H. Demsetz, 'Production, Information Costs, and Economic Organisation', *American Economic Review*, vol. 62 (1972) pp. 777–95.

Aldington, Lord, 'Britain's Manufacturing Industry', *Royal Bank of Scotland Review*, vol. 151 (1986) pp. 3–13.

Alessi, L. de, 'An Economic Analysis of Government Ownership and Regulation: Theory and Evidence from the Electric Power Industry', *Public Choice*, vol. 19 (1974) pp. 1–42.

Alessi, L. de, 'Some Effects of Ownership on the Wholesale Prices of Electric Power', *Economic Inquiry*, vol. 13 (1975) pp. 526–38.

Amato, L. and R. P. Wilder, 'Market Concentration, Efficiency and Antitrust Policy: Demsetz Revisited', *Quarterly Journal of Business and Economics*, vol. 27 (1988) pp. 3–19.

Amel, D. F. and S. A. Rhoades, 'Strategic Groups in Banking', *Review of Economics and Statistics*, vol. 70 (1988) pp. 685–9.

Andersen, O. and M. Rynning, 'An Empirical Illustration of an Alternative Approach to Measuring the Market Power and High Profits Hypothesis', *International Journal of Industrial Organisation*, vol. 9 (1991) pp. 239–49.

Andrews, P. W. S., *On Competition in Economic Theory* (London: Macmillan, 1964).

Andrews, P. W. S. and E. Brunner, *Studies in Pricing* (London: Macmillan, 1975).

Armstrong, H. and J. Taylor, 'Regional Policy', in G. B. J. Atkinson (ed.) *Developments in Economics: An Annual Review*, vol. 1 (Ormskirk: Causeway Press, 1985).

Arrow, K. J., 'The Organisation of Economic Activity', in *The Analysis and Evaluation of Public Expenditure: The PPB System* (Washington, DC: Joint Economic Committee, 91st Congress, 1st Session, 1969).

Arrow, K. J. and F. H. Hahn, *General Competitive Analysis* (San Francisco: Holden-Day, 1971).

271

Atkinson, S. E. and R. Halvorsen, 'Efficiency of Public and Private Firms', *Journal of Public Economics*, vol. 29 (1986) pp. 281–94.

Audit Commission, *Securing Further Improvements in Refuse Collection* (London: HMSO, 1984).

Averch, H. and L. L. Johnson, 'Behaviour of the Firm Under Regulatory Constraint', *American Economic Review*, vol. 52 (1962) pp. 1052–69.

Backman, J., *Advertising and Competition* (New York: University Press, 1967).

Bacon, R. and W. Eltis, *Britain's Economic Problem: Too Few Producers* (London: Macmillan, 1976).

Baden-Fuller, C. and J. M. Stopford, *Rejuvenating the Mature Business: The Competitive Challenge* (London: Routledge, 1992).

Bain, J. S., 'The Profit Rate as a Measure of Monopoly Power', *Quarterly Journal of Economics*, vol. 55 (1941) pp. 271–93.

Bain, J. S., 'Relation of Profit Rate to Industrial Concentration: American Manufacturing 1936–40', *Quarterly Journal of Economics*, vol. 65 (1951) pp. 293–324.

Bain, J. S., *Barriers to New Competition* (Cambridge, Mass.: Harvard University Press, 1956).

Bain, J. S., *Industrial Organisation*, 2nd edn (New York: Wiley, 1968).

Bain, J. S., 'The Comparative Stability of Market Structure', in J. W. Markham and G. F. Papanek (eds), *Industrial Organisation and Economic Development: Essays in Honor of E. S. Mason* (Boston, Mass.: Houghton Mifflin, 1970).

Bank of England, 'Services in the UK Economy', *Bank of England Quarterly Bulletin*, vol. 25 (1985) pp. 404–14.

Bariam, E. I., 'Income Elasticities of Imports and Exports: A Re-examination of the Empirical Evidence', *Applied Economics*, vol. 25 (1993) pp. 71–4.

Barker, T. S. and J. P. Dunne, *The British Economy After Oil: Manufacturing or Services?* (London: Croom Helm, 1988).

Baumol, W. J., 'Contestable Markets: An Uprising in the Theory of Industrial Structure', *American Economic Review*, vol. 72 (1982) pp. 1–15.

Beesley, M. and S. Littlechild, 'Privatisation: Principles, Problems and Priorities', *Lloyds Bank Review*, vol. 149 (1983) pp. 1–20.

Behrman, J. N., *Industrial Policies: International Restructuring and Transnationals* (Lexington, Mass.: Lexington Books, 1984).

Bell, W., 'The Effects of Monopoly Profits and Wages on Prices and Consumers' Surplus in US Manufacturing', *Western Economic Journal*, vol. 6 (1968) pp. 233–41.

Benham, L., 'The Effect of Advertising on the Price of Eyeglasses', *Journal of Law and Economics*, vol. 15 (1972) pp. 337–52.

Berger, A. N. and T. H. Hannan, 'The Price–Concentration Relationship in Banking', *Review of Economic Studies*, vol. 71 (1989) pp. 291–9.

Berger, A. N. and T. H. Hannan, 'The Price–Concentration Relationship in Banking: A Reply', *Review of Economic Studies*, vol. 74 (1992) pp. 376–9.

Bergsten, C. F., T. Horst and T. H. Moran, *American Multinationals and American Interests* (Washington, DC: Brookings Institution, 1978).

Biggadike, E., *Corporate Diversification: Entry, Strategy and Performance*, MA

Thesis (Cambridge, Mass.: Harvard University, 1976).

Binder, J., 'Beta, Firm Size and Concentration', *Economic Inquiry*, vol. 15 (1992) pp. 556–63.

Bishop, M. and J. A. Kay, *The Impact of Privatisation on the Performance of the UK Public Sector*, Paper for the CEPR/IMPG Conference in Milan (1991).

Blaug, M., *Economic Theory in Retrospect*, 2nd edn (London: Heinemann, 1968).

Bloch, H., 'Advertising and Profitability: A Reappraisal', *Journal of Political Economy*, vol. 82 (1974) pp. 267–86.

Bluestone, B. and B. Harrison, *The Deindustrialisation of America* (New York: Basic Books, 1982).

Boardman, A. E. and A. R. Vining, 'Ownership and Performance in Competitive Environments: A Comparison of the Performance of Private, Mixed and State-owned Enterprises, *Journal of Law and Economics*, vol. 32 (1989) pp. 1–33.

Boonekamp, C., 'Industrial Policies of Industrial Countries', *Finance and Development*, vol. 26 (1989) pp. 14–17.

Boonekamp, C., 'Voluntary Export Restraints', in P. King (ed.), *International Economics and International Economic Policy* (New York: McGraw-Hill, 1990).

Borcherding, T. E., W. W. Pommerehne and F. Schneider, 'Comparing the Efficiency of Private and Public Production: The Evidence from Five Countries', *Zeitschrift Für Nationalökonomie*, Supplement 2 (1982) pp. 127–56.

Borden, N. H., *The Economic Effects of Advertising* (Chicago, Ill.: Irwin, 1942).

Bothwell. J. L., C. F. Cooley and T. E. Hall, 'A New View of the Market Structure–Performance Debate', *Journal of Industrial Economics*, vol. 32 (1984) pp. 397–417.

Bound, J., C. Cummins, Z. Griliches, B. H. Hall and A. Jaffe, 'Who Does R&D and Who Patents?', in Z. Griliches (ed.), *R&D Patents and Productivity* (Chicago, Ill.: University Press, 1984).

Bresnahan, T. F., 'Empirical Studies of Industries with Market Power', in R. Schmalensee and R. D. Willig (eds), *Handbook of Industrial Organisation Volume II* (Amsterdam: North-Holland, 1989).

Bresnahan, T. F. and P. C. Reiss, 'Entry and Competition in Concentrated Markets', *Journal of Political Economy*, vol. 99 (1991) pp. 977–1009.

Brittan, S., 'Privatisation: A Comment on Kay and Thompson', *Economic Journal*, vol. 96 (1986) pp. 18–32.

Bronsteen, P., 'A Review of the Revised Merger Guidelines', *Antitrust Bulletin*, vol. 29 (1984) pp. 613–52.

Brown, C. J. F. and T. D. Sheriff, 'Deindustrialisation: A Background Paper', in F. Blackaby (ed.), *Deindustrialisation* (London: Heinemann Educational, 1979).

Brown, R. S., 'Estimating Advantages to Large Scale Advertising', *Review of Economics and Statistics*, vol. 60 (1978) pp. 428–37.

Brozen, Y., 'The Anti-Trust Task Force Deconcentration Recommendation',

Journal of Law and Economics, vol. 13 (1970) pp. 279–92.

Brozen, Y., 'Bain's Concentration and Rates of Return Revisited', *Journal of Law and Economics*, vol. 14 (1971) pp. 351–69.

Brozen, Y., *Is Government the Source of Monopoly? and Other Essays* (New York: CATO Institute, 1980).

Bruggink, T. H., 'Public Versus Private Enterprise in the Municipal Water Industry: A Comparison of Operating Costs', *Quarterly Review of Economics and Business*, vol. 22 (1982) pp. 111–25.

Buchanan, J. M., *Demand and Supply of Public Goods* (Chicago, Ill.: Rand McNally, 1968).

Buckley, P. J. and P. Artisien, 'Policy Issues of Intra-EC Direct Investment: British, French and German Multinationals in Greece, Portugal and Spain, with Special Reference to Employment Effects', in J. H. Dunning and P. Robson (eds), *Multinationals and the European Community* (Oxford: Basil Blackwell, 1988).

Burnett, L., *What Makes a Top Brand* (London: Leo Burnett Ltd, 1979).

Burton, J., *Picking Losers....?* (London: Institute of Economic Affairs, 1983).

Button, K. J. and T. E. Keeler, 'The Regulation of Transport Markets', *Economic Journal*, vol. 103 (1993) pp. 1017–27.

Buzzell, R. D. and P. W. Farris, 'Marketing Costs in Consumer Goods Industries', in H. B. Thorelli (ed.), *Strategy + Structure = Performance* (Bloomington: Indiana University Press, 1977).

Byatt, I., N. Hartley, R. Lomax, S. Powell and P. Spencer, *North Sea Oil and Structural Adjustment*, Government Economic Service Working Paper No. 54 (London: HM Treasury, 1982).

Cabinet Office, *International Comparisons of Research and Development Spending* (London: HMSO, 1992).

Cable, J., 'Market Structure, Advertising Policy, and Intermarket Differences in Advertising Intensity', in K. Cowling (ed.), *Market Structure and Corporate Behaviour* (London: Macmillan, 1972).

Cady, J., 'Advertising Restrictions and Retail Prices', *Journal of Advertising Research*, vol. 16 (1976) pp. 27–30.

Cairncross, A., 'What is Deindustrialisation?', in F. Blackaby (ed.), *Deindustrialisation* (London: Heinemann Educational, 1979).

Cambridge Economic Policy Group, *Cambridge Economic Policy Review No. 2* (Aldershot: Gower, 1976).

Cambridge Economic Policy Group, *Cambridge Economic Policy Review No. 3* (Aldershot: Gower, 1977).

Cambridge Economic Policy Group, *Cambridge Economic Policy Review No. 4* (Aldershot: Gower, 1978).

Cannon, C. M., 'International Trade, Concentration and Competition in UK Consumer Goods Markets', *Oxford Economic Papers*, vol. 30 (1978) pp. 130–7.

Carlsson, B., 'Reflections on "Industrial Dynamics": The Challenges Ahead', Presidential Address to Twelfth EARIE Conference (1985).

Carlsson, B., 'Industrial Dynamics: An Overview', in B. Carlsson (ed.), *Industrial Dynamics* (Dordrecht: Kluwer, 1989).

Carsberg, B., 'Injecting Competition into Telecommunications', in C. Veljanovski (ed.), *Privatisation and Competition: A Market Prospectus* (London: Institute of Economic Affairs, 1989).

Carter, J. R., 'Collusion, Efficiency and Antitrust', *Journal of Law and Economics*, vol. 21 (1978) pp. 435–44.

Casson, M., *The Entrepreneur: An Economic Theory* (Oxford: Robertson/ Blackwell, 1982).

Caves, D. W. and L. R. Christensen, 'The Relative Efficiency of Public and Private Firms in a Competitive Environment: The Case of Canadian Railroads', *Journal of Political Economy*, vol. 88 (1980) pp. 958–76.

Caves, R. E. and M. E. Porter, 'From Entry Barriers to Mobility Barriers', *Quarterly Journal of Economics*, vol. 91 (1977) pp. 241–62.

Caves, R. E. and M. E. Porter, 'Market Structure, Oligopoly and the Stability of Market Shares', *Journal of Industrial Economics*, vol. 26 (1978) pp. 289– 313.

Caves, R. E., 'The Structure of Industry', in M. Feldstein (ed.), *The American Economy in Transition* (Chicago, Ill.: University Press, 1980).

Central Statistical Office, *Standard Industrial Classification, Revised 1968* (London: HMSO, 1968).

Central Statistical Office, *Standard Industrial Classification, Revised 1980* (London: HMSO, 1979).

Chamberlin, E. H., *The Theory of Monopolistic Competition*, 8th edn (Cambridge, Mass.: Harvard University Press, 1962).

Clark, J. M., 'Towards a Concept of Workable Competition', *American Economic Review*, vol. 30 (1940) pp. 241–56.

Clark, J. M., *Competition as a Dynamic Process* (Washington, DC: Brookings Institution, 1961).

Clarke, D. G., 'Econometric Measurement of the Duration of Advertising Effect on Sales', *Journal of Marketing Research*, vol. 13 (1976) pp. 345–57.

Clarke, R., 'Profit Margins and Market Concentration in UK Manufacturing Industry', *Applied Economics*, vol. 16 (1984) pp. 57–71.

Clarke, R., *Industrial Economics* (Oxford: Basil Blackwell, 1985).

Clarke, R. and S. W. Davies, 'Market Structure and Price–Cost Margins', *Economica*, vol. 49 (1982) pp. 277–88.

Clarke, R. and S. W. Davies, 'Aggregate Concentration, Market Concentration and Diversification', *Economic Journal*, vol. 93 (1983) pp. 182–92.

Clarke, R., S. W. Davies and M. Waterson, 'The Profitability–Concentration Relation: Market Power or Efficiency?', *Journal of Industrial Economics*, vol. 32 (1984) pp. 435–50.

Coase, R., 'The Nature of the Firm', *Economica*, vol. 4 (1937) pp. 386–405.

Coase, R., 'The Problem of Social Cost', *Journal of Law and Economics*, vol. 3 (1960) pp. 1–44.

Coate, M. B., 'The Dynamics of Price–Cost Margins in Concentrated Industries', *Applied Economics*, vol. 21 (1988) pp. 261–72.

Coate, M. B., 'Economics, the Guidelines and the Evolution of Merger Policy', *Antitrust Bulletin*, vol. 37 (1992) pp. 997–1024.

Cocks, D., 'Production Innovation and the Dynamic Elements of Competition in the Ethical Pharmaceutical Industry', in R. B. Helms (ed.), *Drug Development and Marketing* (Washington, DC: Center for Health Policy Research of the American Enterprise Institute, 1973).

Cohen, W. M. and R. C. Levin, 'Innovation and Market Structure', in R. Schmalensee and R. D. Willig (eds), *Handbook of Industrial Organisation Volume II* (Amsterdam: North-Holland, 1989).

Colenutt, D. W. and P. P. O'Donnell, 'The Consistency of Monopolies and Mergers Commission Reports', *Antitrust Bulletin*, vol. 20 (1978) pp. 51–82.

Colley, R. H., *Defining Goals for Measuring Advertising Results* (New York: Association of National Advertisers, 1961).

Collyns, C. and S. Dunaway, 'The Cost of Trade Restraints: The Case of Japanese Automobile Exports to the US', in P. King (ed.), *International Economics and International Economic Policy* (New York: McGraw-Hill, 1990).

Comanor, W. S. and T. A. Wilson, *Advertising and Market Power* (Cambridge, Mass.: Harvard University Press, 1974).

Comanor, W. S. and T. A. Wilson, 'The Effect of Advertising on Competition: A Survey', *Journal of Economic Literature*, vol. 17 (1979) pp. 453–76.

Commission of the European Communities, *Memorandum on the Community's Industrial Policy* (Luxembourg: Office for Official Publications of the European Communities, 1970a).

Commission of the European Communities, *Nomenclature Générale des Activités Economiques dans les Communautés Européennes* (Luxembourg: Office for Official Publications of the European Communities, 1970b).

Commission of the European Communities, *First Report on Competition Policy* (Luxembourg: Office for Official Publications of the European Communities, 1972).

Commission of the European Communities, *Treaties Establishing the European Communities* (Luxembourg: Office for Official Publications of the European Communities, 1973).

Commission of the European Communities, *European Regional Development Fund: Ninth Annual Report* (Luxembourg: Office for Official Publications of the European Communities, 1984).

Commission of the European Communities, *Fourteenth Report on Competition Policy* (Luxembourg: Office for Official Publications of the European Communities, 1985).

Commission of the European Communities, *Fifteenth Report on Competition Policy* (Luxembourg: Office for Official Publications of the European Communities, 1986a).

Commission of the European Communities, *Nineteenth General Report on the Activities of the European Communities* (Luxembourg: Office for Official Publications of the European Communities, 1986b).

Commission of the European Communities, *Competition Rules in the EEC and the ECSC Applicable to State Aids* (Luxembourg: Office for Official Publications of the European Communities, 1987).

Commission of the European Communities, *Industrial Policy in an Open and Competitive Environment*, COM (90) 556 (Luxembourg: Office for Official

Publications of the European Communities, 1990a).

Commission of the European Communities, *Official Journal of the European Communities*, L 293 (Luxembourg: Office for Official Publications of the European Communities, 1990b).

Commission of the European Communities, *Improving the Competitiveness of the Community's Textile and Clothing Industry*, COM (91) 399 (Luxembourg: Office for Official Publications of the European Communities, 1991a).

Commission of the European Communities, *The Regions in the 1990s* (Luxembourg: Office for Official Publications of the European Communities, 1991b).

Commission of the European Communities, *Twenty First Report on Competition Policy* (Luxembourg: Office for Official Publications of the European Communities, 1992a).

Commission of the European Communities, *Reform of the Structural Funds: A Tool to Promote Economic and Social Cohesion* (Luxembourg: Office for Official Publications of the European Communities, 1992b).

Commission of the European Communities, *Third Survey on State Aids in the European Community in the Manufacturing and Other Sectors* (Luxembourg: Office for Official Publications of the European Communities, 1992c).

Connor, J. M. and E. B. Petersen, 'Market-Structure Determinants of National Brand–Private Label Price Differences of Manufactured Food Products', *Journal of Industrial Economics*, vol. 40 (1992) pp. 157–71.

Cornell, N. W. and D. W. Webbink, 'Public Utility Rate of Return Regulation: Can it Ever Protect Consumers?', in R. W. Poole (ed.), *Unnatural Monopolies: The Case for Deregulating Public Utilities* (Lexington, Mass.: Lexington Books, 1985).

Cowling, K. (ed.), *Market Structure and Corporate Behaviour: Theory and Empirical Analysis of the Firm* (London: Gray-Mills, 1972).

Cowling, K., 'A New Industrial Strategy', *International Journal of Industrial Organisation*, vol. 8 (1990) pp. 165–83.

Cowling, K. and D. Mueller, 'The Social Costs of Monopoly', *Economic Journal*, vol. 88 (1978) pp. 727-48.

Cowling, K. and M. Waterson, 'Price–Cost Margins and Market Structure', *Economica*, vol. 43 (1976) pp. 267–74.

Cowling, K., J. Cable, M. Kelly and T. McGuiness, *Advertising and Economic Behaviour* (London: Macmillan, 1975).

Cox, S. R., A. C. Deserpa and W. C. Canby, 'The Pricing of Legal Services', *Journal of Industrial Economics*, vol. 30 (1982) pp. 305–18.

Crafts, N., *Can De-Industrialisation Seriously Damage Your Wealth?* (London: Institute of Economic Affairs, 1993).

Crain, W. M and A. Zardkoohi, 'A Test of the Property Rights Theory of the Firm', *Journal of Law and Economics*, vol. 21 (1978) pp. 395–408.

Crain, W. M and A. Zardkoohi, 'Public Sector Expansion: Stagnant Technology or Property Rights', *Southern Economic Journal*, vol. 46 (1980) pp. 1069–82.

Cremer, J. and M. Sirbu, 'Une Analyse Econométrique de l'Effort de Recherche et Developpement de l'Industrie Française', *Revue Economique*, vol. 29 (1978) pp. 940–54.

Cubbin, J. and P. A. Geroski, *The Persistence of Profits in the UK*, Discussion paper no. 8704 (Department of Economics, University of Southampton, 1987a).

Cubbin, J. and P. A. Geroski, 'The Convergence of Profits in the Long Run: Inter-firm and Inter-industry Comparisons', *Journal of Industrial Economics*, vol. 35 (1987b) pp. 427–42.

Cyert, R. M. and J. G. March, *A Behavioural Theory of the Firm* (Engelwood Cliffs, NJ: Prentice-Hall, 1963).

Daniels, P. W. and F. Moulaert, *The Changing Geography of Advanced Producer Services* (London: Belhaven Press, 1991).

Davies, D. G., 'The Efficiency of Public versus Private Firms: The Case of Australia's Two Airlines', *Journal of Law and Economics*, vol. 14 (1971) pp. 149–65.

Davies, D. G., 'Property Rights and Economic Efficiency – The Australian Airlines Revisited', *Journal of Law and Economics*, vol. 20 (1977) pp. 223–6.

Davis, E. H. 'Express Coaching Since 1980: Liberalisation in Practice', *Fiscal Studies*, vol. 5 (1984) pp. 76–86.

Davis, E. H., J. A. Kay and J. Star, 'Is Advertising Rational?', *Business Strategy Review*, vol. 2/3 (1991) pp. 1–23.

Demsetz, H., 'Why Regulate Utilities?', *Journal of Law and Economics*, vol. 11 (1968) pp. 55–65.

Demsetz, H., 'Industry Structure, Market Rivalry, and Public Policy', *Journal of Law and Economics*, vol. 16 (1973) pp. 1–9.

Demsetz, H., 'Advertising in the Affluent Society', in Y. Brozen (ed.), *Advertising and Society* (New York: University Press, 1974a).

Demsetz, H., 'Two Systems of Belief About Monopoly', in H. J. Goldschmid, H. M. Mann and J. F. Weston (eds), *Industrial Concentration: the New Learning* (Boston, Mass.: Little, Brown, 1974b).

Demsetz, H., *Economic, Legal and Political Dimensions of Competition* (Amsterdam: North-Holland, 1982).

Demsetz, H, 'The Theory of the Firm Revisited', in O. E. Williamson and S. G. Winter (eds), *The Nature of the Firm: Origins, Evolution, and Development* (New York: Oxford University Press, 1991).

Demsetz, H., 'How Many Cheers for Antitrust's 100 Years?' *Economic Inquiry*, vol. 30 (1992) pp. 201–17.

Denison, E. F., *Why Growth Rates Differ* (Washington, DC: Brookings Institution, 1967).

Denison, E. F., *Accounting for United States Economic Growth, 1929-1969* (Washington, DC: Brookings Institution, 1974).

Department of Prices and Consumer Protection, *A Review of Monopolies and Mergers Policy: A Consultative Document*, Cmnd 7198 (London: HMSO, 1978).

Department of Trade and Industry, *Regional Industrial Development*, Cmnd 9111 (London: HMSO, 1983).

Department of Trade and Industry, Business Statistics Office, *Industrial*

Research and Development Expenditure and Employment, 1981, Business Monitor MO14 (London: HMSO, 1985).

Department of Trade and Industry, *Recent Trends in UK Concentration* (unpublished, 1986).

Department of Trade and Industry, Business Statistics Office, *Report on the Census of Production: Summary Tables*, Business Monitor, PA1002 (London: HMSO, various years).

Dertouzos, M. L., R. K. Lester, R. M. Solow and the MIT Commission on Industrial Productivity, *Made in America: Regaining the Productive Edge* (Cambridge, Mass.: MIT Press, 1989).

Di Lorenzo, T. J. and R. Robinson, 'Managerial Objectives Subject to Political Market Constraints: Electric Utilities in the US', *Quarterly Review of Economics and Business*, vol. 22 (1982) pp. 113–25.

Dickson, V., 'The Relationship Between Concentration and Prices and Concentration and Costs', *Applied Economics*, vol. 23 (1991) pp. 101–6.

Dixit, A., 'Recent Developments in Oligopoly Theory', *American Economic Review, Papers and Proceedings*, vol. 72 (1982) pp. 12–17.

Domberger, S. and J. Piggott, 'Privatisation Policies and Public Enterprise: A Survey', Economic Record, vol. 62 (1986) pp. 145–62.

Domberger, S., S. A. Meadowcroft and D. J. Thompson, 'Competitive Tendering and Efficiency: The Case of Refuse Collection', *Fiscal Studies*, vol. 7 (1986) pp. 69–87.

Domowitz, I., R. G. Hubbard and B. C. Petersen, 'Business Cycles and the Relationship Between Concentration and Price–Cost Margins', *Rand Journal of Economics*, vol. 17 (1986) pp. 1–17.

Donsimoni, M., P. Geroski and A. Jacquemin, 'Concentration Indices and Market Power: Two Views', *Journal of Industrial Economics*, vol. 32 (1984) pp. 419–34.

Dorfman, R. and P. O. Steiner, 'Optimal Advertising and Optimal Quality', *American Economic Review*, vol. 44 (1954) pp. 826–36.

Dosi, G. and L. Orsenigo, 'Coordination and Transformation: an Overview of Structures, Behaviours and Change in Evolutionary Environments', in G. Dosi, C. Freeman, R. Nelson, G. Silverberg and L. Soete (eds), *Technical Change and Economic Theory* (London: Pinter, 1988).

Downs, A., *An Economic Theory of Democracy* (London: Harper & Row, 1957).

Doyle, P., 'Economic Aspects of Advertising: A Survey', *Economic Journal*, vol. 77 (1968) pp. 570–602.

Duch, R. M., *Privatizing the Economy* (Ann Arbor: University of Michigan Press, 1991).

Dunne, T. and M. J. Roberts, 'Variation in Producer Turnover Across US Manufacturing Industries', in P. A. Geroski and J. Schwalbach (eds), *Entry and Market Contestability* (Oxford: Basil Blackwell, 1991).

Dunning, J. H., 'Japanese Manufacturing Investment and the Restructuring of the United Kingdom Economy', in A. Webster and J. H. Dunning (eds), *Structural Change in the World Economy* (London: Routledge, 1990).

Dyson, K. and S. Wilks (eds), *Industrial Crisis: A Comparative Study of the*

State and Industry (Oxford: Martin Robertson, 1983).

Eckard, E. W. Jnr, 'Advertising, Competition and Market Share Instability', *Journal of Business*, vol. 60 (1987) pp. 539–52.

Eckard, E. W. Jnr, 'Concentration Changes and Large-firm/Small-firm Efficiency Differences: Evidence from US Manufacturing Industries', *Applied Economics*, vol. 22 (1990) pp. 131–42.

Eckard, E. W. Jnr, 'Competition and the Cigarette TV Advertising Ban', *Economic Inquiry*, vol. 29 (1991) pp. 119–33.

Edwards, R. S. and H. Townsend, 'Markets and Industries' in H. Townsend (ed.), *Price Theory*, 2nd edn (Harmondsworth: Penguin, 1980).

Eliasson, G., 'The Micro-Foundations of Industry Policy', in A. P. Jacquemin (ed.), *European Industry: Public Policy and Corporate Strategy* (Oxford: Clarendon Press, 1984).

Eliasson, G., 'Modelling the Experimentally Organised Economy', *Journal of Economic Behaviour and Organisation*, vol. 16 (1991) pp. 153–82.

Ellwood, S., 'Costing and Pricing Health Care', *Management Accounting*, November (1991) pp. 26–8.

Else, P. K., 'The Incidence of Advertising in Manufacturing Industries', *Oxford Economic Papers*, vol. 18 (1966) pp. 88–110.

Eskin, G. J., 'A Case for Test Marketing Experiments', *Journal of Advertising Research*, vol. 15 (1975) pp. 27–33.

Eskin, G. J. and P. H. Baron, 'Effect of Price and Advertising in Test-Market Experiments', *Journal of Marketing Research*, vol. 14 (1977) pp. 499–508.

Estrin, S. and V. Pérotin, 'Does Ownership Always Matter', *International Journal of Industrial Organisation*, vol. 9 (1991) pp. 55–72.

Evans, A., 'Competition and the Structure of Local Bus Markets', *Journal of Transport Economics and Policy*, vol. 24 (1990) pp. 255–81.

Fairburn, J. A., 'The Evolution of Merger Policy in Britain', in J. A. Fairburn and J. A. Kay (eds), *Mergers and Merger Policy* (Oxford: University Press, 1989).

Fairburn, J. A. and J. A. Kay (eds), *Mergers and Merger Policy* (Oxford: University Press, 1989).

Fama, E., 'Agency Problems and the Theory of the Firm', *Journal of Political Economy*, vol. 88 (1980) pp. 288–307.

Färe, R., S. Grosskopf and J. Logan, 'The Relative Performance of Publicly Owned and Privately Owned Electric Utilities', *Journal of Public Economics*, vol. 26 (1985) pp. 89–106.

Farris, P. W. and R. D. Buzzell, 'Variations in Advertising Intensity: Some Cross-Sectional Analysis', *Journal of Marketing*, vol. 43 (1979) pp. 112–22.

Farris, P. W. and D. J. Reibstein, 'How Prices, Advertising Expenditures and Profits are Linked', *Harvard Business Review*, vol. 57 (1979) pp. 173–84.

Fehr, N-H. M. von der and D. Harbord, 'Spot Market Competition in the UK Electricity Industry', *Economic Journal*, vol. 103 (1993) pp. 531–46.

Feigenbaum, S. and R. Teeples, 'Public Versus Private Water Delivery: A Hedonic Cost Approach', *Review of Economics and Statistics*, vol. 65 (1983) pp. 672–8.

Ferguson, P. R., 'The Monopolies and Mergers Commission and Economic

Theory', *National Westminster Bank Quarterly Review*, November (1985) pp. 30-40.

Ferguson, P. R., 'Privatisation Options for Eastern Europe: The Irrelevance of Western Experience', *The World Economy*, vol. 15 (1992) pp. 487–504.

Ferguson, P. R., G. J. Ferguson and R. Rothschild, *Business Economics: The Application of Economic Theory* (Basingstoke: Macmillan, 1993).

Finger, J. M., 'Dumping and Antidumping: The Rhetoric and Reality of Protection in Industrial Countries', *World Bank Research Observer*, vol. 7 (1992) pp. 121–43.

Fisher, F. M. and J. J. McGowan, 'On the Misuse of Accounting Rates of Return to Infer Monopoly Profits', *American Economic Review*, vol. 73 (1983) pp. 82–97.

Forsyth, P. J. and R. D. Hocking, 'Property Rights and Efficiency in a Regulated Environment: The Case of Australian Airlines', *Economic Record* (1980) pp. 182–5.

Forsyth, P. J. and J. A. Kay., 'The Economic Implications of North Sea Oil Revenues', *Fiscal Studies*, vol. 1 (1980) pp. 1–28.

Forsyth, P. J. and J. A. Kay, 'Oil Revenues and Manufacturing Output', *Fiscal Studies*, vol. 2 (1981) pp. 9–17.

Foster, C. D., *Privatization, Public Ownership and the Regulation of Natural Monopoly* (Oxford: Blackwell, 1992).

Frank, R. and R. Freeman, 'The Distributional Consequences of Direct Foreign Investment', in W. Deward (ed.), *The Impact of International Trade and Investment on Employment: A Conference of the US Department of Labour* (Washington, DC: US Government Printing Office, 1978).

Franzmeyer, F., *Approaches to Industrial Policy Within the EC and its Impact on European Integration* (Aldershot: Gower, 1982).

Frazer, T., *Monopoly, Competition and the Law*, 2nd edn (Hemel Hempstead: Harvester Wheatsheaf, 1992).

Freeman, C., *The Economics of Industrial Innovation* (Harmondsworth: Penguin, 1974).

Freeman, C., 'Technical Innovation and British Trade Performance', in F. Blackaby (ed.), *Deindustrialisation* (London: Heinemann International, 1979).

Fulop, C. and K. Warren, 'The Marketing of a Professional Service: Opticians', *International Journal of Advertising*, vol. 11 (1992) pp. 287–305.

Funahashi, K., *Monopoly and Welfare Loss*, unpublished dissertation (Department of Economics, University of Lancaster, 1982).

Funkhouser, R. and P. W. Macavoy, 'A Sample of Observations on the Comparative Prices in Public and Private Enterprises', *Journal of Public Economics*, vol. 11 (1979) pp. 353–68.

Galal, A., L. Jones, P. Tandon and I. Vogelsang, *The Welfare Consequences of Selling Public Enterprises: Cases from Chile, Malaysia, Mexico and the UK* (Papers presented at World Bank Conference, 1992).

Gale, B. T. and B. S. Branch, 'Concentration Versus Market Share: Which Determines Performance and Why Does it Matter?' *Antitrust Bulletin*, vol. 27 (1982) pp. 83–105.

Ganguly, P., 'Lifespan Analysis of Businesses in the UK 1973–82', *British Business*, vol. 11 (1983) pp. 838–45.

Geldens, M., 'Towards Fuller Employment', *The Economist* (28 July 1984) pp. 17–20.

George, K. D., 'Do We Need a Merger Policy', in J. A. Fairburn and J. A. Kay (eds), *Mergers and Merger Policy* (Oxford: University Press, 1989).

George, K. D. and A. Jacquemin, 'Dominant Firms and Mergers', *Economic Journal*, vol. 102 (1992) pp. 148–57.

George, K. D. and J. Shorey, *The Allocation of Resources* (London: Allen & Unwin, 1978).

Geroski, P. A., 'Innovation, Technological Opportunity and Market Structure', *Oxford Economic Papers*, vol. 42 (1990) pp. 586–602.

Geroski, P. A., *Market Dynamics and Entry* (Oxford: Basil Blackwell, 1991a).

Geroski, P. A., 'Domestic and Foreign Entry in the United Kingdom: 1983–4', in P. A. Geroski and J. Schwalbach (eds), *Entry and Market Contestability* (Oxford: Basil Blackwell, 1991b).

Geroski, P. A., 'Some Data-Driven Reflections on the Entry Process', in P. A. Geroski and J. Schwalbach (eds), *Entry and Market Contestability* (Oxford: Basil Blackwell, 1991c).

Geroski, P. A., 'Vertical Relations Between Firms and Industrial Policy', *Economic Journal*, vol. 102 (1992) pp. 138–47.

Geroski, P. A. and A. Jacquemin, 'The Persistence of Profits: A European Comparison', *Economic Journal*, vol. 98 (1988) pp. 375–89.

Geroski, P. A. and A. Murfin, 'Entry and Industry Evolution: The UK Car Industry 1958–83', *Applied Economics*, vol. 23 (1991) pp. 799–810.

Gershuny, J., *After Industrial Society?: The Emerging Self-Service Economy* (London: Macmillan, 1978).

Gershuny, J. and I. Miles, *The New Service Economy* (London: Frances Pinter, 1983).

Gibrat, R., *Les Inequalités Economiques* (Paris: Recueil Sirey, 1931).

Ginsburg, D. H., 'Antitrust as Antimonopoly', *Regulation*, vol. 14 (1991) pp. 91–100.

Gisser, M., 'Price Leadership and Welfare Losses in US Manufacturing', *American Economic Review*, vol. 76 (1986) pp. 756–67.

Gisser, M., 'Advertising, Concentration and Profitability in Manufacturing', *Economic Inquiry*, vol. 29 (1991) pp. 148–65.

Goldin, I. and D. van der Mensbrugghe, *Trade Liberalisation: What's at Stake?* (Paris: Organisation for Cooperation and Development, 1992).

Goldschmid, H. J., H. M. Mann and J. F. Weston (eds), *Industrial Concentration: The New Learning* (Boston, Mass.: Little, Brown, 1974).

Gomez-Ibanez, J. A., J. R. Meyer and D. E. Luberoff, 'The Prospects for Privatising Infrastructure', *Journal of Transport Economics and Policy*, vol. 25 (1991) pp. 259–78.

Good, D. H., L-H Röller and R. C. Sickles, 'US Airline Deregulation: Implications for European Transport', *Economic Journal*, vol. 103 (1993) pp. 1028–41.

Grabowski, H. G. and J. M. Vernon, 'Brand Loyalty, Entry, and Price

Competition in Pharmaceuticals After the 1984 Drug Act', *Journal of Law and Economics*, vol. 35 (1992) pp. 331–50.

Greer, D. F., 'Advertising and Market Concentration', *Southern Economic Journal*, vol. 38 (1971) pp. 10–32.

Griffiths, A. and S. Wall (eds), *Applied Economics*, 5th edn (Harlow: Longman, 1993).

Guerin-Calvert, M. E. and J. A. Ordover, 'The 1992 Agency Horizontal Merger Guidelines and the Department of Justice's Approach to Bank Merger Analysis', *Antitrust Bulletin*, vol. 37 (1992) pp. 667–88.

Guth, L. A., 'Advertising and Market Structure Revisited', *Journal of Industrial Economics*, vol. 19 (1971) pp. 179–98.

Hall, P. (ed.), *Technology Innovation and Economic Policy* (Oxford: Philip Allan, 1986).

Hamberg, D., *R&D: Essays in the Economics of Research and Development* (New York: Random House, 1966).

Hannah, L and J. A. Kay, *Concentration in Modern Industry: Theory, Measurement and the UK Experience* (London: Macmillan, 1977).

Harberger, A., 'Monopoly and Resource Allocation', *American Economic Review Papers and Proceedings*, vol. 44 (1954) pp. 77–87.

Harrison, A. (ed.), *Health Care in the UK 1991*, King's Fund Institute (Newbury: Policy Journals, 1992).

Hart, P. E. and R. Clarke, *Concentration in British Industry 1935–75* (Cambridge: University Press, 1980).

Hart, P. E. and S. J. Prais, 'The Analysis of Business Concentration: A Statistical Approach', *Journal of the Royal Statistical Society*, Series A, vol. 119 (1956) pp. 150–91.

Hawkins, R., *Job Displacement and the Multinational Firm: A Methodological Review* (Centre for Multinational Studies, 1972).

Hay, D. A. and D. J. Morris, *Industrial Economics* (Oxford: University Press, 1979).

Hayek, F. A., *The Road to Serfdom* (London: Routledge, 1944).

Hayek, F. A., 'The Use of Knowledge in Society', *American Economic Review*, vol. 35 (1945) pp. 519–30.

Hazlett, T., 'The Curious Evolution of Natural Monopoly Theory', in R. W. Poole (ed.), *Unnatural Monopolies: The Case for Deregulating Public Utilities* (Lexington, Mass.: Lexington Books, 1985a).

Hazlett, T., 'Private Contracting versus Public Regulation as a Solution to the Natural Monopoly Problem', in R. W. Poole (ed.), *Unnatural Monopolies: The Case for Deregulating Public Utilities* (Lexington, Mass.: Lexington Books, 1985b).

Helm, D. and G. Yarrow, 'The Assessment: The Regulation of Utilities', *Oxford Review of Economic Policy*, vol. 4 (1988) pp. i–xxxi.

Heseltine, P. M. and D. T. Silcock, 'The Effects of Bus Deregulation on Costs', *Journal of Transport Economics and Policy*, vol. 24 (1990) pp. 239–54.

Hippel, E. von, *The Sources of Innovation* (Oxford: University Press, 1988).

Hirschman, A. O., 'The Paternity of an Index', *American Economic Review*, vol. 54 (1964) pp. 761–2.

HM Government, *Opening Markets: New Policy on Restrictive Trade Practices*, Cmnd 727 (London: HMSO, 1989).

HM Government, *Competition and Choice: Telecommunications Policy for the 1990s*, Cmnd 1461 (London: HMSO, 1991).

HM Government, *Realising Our Potential*, Cmnd 2250 (London: HMSO, 1993).

HM Treasury, *The Financial and Economic Obligations of the Nationalised Industries*, Cmnd 1337 (London: HMSO, 1961).

HM Treasury, *Nationalised Industries: A Review of Economic and Financial Objectives*, Cmnd 3437 (London: HMSO, 1967).

HM Treasury, *Evidence on the Financing of Trade and Industry to the Committee to Review the Functioning of Financial Institutions* (London: HMSO, 1977).

HM Treasury, *The Nationalised Industries*, Cmnd 7131 (London: HMSO, 1978).

HM Treasury, *Competing for Quality: Buying Better Public Services*, Cmnd 1730 (London: HMSO, 1991).

HM Treasury, *Offer for Sale: British Telecommunications plc* (London: S. G. Warburg & Co., 1993).

Holstius, K, 'Sales Response to Advertising', *International Journal of Advertising*, vol. 9 (1990) pp. 38–56.

Hughes, A. and M. S. Kumar, 'Recent Trends in Aggregate Concentration in the UK', *Cambridge Journal of Economics*, vol. 8 (1984) pp. 235–50.

International Monetary Fund, *Balance of Payments Statistics Yearbook* (Washington, DC: IMF, various years).

Jackson, W. E., 'The Price–Concentration Relationship in Banking: A Comment', *Review of Economic Studies*, vol. 74 (1992) pp. 373–6.

Jacquemin, A. P., 'Introduction: Which Policy for Industry?', in A. P. Jacquemin (ed.), *European Industry: Public Policy and Corporate Strategy* (Oxford: Clarendon Press, 1984).

Jacquemin, A. P. and H. W. de Jong, *European Industrial Organisation* (London: Macmillan, 1977).

Jaffer, S. M. and D. J. Thompson, 'Deregulating Express Coaches: A Reassessment', *Fiscal Studies*, vol. 7 (1986) pp. 45–68.

Jansson, K. and B. Wallin, 'Deregulation of Public Transport in Sweden', *Journal of Transport Economics and Policy*, vol. 25 (1991) pp. 97–107.

Jenny, F. and A. P. Weber, 'Aggregate Welfare Loss Due to Monopoly Power in the French Economy: Some Tentative Estimates', *Journal of Industrial Economics*, vol. 32 (1983) pp. 113–30.

Jensen, M. C., 'Organisation Theory and Methodology,' *Accounting Review*, vol. 50 (1983) pp. 319–39.

Jensen, M. C. and W. Meckling, 'Theory of the Firm: Managerial Behaviour, Agency Costs and Ownership Structure', *Journal of Financial Economics*, vol. 3 (1976) pp. 305–60.

Jeong, K-Y and R. T. Masson, 'Entry During Explosive Growth: Korea During Take-off', in P. A. Geroski and J. Schwalbach (eds), *Entry and Market Contestability* (Oxford: Basil Blackwell, 1991).

Jewkes, J., D. Sawers and R. Stillerman, *The Sources of Invention*, 2nd edn (New York, W. W. Norton, 1969).

Jimenez, E., M. E. Lockheed and V. Paqueo, 'The Relative Efficiency of Private and Public Schools in Developing Countries', *The World Bank Research Observer*, vol. 6 (1991) pp. 205–18.

Johnson, P. S. (ed.), *The Structure of British Industry* (London: Granada, 1980).

Jones, J. C. H. and L. Laudadio, 'The Empirical Basis of Canadian Antitrust Policy: Resource Allocation and Welfare Losses in Canadian Industry', *Industrial Organisation Review*, vol. 6 (1978) pp. 49–59.

Jones, T. T. and T. A. J. Cockerill, *Structure and Performance of Industries* (Oxford: Philip Allan, 1984).

Jong, H. W. de, 'Sectoral Development and Sectoral Policies in the EC', in A. P. Jacquemin (ed.), *European Industry: Public Policy and Corporate Strategy* (Oxford: Clarendon Press, 1984).

Kaldor, N. and R. A. Silverman, *Statistical Analysis of Advertising Expenditure and Revenue of the Press* (Cambridge: University Press, 1948).

Kamerschen, D., 'An Estimation of the "Welfare Losses" from Monopoly in the American Economy', *Western Economic Journal*, vol. 4 (1966) pp. 221–36.

Kamien, M. I. and N. L. Schwartz, 'Market Structure and Innovation: A Survey', Journal of Economic Literature, vol. 13 (1975) pp. 1–37.

Kamien, M. I. and N. L. Schwartz, *Market Structure and Innovation* (Cambridge: University Press, 1982).

Kay, J. A and D. J. Thompson, 'Privatisation: A Policy in Search of a Rationale', *Economic Journal*, vol. 96 (1986) pp. 18–32.

Kay, N. M., *The Emergent Firm* (London: Macmillan, 1984).

Kay, N. M., 'Markets, False Hierarchies and the Evolution of the Modern Firm', *Journal of Economic Behaviour and Organisation*, vol. 17 (1992) pp. 315–33.

Keating, B., 'An Update on Industries Ranked by Average Rates of Return', *Applied Economics*, vol. 23 (1991) pp. 897–902.

Keeler, T. E., 'Airline Deregulation and Market Performance: The Economic Basis for Regulatory reform and Lessons from the US Experience', in D. Banister and K. J. Button (eds), *Transport in a Free Market Economy* (Basingstoke: Macmillan, 1991).

Keown, C. F., N. E. Synodinos, L. W. Jacobs and R. Worthley, 'Transnational Advertising-to-sales Ratios: Do They Follow the Rules?', *International Journal of Advertising*, vol. 8 (1989) pp. 375–82.

Kessides, I. N., 'Advertising, Sunk Costs and Barriers to Entry', *Review of Economics and Statistics*, vol. 68 (1986) pp. 84–95.

Kessides, I. N., 'Market Concentration, Contestability and Sunk Costs', *Review of Economics and Statistics*, vol. 72 (1990) pp. 614–22.

Kessides, I. N., 'Entry and Market Contestability: The Evidence from the United States', in P. A. Geroski and J. Schwalbach (eds), *Entry and Market Contestability* (Oxford: Basil Blackwell, 1991).

Killick, T., 'Employment in Foreign-owned Manufacturing Plants', *British Business*, vol. 10 (1982) pp. 536–7.

Kim, M., 'The Beneficiaries of Trucking Regulation, Revisited', *Journal of Law and Economics*, vol. 27 (1984) pp. 227–94.

King, M. A., 'The UK Profits Crisis: Myth or Reality?', *Economic Journal*, vol. 85 (1975) pp. 33–54.

Kirzner, I. M., *Competition and Entrepreneurship* (Chicago, Ill.: University Press, 1973).

Kirzner, I. M., *Prime Mover of Progress* (London: Institute of Economic Affairs, 1980).

Kirzner, I. M. (ed.), *Method, Process and Austrian Economics* (Lexington, Mass.: Lexington Books, 1982).

Knight, F. H, Risk, *Uncertainty and Profit* (New York: Hart, Schaffner & Marx, 1921).

Knudsen, C., 'Modelling Rationality, Institutions and Processes in Economic Theory', in U. Mäki, B. Gustafsson and C. Knudsen (eds), *Rationality, Institutions and Economic Methodology* (London: Routledge, 1993).

Koch, J. V., 'Industry Market Structure and Industry Price–Cost Margins', *Industrial Organisation Review*, vol. 2 (1974) pp. 189–94.

Koch, J. V., *Industrial Organisation and Prices*, 2nd edn (London: Prentice-Hall, 1980).

Kuznets, S., *Six Lectures on Economic Growth* (New York: Free Press, 1959).

Kwoka, J. E., 'Advertising and the Price and Quality of Optometric Services', *American Economic Review*, vol. 74 (1984) pp. 211–16.

Lambin, J. J., *Advertising, Competition and Market Conduct in Oligopoly Over Time* (Amsterdam: North-Holland, 1976).

Langlois, R. N., 'The New Institutional Economics: An Introductory Essay', in R. N. Langlois (ed.), *Economics as a Process, Essays in the New Institutional Economics* (Cambridge: University Press, 1986).

Langlois, R. N. and L. Csontos, 'Optimisation, Rule-following and the Methodology of Situational Analysis', in U. Mäki, B. Gustafsson and C. Knudsen (eds), *Rationality, Institutions and Economic Methodology* (London: Routledge, 1993).

Lee, C-F., K. T. Liaw and S. Rahman, 'Impacts of Market Power and Capital–Labour Ratio on Systematic Risk', *Journal of Economics and Business*, vol. 30 (1990) pp. 237–41.

Leff, N. H. and J. U. Farley, 'Advertising Expenditures in the Developing World', *Journal of International Business Studies*, vol. 11 (1980) pp. 64–79.

Leibenstein, H., 'Allocative Efficiency versus X-efficiency', *American Economic Review*, vol. 56 (1966) pp. 392–415.

Lerner, A. P., 'The Concept of Monopoly and the Measurement of Monopoly Power', *Review of Economic Studies*, vol. 1 (1934) pp. 157–75.

Lesourne, J., 'The Changing Context of Industrial Policy: External and Internal Developments', in A. P. Jacquemin (ed.), *European Industry: Public Policy and Corporate Strategy* (Oxford: Clarendon Press, 1984).

Levin, R. C., A. K. Klevorick, R. R. Nelson and S. G. Winter, 'Appropriating the Returns from Industrial R&D', *Brookings Papers on Economic Activity* (1987) pp. 783–820.

Levine, M. E., 'Airline Competition in Deregulated Markets: Theory, Firm Strategy and Public Policy', *Yale Journal of Regulation*, vol. 4 (1987) pp. 393–

494.

Lieberman, M. B. and D. B. Montgomery, 'First-mover Advantages', *Strategic Management Journal*, vol. 9 (1988) pp. 41–58.

Liebermann, Y. and A. Ayal, 'Retailer–Manufacturer Price and Profit Relationships Along the Advertising Life Cycle: An Empirical Examination', *Management and Decision Economics*, vol. 13 (1992) pp. 247–54.

Liebowitz, S. J., 'What Do Census Price–Cost Margins Measure?', *Journal of Law and Economics*, vol. 25 (1982) pp. 231–46.

Lindbeck, A., 'Industrial Policy as an Issue of the Economic Environment', *World Economy*, vol. 4 (1981) pp. 391–405.

Lindbeck, A., 'What is Wrong with the West European Economies?', *World Economy*, vol. 8 (1985) pp. 153–70.

Lintner, J., 'The Valuation of Risk assets and the Selection of Risky Investments in Stock Portfolios and Capital Budgets', *Review of Economics and Statistics*, vol. 47 (1965) pp. 13–37.

Lipsey, R. G. and K. Lancaster, 'The General Theory of the Second Best', *Review of Economic Studies*, vol. 24 (1956) pp. 11–32.

Littlechild, S. C., 'Misleading Calculations of the Social Costs of Monopoly Power', *Economic Journal*, vol. 91 (1981) pp. 348–63.

Littlechild, S. C., *The Fallacy of the Mixed Economy*, 2nd edn (London: Institute of Economic Affairs, 1986a).

Littlechild, S. C., *Economic Regulation of Privatised Water Authorities* (London: HMSO, 1986b).

Littlechild, S. C., 'Myths and Merger Policy', in J. A. Fairburn and J. A. Kay (eds), *Mergers and Merger Policy* (Oxford: University Press, 1989).

Low, P., Trading Free: *The GATT and US Trade Policy* (New York: Twentieth Century Fund Press, 1993).

Lucas, R. E., 'Adaptive Behaviour and Economic Theory', in R. M. Hogarth and M. W. Reder (eds), *Rational Choice – The Contract Between Economics and Psychology* (Chicago, Ill.: University Press, 1987).

Luders, R., 'The Success and failure of State-owned Enterprise Divestitures in a Developing Country: The Case of Chile', *Columbia Journal of World Business*, vol. 28 (1993) pp. 98–121.

Lustgarten, S., 'Gains and Losses from Concentration: a Comment', *Journal of Law and Economics*, vol. 22 (1979) pp. 183–90.

Lynk, W. J., 'Information, Advertising and the Structure of the Market', *Journal of Business*, vol. 54 (1981) pp. 271–303.

McAnneny, J. 'The Justice Department's Crusade Against Price-fixing: Initiative or Reaction?', *Antitrust Bulletin*, vol. 36 (1991) pp. 521–42.

McChesney, F. S., 'Antitrust and Regulation: Chicago's Contradictory Views', *Cato Journal*, vol. 10 (1991) pp. 775–98.

McDonald, K. R., 'Why Privatization is Not Enough', *Harvard Business Review*, vol. 71 (1993) pp. 49–59.

McGee, J. S., 'Patent Exploitation: Some Economic and Legal Problems', *Journal of Law and Economics*, vol. 9 (1966) pp. 135–162.

McKie, J. W., 'Market Structure and Function: Performance versus Behaviour', in J. W. Markham and G. F. Papanek (eds), *Industrial Organisation and*

Economic Development; Essays in Honour of E. S. Mason (Boston, Mass.: Houghton Mifflin, 1970).

Majumdar, B. A., 'Industrial Policy in Action: The Case on the Electronics Industry in Japan', *Columbia Journal of World Business*, vol. 23 (1988) pp. 25–34.

Mäki, U., 'Social Theories of Science and the Fate of Institutionalism in Economics', in U. Mäki, B. Gustafsson and C. Knudsen (eds), *Rationality, Institutions and Economic Methodology* (London: Routledge, 1993).

Mäki, U., B. Gustafsson and C. Knudsen (eds), *Rationality, Institutions and Economic Methodology* (London: Routledge, 1993).

Mann, H. M., 'Seller Concentration, Barriers to Entry, and Rates of Return in Thirty Industries, 1950–1960', *Review of Economics and Statistics*, vol. 48 (1966) pp. 296–307.

Mann, H. M. and J. W. Meehan, 'Advertising and Concentration: New Data and an Old Problem', *Antitrust Bulletin*, vol. 16 (1971) pp. 101–4.

Mansfield, E., *Industrial Research and Technological Innovation* (New York: W. W. Norton, 1968).

Mansfield, E., 'How Rapidly Does New Industrial Technology Leak Out?', *Journal of Industrial Economics*, vol. 34 (1985) pp. 217–23.

Mansfield, E., 'Patents and Innovation: An Empirical Study', *Management Science*, vol. 32 (1986) pp. 173–81.

Mansfield, E., J. Rapoport, A. Romeo, S. Wagner and G. Beardsley, 'Social and Private Rates of Return from Industrial Innovations', *Quarterly Journal of Economics*, vol. 91 (1977) pp. 221–40.

Marfels, C., *Recent Trends in Concentration in Selected Industries of the European Community, Japan and the United States* (Luxembourg: Office for Official Publications of the European Communities, 1988).

Marshall, A., *Principles of Economics*, 8th edn (London: Macmillan, 1920).

Marshall, A., *Memorials of Alfred Marshall*, ed. A. C. Pigou (London: Macmillan, 1925).

Marshall, J. and F. Montt, 'Privatisation in Chile', in P. Cook and C. Kirkpatrick (eds), *Privatisation in Less Developed Countries* (Hemel Hempstead: Harvester Wheatsheaf, 1988).

Marshall, J. N., *Services and Uneven Development* (Oxford: University Press, 1988).

Mason, E. S., 'Price and Production Policies of Large Scale Enterprises', *American Economic Review Supplement*, vol. 29 (1939) pp. 61–74.

Masson, R. T. and J. Shaanan, 'Social Costs of Oligopoly and the Value of Competition', *Economic Journal*, vol. 94 (1984) pp. 520–35.

Maurizi, A. R., 'The Effect of Laws Against Price Advertising: The Case of Retail Gasoline', *Western Economic Journal*, vol. 10 (1972) pp. 321–9.

Maurizi, A. R., R. L. Moore and L. Shepherd, 'The Impact of Price Advertising: The California Eyewear Market After One Year', *Journal of Consumer Affairs*, vol. 15 (1981).

Mayes, D. and Y. Ogiwara, 'Transplanting Japanese Success in the UK', *National Institute Economic Review*, vol. 142 (1992) pp. 99–105.

Mears, K., 'The New United Kingdom Standard Industrial Classification of

Economic Activities – SIC (92), *Economic Trends,* No. 468 (1992) pp. 165–70.

Meisel, J. B., 'Entry, Multiple Brand Firms and Market Share Instability', *Journal of Industrial Economics*, vol. 29 (1981) pp. 375–84.

Meyer, R. A., 'Publicly Owned Versus Privately Owned Utilities: A Policy Choice', *Review of Economics and Statistics*, vol. 57 (1975) pp. 391–9.

Mill, J. S., *Principles of Political Economy*, ed. W. J. Ashley (London: Longmans Green, 1909).

Millward, R. and D. Parker, 'Public and Private Enterprise: Comparative Behaviour and Relative Efficiency', in R. Millward, D. Parker, L. Rosenthal, M. T. Sumner and N. Topham (eds), *Public Sector Economics* (London: Longman, 1983).

Mises, L. von, *Human Action: A Treatise on Economics* (Newhaven, Conn.: Yale University Press, 1949).

Molyneux, R. and D. Thompson, 'Nationalised Industry Performance: Still Third Rate?', *Fiscal Studies*, vol. 8 (1987) pp. 48–82.

Monopolies and Mergers Commission, *Contraceptive Sheaths*, HC135 1974-5 (London: HMSO, 1975).

Monopolies and Mergers Commission, *Cat and Dog Foods*, HC447 1976-7 (London: HMSO, 1977).

Monopolies and Mergers Commission, *Insulated Electric Wires and Cables*, HC243 1978-9 (London: HMSO, 1979).

Monopolies and Mergers Commission, *The Inner London Letter Post*, HC515 1979-80 (London: HMSO, 1980).

Monopolies and Mergers Commission, *Contraceptive Sheaths*, Cmnd 8689 (London: HMSO, 1982).

Monopolies and Mergers Commission, Gas: *A Report on the Existence or Possible Existence of a Monopoly Situation in Relation to the Supply in Great Britain of Gas Through Pipes to Persons Other Than Tariff Customers*, Cmnd 500 (London: HMSO, 1988).

Monopolies and Mergers Commission, *Kingfisher plc and Dixons Group plc: A Report on the Proposed Merger*, Cmnd 1079 (London: HMSO, 1990).

Monopolies and Mergers Commission, *Soluble Coffee*, Cmnd 1459 (London: HMSO, 1991).

Monopolies and Mergers Commission, *The Gillette Company and Parker Pen Holdings Ltd: A Report on the Proposed Merger*, Cmnd 2221 (London: HMSO, 1993a).

Monopolies and Mergers Commission, *Contact Lens Solutions: A Report on the Supply Within the United Kingdom of Contact Lens Solutions*, Cmnd 2243 (London: HMSO, 1993b).

Moore, B. C., J. Rhodes and P. Tyler, *The Effect of Government Regional Economic Policy* (London: HMSO, 1986).

Moore, T. G., 'The Effectiveness of Regulation of Electric Utility Prices', *Southern Economic Journal*, vol. 36 (1970) pp. 365–75.

Moore, T. G., 'The Beneficiaries of Trucking Regulation', *Journal of Law and Economics*, vol. 21 (1978) pp. 327–43.

Moore, T. G., 'US Airline Deregulation: Its Effects on Passengers, Capital and

Labor', *Journal of Law and Economics*, vol. 29 (1986) pp. 1–28.

Morrison, S. and C. Winston, 'Enhancing the Performance of the Deregulated Air Transportation System', in M. N. Baily and C. Winston (eds), *Brookings Papers In Economic Activity: Microeconomics 1989* (Washington, DC: Brookings Institution, 1989).

Mueller, D. C., *Profits in the Long Run* (Cambridge: University Press, 1986).

Mueller, D. C., 'Entry, Exit and the Competitive Process', in P. A. Geroski and J. Schwalbach (eds), *Entry and Market Contestability* (Oxford: Basil Blackwell, 1991).

Nash, C. A., 'British Bus Deregulation', *Economic Journal*, vol. 103 (1993) pp. 1042–9.

National Audit Office, *Efficiency of Nationalised Industries: References to the Monopolies and Mergers Commission* (London: HMSO, 1986).

National Economic Development Office, *A Study of UK Nationalised Industries* (London: HMSO, 1976).

National Economic Development Office, *International Price Competitiveness, Non-Price Factors and Export Performance* (London: HMSO, 1977).

National Institute for Economic and Social Research, *National Institute Economic Review*, vol. 114 (1985).

Needham, D., *The Economics of Industrial Structure, Conduct and Performance* (London: Holt, Reinhart & Winston, 1978).

Nelson, P., 'Information and Consumer Behaviour', *Journal of Political Economy*, vol. 78 (1970) pp. 311–29.

Nelson, P., 'The Economic Value of Advertising', in Y. Brozen (ed.), *Advertising and Society* (New York: University Press, 1974a).

Nelson, P., 'Advertising as Information', *Journal of Political Economy*, vol. 82 (1974b) pp. 729–54.

Nelson, P., 'The Economic Consequences of Advertising', *Journal of Business*, vol. 48 (1975) pp. 213–41.

Nelson, P., 'Advertising as Information Once More', in D. G. Tuerck (ed.), *Issues in Advertising: the Economics of Persuasion* (New York: University Press, 1978).

Nelson, R. A., 'The Effects of Competition on Publicly-owned Firms', *International Journal of Industrial Organisation*, vol. 8 (1990) pp. 37–51.

Nelson, R. R. and S. G. Winter, *An Evolutionary Theory of Economic Change* (Cambridge, Mass.: Harvard University Press, 1982).

Nerlove, M. and K. J. Arrow, 'Optimal Advertising Policy Under Dynamic Conditions', *Economica*, vol. 29 (1962) pp. 129–42.

Neuberg, L. G., 'Two Issues in the Municipal Ownership of Electric Power Distribution Systems', *Bell Journal of Economics and Management Science*, vol. 8 (1977) pp. 303–23.

Neumann, M., 'Industrial Policy and Competition Policy', *European Economic Review*, vol. 34 (1990) pp. 562–7.

Nissan, E and R. Caveny, 'Concentration of Sales and Assets of the Top 25 Fortune 500 Firms: 1967–90', *Applied Economics*, vol. 25 (1993) pp. 191–7.

Nogués, J. J., A. Olechowski and L. A. Winters, 'The Extent of Nontariff Barriers to Industrial Countries' Imports', *World Bank Economic Review*, vol. 1 (1986) pp. 181–99.

Nordhaus, W. D., *Invention, Growth and Welfare* (Boston: Massachusetts Institute of Technology, 1969).

Nordhaus, W. D. and J. Tobin, 'Is Growth Obsolete?' in R. J. Gorden (ed.) *Economic Research: Retrospect and Prospect – Economic Growth* (National Bureau of Economic Research, 1972).

North, D. C., Institutions, *Institutional Change and Economic Performance* (Cambridge: University Press, 1990).

North, D. C., 'Institutions and Economic Performance', in U. Mäki, B. Gustafsson and C. Knudsen (eds), *Rationality, Institutions and Economic Methodology* (London: Routledge, 1993).

Office of Fair Trading, *Opticians and Competition* (London: HMSO, 1982).

Oh, S. J., 'The Magnitude of Welfare Losses from Monopoly in the Korean Economy', *Economic Research*, vol. 7 (1986) pp. 219–34.

Oliver, N. and B. Wilkinson, *The Japanization of British Industry: New Developments in the 1990s* (Oxford: Basil Blackwell, 1992).

Ong'olo, D. O., *The Welfare Costs of Monopoly: An Inter-sectoral Analysis for Kenya's Manufacturing Industry*, unpublished dissertation (Department of Economics, University of Lancaster, 1987).

Organisation for Economic Cooperation and Development, *Costs and Benefits of Protection* (Paris: OECD, 1985).

Organisation for Economic Cooperation and Development, *Economies in Transition: Structural Adjustment in OECD Countries* (Paris: OECD, 1989).

Organisation for Economic Cooperation and Development, *Main Economic Indicators: Historical Series 1969–88* (Paris: OECD, 1990).

Organisation for Economic Cooperation and Development, *Industrial Policy in OECD Countries: Annual Review 1992* (Paris: OECD, 1992).

Organisation for Economic Cooperation and Development, *Main Economic Indicators: January 1993* (Paris: OECD, 1993).

Organisation for Economic Cooperation and Development, *Economic Surveys* (Paris: OECD, various years).

Ornstein, S. I., 'Empirical Uses of the Price–Cost Margin', *Journal of Industrial Economics*, vol. 24 (1975) pp. 105–17.

Orr, D., 'An Index of Entry Barriers and its Application to the Market Structure–Performance Relationship', *Journal of Industrial Economics*, vol. 23 (1974) pp. 39–50.

Panic, M., 'Why the UK's Propensity to Import is High', *Lloyds Bank Review*, vol. 115 (1975) pp. 1–12.

Parker, D., 'The 1988 Local Government Act and Compulsory Competitive Tendering', *Urban Studies*, vol. 27 (1990) pp. 653–68.

Parker, D. 'Privatisation Ten Years On: A Critical Analysis of its Rationale and Results', *Economics*, vol. 27 (1991) pp. 154–63.

Parker, S. C., 'Significantly Concentrated Markets', *International Journal of Industrial Organisation*, vol. 9 (1991) pp. 585–90.

Paterson, A., 'Advertising by Lawyers: The American Experience', *Journal of the Law Society of Scotland* (1984).

Pavitt, K., M. Robson and J. Townsend, 'The Size Distribution of Innovating

Firms in the UK: 1945–1983', *Journal of Industrial Economics*, vol. 35 (1987) pp. 297–316.

Peles, Y., 'Economies of Scale in Advertising Beer and Cigarettes', *Journal of Business*, vol. 44 (1971) pp. 32–7.

Peltzman, S., 'Towards a More General Theory of Regulation', *Journal of Law and Economics*, vol. 19 (1976) pp. 211–40.

Peltzman, S., 'The Gains and Losses from Industrial Concentration', *Journal of Law and Economics*, vol. 20 (1977) pp. 229–63.

Peltzman, S., 'The Causes and Consequences of Rising Industrial Concentration: a Reply', *Journal of Law and Economics*, vol. 22 (1979) pp. 209–11.

Peltzman, S., 'The Economic Theory of Regulation After a Decade of Deregulation', in M. N. Baily and C. Winston (eds), *Brookings Papers In Economic Activity: Microeconomics 1989* (Washington, DC: Brookings Institution, 1989).

Pescatrice, D. R. and J. M. Trapani, 'The Performance and Objectives of Public and Private Utilities Operating in the US', *Journal of Public Economics*, vol. 13 (1980) pp. 259–75.

Petit, P., *Slow Growth and the Service Economy* (London: Frances Pinter, 1986).

Pezzoli, A., *The Measurement of Monopoly Welfare Loss: Theory, and Evidence from the Italian Economy 1982–83*, unpublished dissertation (Department of Economics, University of Lancaster, 1985).

Porter, M. E., 'Optimal Advertising: an Intra-Industry Approach', in D. G. Tuerck (ed.), *Issues in Advertising: the Economics of Persuasion* (Washington, DC: American Enterprise Institute for Public Policy Research, 1978).

Porter, M. E., *Competitive Strategy* (New York: Free Press, 1980).

Primeaux, W. J., 'Total Deregulation of Electric Utilities: A Viable Policy Choice', in R.W. Poole (ed.), *Unnatural Monopolies: The Case for Deregulating Public Utilities* (Lexington, Mass.: Lexington Books, 1985).

Primeaux, W. J., 'Electricity Supply: an End to Natural Monopoly', in C. Veljanovski (ed.), *Privatisation and Competition: A Market Prospectus* (London: Institute of Economic Affairs, 1989).

Pryke, R., 'The Comparative Performance of Public and Private Enterprise', *Fiscal Studies*, vol. 3 (1982) pp. 68–81.

Pryke, R., 'Airline Deregulation and European Liberalisation', in D. Banister and K. J. Button (eds), *Transport in a Free Market Economy* (Basingstoke: Macmillan, 1991).

Qualls, D., 'Stability and Persistence of Economic Profit Margins in Highly Concentrated Industries', *Southern Economic Journal*, vol. 40 (1974) pp. 604–12.

Ravenscraft, D. J., 'Structure–Profit Relationships at the Line of Business and Industry Level', *Review of Economics and Statistics*, vol. 65 (1983) pp. 22–31.

Ravenscraft, D. J. and C. L. Wagner, 'The Role of the FTC's Line of Business Data in Testing and Expanding the Theory of the Firm', *Journal of Law and Economics*, vol. 34 (1991) pp. 703–39.

Ray, G. F., 'Productivity in Services', *National Institute Economic Review*, vol. 115 (1986a) pp. 44–7.

Ray, G. F., 'The Changing Structure of the UK Economy', *National Institute Economic Review*, vol. 118 (1986b) pp. 82–8.

Reder, M. W., 'Chicago Economics: Permanence and Change', *Journal of Economic Literature*, vol. 20 (1982) pp. 1–38.

Reekie, W. D., 'Some Problems Associated with the Marketing of Ethical Pharmaceutical Products', *Journal of Industrial Economics*, vol. 19 (1970) pp. 33–49.

Reekie, W. D., 'Advertising and Market Structure: Another Approach', *Economic Journal*, vol. 85 (1975) pp. 165–74.

Reekie, W. D., *Advertising and Price* (London: The Advertising Association, 1979).

Reekie, W. D., 'Advertising and Price', *Journal of Advertising*, vol. 1 (1982) pp. 131–41.

Reekie, W. D., *Markets, Entrepreneurs and Liberty: An Austrian View of Capitalism* (Brighton: Wheatsheaf, 1984).

Reich, R., *The Next American Frontier* (New York: Times Books, 1983).

Reich, R., 'Toward a New Economic Development', *Industry Week*, vol. 241 (1992) pp. 37–44.

Reid, G., *Theories of Industrial Organisation* (Oxford: Basil Blackwell, 1987).

Rhodes, J., 'Regional Dimensions of Industrial Decline', in R. Martin and B. Rowthorn (eds), *The Geography of Deindustrialisation* (Basingstoke: Macmillan, 1986).

Rizzo, J. A. and R. J. Zeckhauser, 'Advertising and Entry: The Case of Physician Services', *Journal of Political Economy*, vol. 98 (1990) pp. 476–50.

Rizzo, J. A. and R. J. Zeckhauser, 'Advertising and the Price, Quantity and Quality of Primary Care Physician Services', *Journal of Human Resources*, vol. 27 (1992) pp. 381–421.

Robinson, E. A. G., *The Structure of Competitive Industry* (Cambridge: University Press, 1958).

Robinson, J., *The Accumulation of Capital* (London: Macmillan, 1956).

Rodwin, L. and H. Sazanami (eds), *Deindustrialisation and Regional Economic Transformation: The Experience of the United States* (Boston, Mass.: Unwin Hyman, 1989).

Rosenbaum, D. I. and F. Lamort, 'Entry, Barriers, Exit, and Sunk Costs: An Analysis', *Applied Economics*, vol. 24 (1992) pp. 297–304.

Rumelt, R., 'How Much Does Industry Matter' *Strategic Management Journal*, vol. 12 (1991) pp. 167–86.

Salinger, M., 'The Concentration–Margins Relationship Reconsidered', in M. N. Baily and C. Winston (eds), *Brookings Papers In Economic Activity: Microeconomics 1990* (Washington, DC: Brookings Institution, 1990).

Sant, M. C., *Industrial Movement and Regional Development: The British Case* (Oxford: Pergamon, 1975).

Sargent, J. R., 'UK Performance in Services', in F. Blackaby (ed.) *Deindustrialisation* (London: Heinemann Educational, 1979).

Savas, E. S., 'An Empirical Study of Competition in Municipal Service Delivery',

Public Administration Review, vol. 37 (1977) pp. 717–24.

Scherer, F. M., A. Beckenstein, E. Kaufer and R. D. Murphy, *The Economics of Multi-Plant Operation: an International Comparisons Study* (Cambridge, Mass.: Harvard University Press, 1975).

Scherer, F. M., 'The Causes and Consequences of Rising Industrial Concentration', *Journal of Law and Economics*, vol. 22 (1979) pp. 191–208.

Scherer, F. M., *Industrial Market Structure and Economic Performance*, 2nd edn (Chicago, Ill.: Rand McNally, 1980).

Schmalensee, R., *The Economics of Advertising* (Amsterdam: North-Holland, 1972).

Schmalensee, R., 'Collusion Versus Differential Efficiency: Testing Alternative Hypotheses', *Journal of Industrial Economics*, vol. 35 (1987) pp. 399–425.

Schmookler, J., *Invention and Economic Growth* (Cambridge, Mass.: Harvard University Press, 1966).

Schumpeter, J., *The Theory of Economic Development* (Cambridge, Mass.: Harvard University Press, 1934).

Schumpeter, J., *Capitalism, Socialism and Democracy* (New York: Harper & Row, 1942).

Schumpeter, J., *History of Economic Analysis* (New York: Oxford University Press, 1954).

Schwalbach, J., 'Entry, Exit, Concentration, and Market Contestability', in P. A. Geroski and J. Schwalbach (eds), *Entry and Market Contestability* (Oxford: Basil Blackwell, 1991).

Schwartzman, D., 'The Burden of Monopoly', *Journal of Political Economy*, vol. 68 (1960) pp. 627–30.

Shackle, G. L. S., *Expectation in Economics* (Cambridge: University Press, 1949).

Shand, A. H., *The Capitalist Alternative* (Brighton: Wheatsheaf, 1984).

Sharpe, W. F., 'Capital Asset Prices: A Theory of Market Equilibrium Under Conditions of Risk', *Journal of Finance*, vol. 19 (1964) pp. 425–42.

Shepherd, W. G., *Market Power and Economic Welfare* (New York: Random House, 1970).

Siegfried, J. J. and T. K. Tiemann, 'The Welfare Costs of Monopoly: an Interindustry Analysis', *Economic Inquiry*, vol. 12 (1974) pp. 190–202.

Silberston, Z. A. and M. Ledic, *The Future of the Multifibre Agreement: Implications for the UK Economy* (London: HMSO, 1989).

Simon, H. A., *Models of Man* (New York: Wiley, 1957).

Simon, J. L., *Issues in the Economics of Advertising* (Urbana: University of Illinois Press, 1970).

Singh, A., 'UK Industry and the World Economy: A Case of Deindustrialisation?', *Cambridge Journal of Economics*, vol. 1 (1977) pp. 113–36.

Singh, A., 'North Sea Oil and the Reconstruction of UK Industry', in F. Blackaby (ed.), *Deindustrialisation* (London: Heinemann Educational, 1979).

Sleuwaegen, L. E., R. R. de Bondt and W. V. Dehandschutter, 'The Herfindahl Index and Concentration Ratios Revisited', *Antitrust Bulletin*, vol. 34 (1989) pp. 625–40.

Smith, A., *The Wealth of Nations*, ed. E. Cannan (London: Methuen, 1961).

Smith, A. D., *The Measurement and Interpretation of Service Output Changes* (London: National Economic Development Office, 1972).

Solow, R. M., 'Technical Change and the Aggregate Production Function', *Review of Economics and Statistics*, vol. 39 (1957) pp. 312–20.

Sosnick, S. H., 'A Criticism of the Concepts of Workable Competition', *Quarterly Journal of Economics*, vol. 72 (1958) pp. 380–423.

Spence, A. M., 'Entry, Capacity, Investment and Oligopolistic Pricing', *Bell Journal of Economics and Management Science*, vol. 8 (1977) pp. 534–44.

Steiner, R. L., 'Does Advertising Lower Consumer Prices?', *Journal of Marketing*, vol. 37 (1973) pp. 19–27.

Steiner, R. L., 'Learning from the Past – Brand Advertising and the Great Bicycle Craze of the 1890s', in S. E. Permut (ed.), *1978 Proceedings of the Annual Conference of the American Academy of Advertising* (Columbia: American Academy of Advertising, 1978a).

Steiner, R. L., 'A Dual Stage Approach to the Effects of Brand Advertising on Competition and Price', in J. F. Cady (ed.), *Marketing and the Public Interest*, Report No. 78–105 (Cambridge, Mass.: Marketing Science Institute, 1978b).

Stevens, B. 'Prospects for Privatisation in OECD Countries', *National Westminster Bank Review*, August (1992) pp. 2–21.

Stigler, G. J., 'The Statistics of Monopoly and Merger', *Journal of Political Economy*, vol. 64 (1956) pp. 33–40.

Stigler, G. J., 'The Economics of Information', *Journal of Political Economy*, vol. 69 (1961) pp. 213–25.

Stigler, G. J., *Capital and Rates of Return in Manufacturing Industries* (Princeton, NJ: National Bureau of Economic Research, 1963).

Stigler, G. J., 'A Theory of Oligopoly', *Journal of Political Economy*, vol. 72 (1964) pp. 44–61.

Stigler, G. J., *Theory of Price*, 3rd edn (New York: Macmillan, 1966).

Stigler, G. J., *The Organisation of Industry* (Homewood, Ill.: R. D. Irwin, 1968).

Stigler, G. J., 'The Theory of Economic Regulation', *Bell Journal of Economics and Management Science*, vol. 2 (1971) pp. 3–21.

Stigler, G. J., *The Economist as Preacher* (Oxford: Basil Blackwell, 1982).

Stoneman, P., *The Economic Analysis of Technological Change* (Oxford: University Press, 1983).

Stopford, J. M. and L. Turner, *Britain and the Multinationals* (Chichester: Wiley, 1985).

Stout, D. K., 'Deindustrialisation and Industrial Policy', in F. Blackaby (ed.), *Deindustrialisation* (London: Heinemann Educational, 1979).

Stout, D. K., 'The Case for Government Support of R and D and Innovation', in C. F. Carter (ed.), *Industrial Policies and Innovation* (London: Heinemann, 1981).

Sullivan, T. G., 'The Cost of Capital and the Market Power of Firms', *Review of Economics and Statistics*, vol. 60 (1978) pp. 209–17.

Sutherland, A., *The Monopolies Commission in Action* (Cambridge: University Press, 1969).

Swann, D., *Competition and Industrial Policy in the European Community* (London: Methuen, 1983).

Taussig, F. W., *Inventors and Moneymakers* (London: Macmillan, 1915).

Telser, L. G., 'Advertising and Competition', *Journal of Political Economy*, vol. 72 (1964) pp. 537–62.

Thirlwall, A. P., 'Deindustrialisation in the United Kingdom', *Lloyds Bank Review*, vol. 144 (1982) pp. 22–37.

Thirlwall, A. P., 'The Balance of Payments and Economic Performance', *National Westminster Bank Quarterly Review*, May (1992) pp. 2–11.

Thomson, I., 'Urban Bus Deregulation in Chile', *Journal of Transport Economics and Policy*, vol. 26 (1992) pp. 319–26.

Thurow, L. C., *The Zero-Sum Society* (New York: Basic Books, 1980).

Tirole, J., *The Theory of Industrial Organization* (Cambridge, Mass.: MIT Press, 1988).

Tischler, M. and Denkewalter, R. D., 'Drug Research – Whence and Whither' in E. Jucker (ed.) *Progress in Drug Research* (Basel, 1966).

Townroe, P. M., *Industrial Location Decisions* (Birmingham: University Press, 1971).

Tremblay, V. J., 'Strategic Groups and the Demand for Beer', *Journal of Industrial Economics*, vol. 34 (1985) pp. 183–97.

Tullock, G., *The Politics of Bureaucracy* (Washington, DC: Public Affairs Press, 1965).

Tullock, G., *The Vote Motive* (London: Institute of Economic Affairs, 1976).

United Nations Conference on Trade and Development, *Review of the Country Presentations in the Light of a Cross-country Analysis by the Secretariat on the Design Implementation and Results of Privatization Programmes*, GE. 93–51871, 7 May (Geneva: UNCTAD, 1993).

United Nations Industrial Development Organisation, *Handbook of Industrial Statistics* (New York: United Nations, 1982).

United Nations Industrial Development Organisation, *Industry in a Changing World* (New York: United Nations, 1983).

United Nations, *International Standard Industrial Classification of All Economic Activities*, Statistical Paper Series M No. 4 Rev. 3 (New York: United Nations, 1989).

United Nations, *International Trade Statistics Yearbook 1988* (New York: United Nations, 1990).

United States Department of Commerce, Bureau of the Census, *Statistical Abstract of the United States* (Washington, DC: Government Printing Office, various years).

United States International Trade Commission, *A Review of Recent Developments in the US Automobile Industry Including an Assessment of the Japanese Voluntary Restraint Agreements* (United States International Trade Commission, 1985).

United States Office of Management and Budget, *Standard Industrial Classification Manual; 1977 Supplement* (Washington, DC: Government Printing Office, 1977).

United States Tariff Commission, *Implications of Multinational Firms for*

World Trade and Investment and for US Trade and Labor, Report to the Senate Committee on Finance (Washington, DC: Government Printing Office, 1973).

Utton, M.A., 'Domestic Concentration and International Trade', *Oxford Economic Papers*, vol. 34 (1982) pp. 479–97.

Utton, M. A. and A. D. Morgan, *Concentration and Foreign Trade* (Cambridge: University Press, 1983).

Veljanovski, C., 'Privatisation: Monopoly Money or Competition?', in C. Veljanovski (ed.), *Privatisation and Competition: A Market Prospectus* (London: Institute of Economic Affairs, 1989).

Vickers, J. and G. Yarrow, *Privatization: An Economic Analysis* (Cambridge. Mass.: MIT Press, 1988).

Vogel, E. F., *Japan as Number One – Lessons for America* (Cambridge, Mass.: Harvard University Press, 1979).

Waelbroeck, J., 'The Logic of EC Commercial and Industrial Policy Making', in A. P. Jacquemin (ed.), *European Industry: Public Policy and Corporate Strategy* (Oxford: Clarendon Press, 1984).

Wahlroos, B., 'Monopoly Welfare Losses under Uncertainty', *Southern Economic Journal*, vol. 51 (1984) pp. 429–42.

Waterman, R. H. Jnr and T. Peters, *In Search of Excellence* (New York: Harper Collins, 1982).

Waterson, M., *Economic Theory of the Industry* (Cambridge: University Press, 1984).

Waterson, M. J., 'International Advertising Expenditure Statistics', *International Journal of Advertising*, vol. 11 (1992) pp. 14–67.

Weir, C, 'Merger Policy and Competition: An Analysis of the Monopolies and Mergers Commission's Decisions', *Applied Economics*, vol. 25 (1993) pp. 57–66.

Weiss, L. W., 'Factors in Changing Concentration', *Review of Economics and Statistics*, vol. 45 (1963) pp. 70–7.

Weiss, L. W., 'The Concentration–Profits Relationship and Antitrust', in H. J. Goldschmid, H. M. Mann and J. F. Weston (eds), *Industrial Concentration: The New Learning* (Boston, Mass.: Little, Brown, 1974).

Weiss, L. W. (ed.), *Concentration and Price* (Cambridge, Mass.: MIT Press, 1989).

Weiss, L. W., R. Geithman and H. Marvel, 'Concentration, Price and Critical Concentration Ratios', *Review of Economics and Statistics*, vol. 63 (1981) pp. 346–53.

Weiss, L. W. and G. A. Pascoe Jnr, *Adjusted Concentration Ratios in Manufacturing 1972 and 1977* (Washington, DC: Federal Trade Commission, 1986).

White, L. J., 'What Has Been Happening to Aggregate Concentration in the US?', *Journal of Industrial Economics*, vol. 29 (1981) pp. 223–30.

White, P. J., 'Bus Deregulation: A Welfare Balance Sheet', *Journal of Transport Economics and Policy*, vol. 24 (1990) pp. 311–32.

Whitehead, C. (ed.), *Reshaping the Nationalised Industries* (Newbury: Policy Journals, 1988).

White House Task Force on Antitrust Policy, 'Report 1' in *Trade Regulations Report Supplement 10 No. 415* (1969).

Whittington, G., 'Changes in the Top 100 Quoted Firms, 1948–1968' *Journal of Industrial Economics*, vol. 21 (1972) pp. 17–34.

Williamson, O. E., 'Managerial Discretion and Business Behaviour', *American Economic Review*, vol. 53 (1963) pp. 1032–57.

Williamson, O. E., 'Economies as an Antitrust Defense: the Welfare Trade-offs', *American Economic Review*, vol. 58 (1968) pp. 18–31.

Williamson, O. E., *Markets and Hierarchies: Analysis and Antitrust Implications* (New York: Free Press, 1975).

Williamson, O. E., 'Franchise Bidding for Natural Monopolies – In General and with Respect to CATV', *Bell Journal of Economics*, vol. 7 (1976) pp. 73–104.

Williamson, O. E., *The Economic Institutions of Capitalism* (New York: Free Press, 1985).

Williamson, O. E., *Economic Organisation: Firms, Markets and Policy Control* (Brighton: Wheatsheaf, 1986).

Willig, R. D., 'Merger Analysis, Industrial Organisation Theory, and Merger Guidelines', in M. N. Baily and C. Winston (eds), *Brookings Papers on Economic Activity: Microeconomics 1991* (Washington, DC: Brookings Institution, 1991).

Willott, W. B., 'Industrial Innovation and the Role of Bodies like the National Enterprise Board', in C. F. Carter (ed.), *Industrial Policies and Innovation* (London: Heinemann, 1981).

Wittink, D. R., 'Advertising Increases Sensitivity to Price', *Journal of Advertising Research*, vol. 17 (1977) pp. 39–42.

Worcester, D. A. Jnr, 'New Estimates of the Welfare Loss to Monopoly in the United States 1956–1969', *Southern Economic Journal*, vol. 40 (1973) pp. 234–45.

World Bank, *World Development Report 1986* (Oxford: University Press, 1986).

World Bank, *World Development Report 1991* (Oxford: University Press, 1991).

World Bank (Country Economics Division), *Privatisation: The Lessons of Experience* (Washington, DC: World Bank, 1992).

Yarrow, G., 'Does Ownership Matter?', in C. Veljanovski (ed.), *Privatisation and Competition: A Market Prospectus* (London: Institute of Economic Affairs, 1989).

Author Index

Subject Index

advertising
- and market share 76–7
- and market structure 67–9
- and price 79–81
- and product quality 67
- and profits 77–8
- and search 65–6, 72
- and type of good 63–7
- as information 72–4, 75, 78, 79, 82
- as persuasion 70–2, 74, 75–6, 77, 78, 79, 81
- Austrian view of 62, 72
- costs of 69–70, 81
- defined 61–2
- Dorfman–Steiner condition 67, 68, 265–7
- economies of scale in 69–70, 72
- empirical evidence 75–81
- expenditure on 60, 61, 63–7
- threshold effect 69, 72
- with a retail sector 74–5

allocative efficiency 15, 16, 29, 201, 202, 217

antitrust *see* competition policy

asset specificity 21, 24, 34, 35

Austrian School
- and competition policy 163, 169, 173
- and industrial dynamics 2
- and industrial economics 259–60
- and industry policy 150, 156
- and innovation 113–16
- and market concentration 58
- critique of neoclassical theory 31–2
- defined 4, 8–9
- view of competition 29, 31–4, 236–7
- view of monopoly 104–7, 205, 215

Averch–Johnson effect 201

beta 23, 97

catallactics 31

Chicago School
- and competition policy 162, 164
- and entry barriers 20
- and monopoly 19, 86, 95–6, 99–100, 104
- defined 4, 6, 9

competition
- as a process 9, 28–9, 31–4, 62, 72, 105, 156, 205, 237

competition policy
- and industry policy 137
- and innovation 183, 185, 190–1
- and market concentration 53
- and regional policy 190
- and trade policy 191
- Austrian view of 163, 169, 173
- Chicago view of 162, 164
- defined 162–3
- in the European Community 163–4, 165, 166–7, 169, 170, 171, 171–2, 173
- market definition 25
- neoclassical view of 162–3, 164, 165, 169, 172
- UK 165, 166, 167, 168, 170–1, 171, 173–4
- US merger guidelines 41, 44, 167–8
- USA 164–5, 165–6, 167–8, 169–70

concentration *see* market concentration

concentration curve 39–40, 45

concentration ratio 40–1, 43, 45, 48, 51–2, 53, 55, 56, 58, 97–9

304